# POSITANO

## LIFE ON THE
## AMALFI COAST

# SUSI BELLA WARDROP

Illustrations by Ian Wardrop

Positano
Life on the Amalfi Coast

ISBN: 879-1-4860-1912

Printed by On Demand Pty. Ltd.
Melbourne, Australia. 2008.

Cover creation and formatting   : RW Marketing
Front cover pony image          : 'Positano' by  A. B. Babbicola

# CONTENTS

# INTRODUCTION

It was time for coffee and reminiscing. Sitting over dinner in one of Melbourne's Italian restaurants, I started to think back, to recall similar evening long past. We always celebrate family birthdays, and now another year had gone by, and it was my birthday once again.

"Do you remember our Positano dinners?" I asked my daughters. "The *trattoria* on the beach at Fornillo; the warm and affectionate couple who owned it."

Born in Italy, the girls had spent their early childhood in Positano. Although both had returned several times, the visits had been brief, and I was aware that their recollections were becoming more and more hazy.

"It's a shame you know so little about those years," I said. "You were so young when we left."

Then they started to tell me, as they always do on such occasions, that it was really up to me.

"You can't expect us to remember all that happened. We love hearing your stories, you know that. Why don't you write it all down? Write a book about life in Positano."

It was not the first time the girls had made this suggestion. Like most families, we had a fund of anecdotes, of shared recollections, of incidents and events that had occured over the years. Listening to my tales about the daily routine, the local culture and way of life, the characters who lived in the mountain villages, they often encouraged me to record my memories.

I'd always laughed at the idea. I didn't have the time, I was far too busy, I couldn't possibly write the book. Now, for the first time, I seriously considered the prospect. Why not? Although thirty years had passed since I'd returned to Australia, my memories of the preceding period were surprisingly fresh and vivid. Maybe I really should write them down before it was too late.

A further impetus was provided by the publication of a research study I had recently conducted on Italian proxy brides in Australia. These were women who had ventured forth, young and alone, to join a new husband in an unknown country. They absolutely must tell their stories, I insisted. It was so important that their children and grandchildren should know their past. Now I began to apply a similar argument to myself.

And so I started to tell my story.

# PREFACE

The ferry blew a farewell salute on its siren; a long low wail which echoed over the land and out to sea. It echoed through the houses, reverberated against the wall, resonated as far as the mountains which towered high above the town.

We all knew what this meant. It was a farewell to summer. The season was coming to an end. Soon the tourists would be gone, the hotels would close, the shops would empty.

I had been living in Positano for several years, and I understood the significance of the change in seasons. Here we alternated between two worlds. Summer was a time of sunlight and colour, of glamour, of exuberant activity. Winter was a time of tranquility; of calm days and quiet evenings.

Visitors came from many countries. "You must go to Positano," they told their friends, describing the yachts and fishing boats, the restaurants and beach bars, the endless round of social occasions. But there perceptions were of the summer Positano.

The winter Positano was a completely different place; the streets empty of people and traffic, the town semi-deserted. The tempo of daily life fell back into the slow, ageless rhythm of bygone days. It was as though someone had waved a magic wand, causing the sophisticated town to be transformed, for a few months, into the small Amalfi coast village it had been before the advent of tourism.

Every year, thousands of travellers come and go. Some stay for a few days, other remains for a week or a month. Eventually most move on, content with memories and photographs of a fashionable beach resort thronged with people. But some who come never leave. Like me, they learn to adapt, to adjust, to understand that each season has its own charm. The local inhabitants recognise that life must follow its annual cycle. And I was now included among their number, for Positano had become my home.

# SUMMER HOLIDAY

I came to Positano by accident. I hadn't planned to go there. I didn't even know it existed. And yet this little Italian village, perched on the side of a mountain overlooking the Mediterranean, captured my heart and my life for years to come.

\*　　\*　　\*　　\*　　\*

It was raining in London. It had been raining for weeks. The days were short, the wind blew in cold gusts, people hurried along the streets, thick woollen scarves clutched tightly around their necks. The bleak, dismal winter had gone on and on. Now the long and eagerly awaited spring had come at last, but I could see little improvement.

When, after several years research work in Australia, I'd been offered a job at a well-known London institute, I jumped at the opportunity. It couldn't have come at a better time. I was young, I had no commitments. For years I'd wanted to travel in Europe; to go skiing in winter, sightseeing in summer, to holiday in France and Italy, to meet people from all over the world. It was time for a change, and change it did.

A year had passed since my arrival, a stimulating, exciting year. I'd been living in London, working at the research institute, and sharing a house in Hampstead with an English biochemist. London in the swinging sixties was a vibrant, dynamic city; my job was interesting and absorbing; my evenings and weekends filled with activity. What more could anyone want? But I did want more. I wanted an end to the foggy mornings, to the short days and continuous rain. I wanted to see the sun, to feel warm, to look up at a sky that was blue, not grey.

Now, on a Saturday morning in May, my housemate Janet and I were sitting in the kitchen of our red-brick terrace house, watching as the early morning drizzle developed into a steady, driving downpour.

"Why does it have to rain every weekend?"

Gathering up the breakfast dishes, Janet paused for a moment.

"I suppose you're going to tell me you need a holiday," she said with a sigh.

Poor Janet, she'd heard it all before. I knew that. But I couldn't help myself. I was so looking forward to the summer, to a holiday in the sun. And to my surprise, my long-suffering housemate actually agreed with me for once. Winter had been worse than usual, she admitted. She could do with a change herself. Suddenly I had a brainwave. Why didn't we take our holidays at the same time and head off to southern Europe?

That morning, while the wind blew and the rain battered at our windows, we started to make plans. My enthusiasm must have been infectious; for by the time we'd finished our second cup of coffee, I could sense that Janet was beginning to share my excitement. By the end of the morning we'd decided to go to southern Italy. And over the next few weeks we talked, planned and dreamed about our Italian trip.

"We could go to Sicily. Or perhaps to Ischia."

Where was Ischia exactly? I knew it was an island south of Naples. I'd better buy a map. But did it really matter if we had no fixed agenda, no travel itinerary, no clearly defined destination? We were looking for sunlight, beautiful beaches, and wondrous food. There was plenty of time, we'd find out more when we got there.

I wasn't worried about the details. I knew I'd love Italy, no matter where we decided to go. Because I'd been hearing about Italy all my life. Although I'd grown up in Australia, my background was European. My mother was Czech, my father Hungarian. They had met in Italy. My mother's sister had married an Italian; for years I'd heard stories about my far-away uncle and his family. A few years earlier I'd visited Italy with my mother and met some of these unknown relatives. I'd discovered delightful cousins in Rome. They'd know the best place for a summer holiday.

In late June, we packed our bags, locked up the house, and set off for Heathrow airport and our flight to Italy. What a joy it was to leave my well-worn winter clothes behind, hanging in their accustomed place in the wardrobe. I never wanted to see them again.

Our first stop was Rome, my favourite city. To me it's a city of wonders, an exciting, fascinating capital. Rome is where the streets echo with history, the monuments are splendid, and the people exuberant. I never know what I'll find around the next corner, but I do know it's good to be alive. Whenever I go there I want to stay forever. This time, however, we had other ideas. We were really excited about our forthcoming holiday. We couldn't afford to linger. Rome would have to wait.

*    *    *    *    *

Twilight was falling on our first night in Italy.

"You can't go to Sicily in July. It's far too hot."

On this balmy summer evening, we sat over dinner in a tiny *trattoria* with my cousin Luisa and her friends. Discussing our sketchy travel plans, we asked for advice. Our companions were amazed that anyone would even consider going so far south in the middle of summer.

"Why don't you start with the Amalfi coast? You could spend a few days in Amalfi and Sorrento, then move on to the islands, to Capri or Ischia."

The names resonated in my mind, conjuring up images of light-filled days, sophisticated hotels, and glamorous people. Sorrento presented a different picture, evoking childhood memories. Because we used to spend our summer holidays at another Sorrento, a small town on the coast not far from Melbourne.

3

Listening as Luisa painted a glowing picture of the coastal area south of Naples, Janet and I became more and more enthusiastic. It sounded fantastic, exactly what we wanted. Now at last we had a plan. We would leave early next morning. Hopefully we'd be out of the city before the traffic became too heavy. We had yet to learn that the traffic in Rome never stops.

But what did it matter? The sky was blue, the morning warm and full of promise. Shopkeepers pulled up shutters and arranged window displays, people hurried to work, piling onto overcrowded buses. The city was starting its day.

We managed, with difficulty, to find a taxi. Of course it took forever to get to the central railway station. But again, we didn't really care. Our driver talked non-stop in broken English, expounding his views on the political and social situation in Italy while manoeuvring us through endless traffic tangles.

Eventually we arrived at the station. My first impression was one of utter confusion, of noise and general pandemonium. But it wasn't as bad as it looked, and in a surprisingly short time we found our way to a ticket office. Thousands of *lire* later, we were ready to go. Gathering up our bags, we joined the crush of people heading towards the platforms. Loudspeakers crackled, whistles blew, passengers hurried up and down steps lugging heavy suitcases. We pushed our way through the crowd. Soon we were on a train speeding south towards Naples.

I wondered why we'd thought Rome was noisy. Naples was infinitely worse. *Napoli* must be one of the most chaotic, hectic and bewildering cities in the world. Somehow we had to find the ferry to Capri and Amalfi. It wasn't going to be easy, but it must be possible. If everyone else could manage, so would we. I'd done a short course in Italian before leaving Australia. Now, at this rowdy railway station, I launched forth in my limited vocabulary.

*"Scusate, dove si trova il battello per Capri?"* Excuse me, where do you find the Capri ferry? The first few people I asked

4

ignored me, then a kind man looked at me sympathetically. "*Prego?*" pardon? he said. I tried again, but he still didn't understand. Janet, always so polite and patient, now took over. I could understand her frustration.

"Can you tell us where to catch the Capri ferry," she said in English.

This was a great success, his face lit up.

"Of course, follow me and I'll show you." So much for my language skills! His English was far from perfect, but it was obviously better than my Italian.

Carrying our bags we hurried after our new friend, who conducted us to the harbour, pointing us in the general direction of the ferry terminal. Accustomed to England, we expected to stand in line, but the concept of forming a queue was, we soon discovered, totally foreign to Neapolitans. Again we found ourselves at the centre of a pushing, shoving throng, all jostling to be first on board.

The *vaporetto* slid off smoothly, taking us across the beautiful bay of Naples. Vesuvius towered majestically in the background. The volcano was dormant, but according to reports, a number of vulcanologists believed it was just waiting to erupt.

The sea was unusually rough that day, so the boat stopped at Capri only long enough to let off a few people, before setting off again for Amalfi. Our route followed the wild and ruggedly beautiful coastline. We stood on the boat-deck, admiring the outlook as we passed little villages scattered here and there, some on the coast, others up in the hills. Then in the distance, appearing and disappearing like a mirage as the boat rose and fell with the waves, we saw a breathtaking sight. A cluster of mountains rose steeply from the sea, and on the nearest mountain, a series of brightly coloured houses with domed roofs and Moorish architecture were seemingly perched one on top of the other. It was a picture of spectacular beauty.

5

"Just look at that incredible place," Janet and I said at the same moment.

"Isn't it lovely? Positano has always been one of my favourite places." A man standing right behind us had heard our excited comments.

We headed for the gangway, ready to disembark and investigate this delightful little town. Quite a few people wanted to get off, but, to our dismay, the boat showed no sign of slowing down. I couldn't believe it. Why wouldn't the ferry let us off, when we'd just discovered our ideal destination? An attendant told us it was impossible to pull in close enough to unload passengers. *"Il mare è troppo mosso."* He was right, the sea really was too rough and choppy. And so we rocked along on our way towards Amalfi, passing lovely villas dotted along the coastline, and other small villages overlooking the sea. None captivated us as much as Positano. "We'll just have to go back." There was no argument. Having seen this picturesque township hugging the cliff-side, we were absolutely determined to get there as quickly as possible.

The moment we set foot in Amalfi, we set about finding a bus to take us back. Ignoring the fact that we were in a historic, fascinating city, we didn't stop to look around. We'd made up our minds. Positano was the place for us.

What an extraordinary trip it was. The road was perilous, winding its way high above sea-level by means of serpentine curves amazingly cut into the cliffs. At each turn, I looked down onto the rocks far below, holding what might easily be my last breath. Beneath us was a sheer drop to the ocean; above, should anyone be foolish enough to look up, a towering precipice appeared about to fall on top of the bus. At first I thought the wisest option was to keep my eyes tightly shut. After a while I decided it was better to stare straight ahead, fixed and unwavering, looking neither to left or right. In fact this wasn't such a bad idea; the view in front was quite spectacular! It was frightening, though, there must have been a thousand hairpin bends and curves.

As we approached each curve, the driver sounded his horn. The noise was deafening, a long, low wail, piercing, melodious, penetrating; it could surely be heard miles away. The horn gave me comfort, I felt relieved to know that all approaching traffic must be well aware we were coming. Every now and then an answering blast came from around the bend, leading to a series of intricate manoeuvres. We realized that these drivers were very skilled, they had to be, because the road between Amalfi and Positano was just wide enough for one bus, definitely not for two! And yet, amid much cursing and swearing, the seemingly impossible occurred; two buses managed to squeeze past one another, navigate the curve, and continue on their way. We proceeded, with a series of stops and starts each time we encountered approaching traffic, passing through several small villages, all picturesque, and all apparently suspended on cliffs between sea and sky. Finally, as dusk was falling, we saw in the distance a little fairy-tale cluster of lights. And then we heard the singsong voice of the driver calling, "*Scendete per Positano*".

# ARRIVAL

It was almost dark. Janet and I were standing by the side of the main Amalfi road. Now where did we go? People were bustling around, porters collected luggage, tourists wandered in and out of an unpretentious looking bar with the grandiose name '*Bar Internazionale*' inscribed over the entrance. By now I was feeling quite weary. Why was it so difficult to actually reach Positano?

Only one road went through the town, we discovered, a *senso unico*, one-way road. We'd have to wait for the local bus. When it eventually came it was really crowded. But we were certainly not going to wait any longer; we'd been travelling all day. We pushed our way on, and at long last arrived at the town centre.

Getting off the bus, we collected our bags and looked around. We were in a small *piazza*, an irregularly shaped junction through which all traffic had to pass. Narrow lanes branched off at unexpected angles, ahead a passageway led to the waterfront. A policeman stood directing traffic. This was the central hub of Positano.

We tried to get our bearings. A jumble of churches, shops, houses, and tiny squares, Positano predated town planning. The main square, *la Piazza dei Mulini*, was bordered on one side by an old stone church. Diagonally opposite, people sat at tables on a terrace overlooking the *piazza;* waiters zipped in and out of a bar on the other side of the road, dodging traffic to serve their customers. Back and forth they scurried, taking orders and returning with trays piled high with coffee, cocktails, and the popular campari soda, a bright red drink in triangular-shaped bottles. As soon as I had a chance I'd order one, I decided, looking on enviously as a young couple, cool and relaxed, clinked crimson-coloured glasses of campari.

Shops were everywhere, in the square, lining each side of the road, extending out in every direction. Boutiques sold smart Italian beachwear; racks of designer clothes were on display wherever an

8

inch of space could be found. I determined to do some serious browsing next day, and start this holiday by getting into the fashion stakes. My supply of casual summer clothes could do with updating; there hadn't been much demand for such items in London.

The place was a hive of activity, I'd never seen so many people concentrated in such a small space. Holiday makers were coming up from the beach, looking relaxed and sporting wonderful suntans; others were dressed for dinner and a night out. A stone bench attached to the church wall served as a bus stop. There was a resigned air about those who sat waiting, I guessed they were locals, accustomed to the vagaries of the daily timetable. Holding shopping bags filled with the day's groceries, they passed the time chatting among themselves, talking in what I came to recognize as Neapolitan dialect.

Walking around the square, we came upon a tourist information office. I tried my Italian again. I wanted to ask where we could stay, where to have dinner, what to do next, but by this time I was so tired I had trouble saying anything at all. But we had no problem finding accommodation, as a group of friendly, helpful people came to our aid. We immediately felt better, how nice everyone was. It confirmed our first impression; we'd been right to come here. In no time we found ourselves in a delightful little *pensione*.

It was one of the old houses, full of long, winding passages. Recessed into the walls were small niches, some holding a Madonna, others a patron saint. The rooms were large, with tall arched doors and domed ceilings. Ours was bright and cheerful, the floor tiles emerald-green, the prints and wall hangings brilliant splotches of colour. It was simply but adequately furnished. Double doors led onto a large terrace overlooking the sea. A myriad of fishing boats bobbed up and down in the water, their overhead lights creating an illusion of fairyland.

We found a couple of lounge chairs and sat down thankfully, gazing enthralled at the view. Clusters of whitewashed villas

9

stretched out in front of us, their rooftops rounded cupolas, their walls overgrown with exuberantly flowering plants. As we watched, a family came out of a bright green door immediately below our balcony, strolled across a flower-filled courtyard, then unlocked wrought-iron gates to emerge in a narrow winding passageway. Off they went, up steps and down, stopping to chat as they encountered friends along the way. Was this the only entrance to their home, we wondered. How did they manage to go about their everyday business?

I don't know how long we sat there. After a time we heard a knock at the door. There stood a slim, smiling girl of about twenty. Dressed in blue shorts and matching top, dark hair pulled back in a pony tail, she looked suntanned, healthy and friendly.

"Welcome to Positano," she said. "I'm Maria."

Maria's father owned our *pensione*. She welcomed us in excellent English. Her family had migrated to New Zealand when she was a child, she told us, and she'd gone to school in Auckland.

We must have looked as though we needed organizing, for she went on:

"Why don't you have a shower, change your clothes, and come with me. I'll show you some of the sights."

We did as she suggested, and soon Maria was guiding us down innumerable flights of steps to the waterfront.

Here the life of Positano was concentrated. What a beautiful sight it was. Boats were drawn up on the beach; fishing boats, excursion vessels, motor launches with painted signs advertising day-trips, and small pleasure craft. Riding at anchor beautiful yachts, slim and elegant with tall masts, stood side by side with an impressive array of large seagoing private vessels. And further out still, strong overhead lights illuminated fishermen plying their trade.

Brightly lit shops and restaurants lined the promenade. Tables and chairs faced the beach in a long and continuous chain. Adjoining restaurants were separated from their neighbours by elaborate wrought-iron railings, or by a row of flowering plants. A delicious smell of cooking emanated from this endless stream of eating places. I suddenly realised that we hadn't eaten for hours.

Deciding on what looked to be the smallest and most inviting *trattoria*, we selected a table overlooking the waterfront. We could see the anchored boats, the passing parade of people, and an impressive pair of antique bronze lions presiding majestically over the harbour. It was the hour of the *passeggiata,* an Italian ritual. Couples strolled along arm in arm, chatting, looking at the shops, taking the night air. Mothers and daughters, arms linked, walked past; young men sauntered by, appreciatively admiring the pretty daughters, or looking into restaurants to determine whether it was worth their while to go in.

We sat down thankfully, admiring the brightly checked tablecloths and overall decor. Pictures of local scenery decorated the walls, strings of onions and garlic hung from overhead beams, bottles of every conceivable shape tempted the eye with vividly coloured liqueurs. We examined our fellow diners - what language were they speaking; were they all tourists? There was so much to discuss. But before we had time to talk, a waiter approached our table. He brought us each a glass of anise, courtesy of the proprietor. It was, we learned, the traditional form of welcome. I'd never tasted this *aperitif* before, one sip and my head was suffused with a concentrated flavour of aniseed. It certainly created a warm glow. I felt I'd better have something to eat before drinking any more of this potent brew.

The proprietor was a big man with an infectious grin. Now he came over to greet us, shaking hands and wishing us *buon appetito.* "You English?" he asked. Since English girls were no longer a novelty in Positano, he accepted Janet without too much excitement. When I introduced myself as Australian, however, his reaction was surprising.

"Australia, but that must be paradise!" he exclaimed. "Why would you come to Italy when you live in such a wonderful country?"

"Australia's certainly a great country," I agreed, "but Italy's wonderful too."

"Perhaps you're right," he said, with a laugh. "Have another drink and we'll toast our two countries." He called the waiter, telling him to bring three more glasses of anise. We raised our glasses while he proposed a *brindisi,* a toast, to Australia and to Italy. As an afterthought he included England so Janet wouldn't feel left out. Then he wished us a good holiday, promised an excellent dinner, and moved on to look after other guests.

We were enjoying our drinks when another waiter appeared, carefully balancing a bowl of *cannelloni.* Even if I hadn't been so hungry, I'd have been impressed. Pasta *fatta in casa,* homemade, and beautifully presented, the filling spinach and ricotta, the tomato sauce aromatic with oregano and basil. A raffia basket on our table was piled high with crusty bread and *grissini.* I noticed diners at other tables dipping hunks of bread into the sauce, then wiping their bowl clean so not a drop was wasted. Much to Janet's horror, I finished my *cannelloni* and followed their example.

We'd hardly managed to digest the last mouthful when the waiter reappeared. With a graceful flourish, he placed a magnificent grilled fish in front of us. A moment later he was back with chips and salad. He proceeded to fillet the fish. We could only admire the skill and dexterity, obviously born of years of practice, with which he managed in a few seconds to provide us with perfect boneless fillets.

I asked him how the fish was cooked. He seemed surprised, I suppose most people don't ask waiters how the food's been prepared. But I was really interested. Obviously he was an expert.

"First we make up a marinade," he said. I think he was really pleased I'd asked. "Olive oil and vinegar, a little mint and parsley, some garlic and a few lemon leaves. We marinate the fish for an hour or so, then grill it on an open fire. It's important to baste with marinade now and then so it stays moist. *Perfetto, no?*" he said, smacking his lips.

I had to agree, it really was perfect. I ate very slowly, savouring each mouthful, to make my delicious meal last as long as possible. Helping ourselves to salad, we dressed it with oil and vinegar provided in decorative cruets on our table. Again our waiter arrived, this time with a jug of peaches in red wine.

"We don't have a menu," he told us, "visitors are served the specialties of the house." It seemed a great idea, I couldn't have made a better choice.

We'd noticed a group of people of mixed nationalities sitting at the next table. Now an American girl came over and invited us to join her friends. And so we began to meet some of the unusual and interesting people who lived in Positano. The American girl, tall, slim and most attractive, told us she'd trained as a psychologist in New York. Her boyfriend was a local fisherman with the fresh-faced good looks, flashing dark eyes, and stocky figure typical of many southern Italians. Gino was perfectly charming, welcoming us and offering suggestions about things we might enjoy doing over the next few days.

Included among their companions were two young painters, one French, the other English. Both were dressed in the latest, colorful fashions I'd seen in the boutiques. They'd been discussing surrealism. Now they included me in the conversation, asking about trends in Australian art. But after a long day travelling and a host of new experiences, I felt unable to do justice to such an intellectual topic, and proposed we postpone our discussion for another time.

"In a moment I'll introduce you to Peter," said Carol, our new American friend. "I'm sure he'll tell you he was one of the 'pioneer' artists who discovered Positano in the 1920s. He's so proud he was one of the first northern Europeans to recognise the charms of this place. And, no doubt, you'll hear about his book. For years he's been working on an interminable study. I think it describes the life and mating habits of butterflies." She made a face. "See that girl sitting next to him. That's Trudi, his German friend."

I glanced around in the direction Carol was indicating, feeling a little embarrassed. What if they heard what she was saying? Fortunately they seemed absorbed in some other conversation.

"Trudi's the latest in a long line of girlfriends. Peter employs them on the pretext of needing a secretary to help with his book."

After that rather negative preamble, we were introduced to Peter and Trudi. Peter was a Dutchman with a thick bushy beard and moustache. I guessed he was about sixty. His friend Trudi, short, blonde, and a little overweight, wore a frilly white blouse tucked into a gathered skirt featuring flowers in blobs of shocking pink. She certainly hadn't bought her clothes in Italy.

When Peter started talking, his conversation followed the lines Carol had predicted. It was hard not to laugh. But he was really an interesting person. I felt that Carol had been a bit unfair. Both Peter and Trudi were good company; I hoped we'd meet them again.

After dinner we sat on, chatting over coffee, watching the passing parade on land and activity out to sea. Our dinner companions knew all about local history and customs. We learned the reason for the powerful overhead lights on the fishing boats we'd seen; apparently the glaring beam served to attract anchovies, squid, and a local species of mollusc known as *totani*. The effect was stunning; the shimmering rays cast a silvery reflection over the sea like strings of fairy lights set up for a celebration.

I asked Peter about his early years in Positano, what it was like when he first arrived.

"It's a long story," he said, "and you're far too tired to hear about it now. So I'll just say that this little town on the Amalfi coast has had a long and fascinating history. Although it's known moments of glory, it's also been through long periods of decline." He paused for a moment.

"By the beginning of the twentieth century Positano had been reduced to the status of a small fishing village. But then it was 'discovered', or perhaps I should say 'rediscovered', by Scandinavian artists in the 1920s. Now it's one of the best-known tourist resorts in Italy."

# POSITANO

All the houses are built on the side of a mountain so steep it could almost be described as a cliff. A multi-coloured, riotous confusion of buildings cling together haphazardly on the hillside; under the intense summer sun their variegated facades shine and shimmer in a dazzling kaleidoscope of colour. White is the predominant colour, luminous and glowing, offset here and there with pastel patches; Pompeii reds and pinks, delicate amber, soft and limpid coral-peach.

Slowly wandering through the maze of narrow lanes, Janet and I examined our surroundings. How was this picture postcard effect achieved? How was it possible that row after row of hotels and houses, each distinctly individual, could blend together to form such a harmonious whole? A painter's delight; the majolica dome of the church; the shutters, blue, green, and faded brown; the terracotta pots and vases, the balconies and courtyards paved with multi-coloured tiles and surrounded by fences and gates of exquisitely worked wrought iron.

And the flowers! A profusion of bougainvillea, purple, pink and crimson, red and white oleanders, drooping mauve wisteria, fragrantly perfumed jasmine. A climbing plant grows rampant - a creeper with enormous showy flowers, striped, mottled, extravagant. Humming insects dart about, butterflies hover and flutter in the still air.

We stopped to visit glamorous hotels, large and small, peered curiously into the entrance foyers of small *pensioni,* investigated tiny, intimate churches. Villas, hotels, restaurants, guest houses, all are positioned to take advantage of the spectacular panorama; windows and terraces look out over the calm, silvery Mediterranean to nearby islands. "How many places have such a view," I said aloud, taking in the rugged coastline, the cliffs plunging down to the sea, the sky of brilliant blue, and the distant island of Capri, flanked by its characteristic giant rocks, *i faraglioni.*

The one and only road traverses the town, but as we soon discovered, most of the houses are nowhere near this road. Access is provided via small laneways, curving, ascending, descending. The route from the main beach to the centre, the most travelled area of the town, is an example, composed entirely of narrow passageways alternating with never-ending flights of steps. At every angle the view is different, providing a constant temptation to stop and admire the outlook. And a good excuse to rest and breathe deeply after the steep and tiring climb. There is no shortage of reasons to stop and linger. Fashion boutiques turn up at strategic intervals along the way; shops sell locally made ceramics and other artefacts. I was particularly enchanted at the little shrines that appear unexpectedly here and there in honour of the Madonna or some patron saint. Never once did I see an altar without freshly picked flowers and lighted candles.

*　　　*　　　*　　　*　　　*

Life in Positano was idyllic. What a joy it was to wake up in the morning to see sunlight streaming through chinks in the louvred shutters. After a long and leisurely breakfast on the enormous terrace of our *pensione*, Janet and I sat lazily sipping coffee. A light breeze gently stirred the leaves of an overhanging tree. A tiny lizard peeped out from behind a flowerpot, before scurrying away on some important lizard business. We watched the buzz of activity on the beach below; beach boys arranging deck-chairs in neat rows; fishermen bringing in the morning's catch; restaurant owners unloading market supplies along the waterfront.

Our original plan had been to spend a few days in Positano, then move on to the island of Ischia. On the second day, however, our program began to change, as, at a cocktail party given by an American couple, I met Stenio, a young Italian lawyer. Little did I know that this fateful meeting would have unforeseen consequences. Nor that my life was about to take off in unexpected directions.

My new friend Stenio kept thinking up fascinating things to do and see. He was determined that we should never be bored. Not a day passed without some new and exciting adventure. Stenio had a

17

boat, a little white runabout with an outboard motor, which was put to good use that year. It chugged along the coast taking us to picturesque beaches, heading off to surrounding inlets where the snorkelling was good, or stopping at sheltered bays for a picnic lunch.

Friends appeared, Riccardo in particular was much in demand as he came with a dashing speedboat. Riccardo conducted a thriving business manufacturing and selling beachwear. Summer was his busy time, but whenever he decided to take a few hours off we were delighted, because he took us further afield. Together we visited villages along the coast and nearby islands, even motoring as far as Capri.

A few miles out to sea, a group of three islands known as '*Li Galli*' or '*Le Sirenuse*' could be glimpsed through the summer haze. These were the islands of the sirens, made famous in Homer's Odyssey. We water-skied around them, amazed at the thought that the sirens of Greek mythology, whose role was to bewitch passing sailors, had allegedly inhabited these islands.

"Some years ago they were bought by Leonide Massine, the famous ballet dancer and choreographer," Stenio told us. "He planned to establish a ballet school and study centre there. We thought it was a great idea, but unfortunately the school never eventuated." After Massine died, another famous Russian dancer, Rudolf Nureyev bought '*Li Galli*'.

Stenio was a great organiser, and regularly gathered his mates to join in whatever activity he'd planned for the day. Janet and I had never been so well looked after; no decisions to make, we just did as we were told. Long lazy days at the beach, swimming, water-skiing, sunbathing, and of course fishing, were a highlight of that first summer. After an early morning start, we collected all we needed for the day's activity, piled into the little boat, and headed out to sea. Several of the group were skilled at spearfishing; they dived from the side and came up with an incredible variety of seafood. When enough fish had been caught, we looked for an isolated beach. Our favourite was one where ruins of a fishing village, deserted hundreds of years ago, lent an air of enchantment to the surroundings.

The men built a barbecue with stones found lying on the beach, the girls collected firewood. Stenio and his friends enjoyed cooking, so we sat in the sun while they cleaned the fish, stuffed them with lemon leaves and parsley, and grilled them on the open fire. Certain varieties were better filleted, they told us, and cooked with tomatoes, garlic, and oregano. I didn't care what recipe they used. It was all the same to me, I knew the end result would be excellent. All we had to do was compliment the cook. "*Buonissimo*, this must be the best meal I've ever eaten." I taught Janet to say this in Italian, and everyone was happy. Now and then local people appeared, looking on curiously, sometimes commenting on the food and cooking. They provided us with potatoes to place in the hot ashes. And they brought good local wine.

Some evenings we prepared a picnic dinner and took it with us. *Prosciutto* with home grown figs. A selection of cheeses, the wonderful *bufalini*, moist white mozzarella made with buffalo milk, and other local specialties produced from sheep or goat's milk. And the salads. Tomatoes in Southern Italy are incredibly sweet. A favourite was *peperonata* - a tasty salad of peppers red and green; roasted, the skin peeled off, the peppers cut in strips and tossed in oil, capers and garlic. We always finished with fruit; delicious juicy peaches, grapes, red and white, melons, tiny sweet pears.

*    *    *    *    *

Stenio told us that the origins of Positano are so lost in antiquity that it's difficult to distinguish between fact and mythology. A popular legend holds that Poseidon, god of the sea, founded Positano as a gift for his beloved, the nymph Pasitea.

"Some historians believe Positano was inhabited by the Greeks and Phoenicians." You could see that Stenio loved explaining the history of his town. "We're situated between Paestum, where the ancient Greeks built magnificent temples, and Pompeii, a living testimony to Imperial Rome. If you stay long enough, I'll take you to visit these places. We know that Romans inhabited Positano, archaeologists have excavated ruins of a grand Roman villa to prove it."

"How fascinating. Do you ever wonder what ancient travellers did here, centuries ago? Do you think they came for a beach holiday like us?" I asked.

"Who knows," Stenio laughed. "We do know that the Emperor Tiberius lived on Capri for many years. According to folklore, he was afraid his courtiers were trying to poison him, so he refused to eat bread made from local flour. Instead, he regularly sent his galley to buy food in Positano. The mill which ground flour in Roman times is still used today. I suppose it's been modernized from time to time over the centuries."

"I certainly hope the mill's been updated since the days of the ancient Romans," I said, even though I suspected this might not be the most diplomatic of comments. And sure enough, Stenio didn't seem at all amused.

Arabic influences are apparent in a large number of buildings. This, we were told, is probably a legacy of the many invasions by Saracen pirates. Fortified towers were built along the coast and in the town as a defence against Saracen raids. Stenio showed us where three such towers still stand in place today, guarding the coastline. I was surprised to hear that quite a few of these historic edifices are privately owned. Strange to think that an ancient fortress can become private property. Several of the impressive Saracen towers have been individually acquired, and we were indeed fortunate to meet one of the present owners. To my delight, he invited us to visit him, offering to show us around. According to Stenio this ancient masterpiece had been beautifully restored; now I'd have the opportunity to see for myself.

With a sense of living in the past, Janet, Stenio and I listened as the clang of the door-knocker resounded through the medieval fortress. A key turned in an enormous lock and the door opened. I felt as though a knight in shining armour might appear in the portal, but all we saw was a maid in a long-sleeved black dress. "Follow me" she said. We stood back as she secured the entrance, then followed her up a spiral staircase set between massive circular stone walls.

We found ourselves in an extensive foyer, where our host, a charming Roman count, welcomed us warmly. He showed us around the castle, which had been refurbished with impeccable taste. Dinner was served at a curved marble table, meticulously sculpted to fit the available space. How this table had been delivered to the site and set in its appropriate place remains a mystery to me.

"I'm so thrilled you invited us to visit your magnificent fort," I said to our host. "How did you manage to restore it so perfectly."

"I was lucky enough to find a brilliant architect," he replied. "As you can imagine, it wasn't easy to adapt living quarters to such an unusual environment. Or to find furnishings to fit circular walls. All the furniture had to be specially designed and custom-made."

The count was an avid collector of ancient weaponry, and had, over many years, accumulated a wonderful array of finely crafted examples. Sadly, a number of invaluable pieces had recently been stolen. He told us about his collection. "If you'd come six months ago I could have shown you some wonderful pieces. I still can't believe I'll never see them again. It was such a shock." He paused, reliving the scene. "I'd spent a few weeks in Rome, and came back to find, to my horror, that thieves had broken into my ancient fortress. I believed the weapons were completely safe here, and I'd taken the extra precaution of employing a local caretaker to watch over the property. But nobody ever expected that burglars would approach from the sea. They came in motor boats, and somehow managed to climb through the small window high up in the walls. They took everything."

"Is there any hope of catching them?" we asked.

"I'm afraid not," said the count. "They're obviously extremely well organised. And resourceful. I get the impression the police haven't the faintest idea where to start."

*     *     *     *     *

On one of our picnics, Stenio and his friends told us about the Saracen invasions, an important part of local mythology. Pirate stories abound. Riccardo was a good story teller, and he spoke excellent English. He gave us this colourful version:

'Saracen pirates had sacked the church and stolen a treasured Byzantine painting of the Virgin Mary known as the 'Black Virgin'. As they were leaving in sailing boats with their prize, a violent storm blew up. The wind blew at gale force, the fury of the sea and torrents of rain threatened to sweep the men and their belongings overboard. Helpless and frantic, the sailors were facing shipwreck when a mysterious voice was heard from above. "*Posa, posa*", it said, 'put me down'. Terrified, the pirates returned the miraculous image. As soon as the Byzantine Madonna was restored to her proper place, the storm abated and all was calm.'

Janet and I later visited the church of Our Lady of the Assumption, which still stands in its original position. The painting rescued from the pirates has pride of place; Mary looks down from the high altar at her faithful flock. The local people have great devotion to this Madonna, and pray to her in times of need. They firmly believe their miraculous 'Black Virgin' will look after her children. Stories are told of her intervention in times of need. Whenever we passed the church, we saw parishioners kneeling reverently before the special image, deep in contemplation and prayer.

Our companions went on with stories of early Positano. During the period of the Maritime Republic of Amalfi, from the ninth to the eleventh centuries, the Amalfi region had been one of the most important mercantile centres of the world, rivalling the celebrated republic of Venice. "Evidence of its days of glory is everywhere in Amalfi. I'll take you there," Stenio promised. "It's

22

fascinating. You can spend hours wandering around the famous arsenal. There are museums with traditional costumes, illustrated manuscripts and so many relics of the past."

Positano was actively involved in commerce with other Mediterranean countries. It can't have been easy; since there was no harbour, galleys had to be pulled up the beach by the townsfolk. Everyone took part.

Riccardo had another tale, this time about a fateful Easter Sunday. On that morning, so the story goes, a ship was about to founder during a wild storm. Hearing the news, the bishop interrupted solemn High Mass, instructing his congregation to hurry to the waterfront and assist the struggling crew. Dressed in splendidly embroidered vestments, he joined in as everyone heaved and strained against the fury of the waves. Finally they succeeded in pulling the ship ashore. Then the people, wet and exhausted, returned to the Church, waiting patiently until their bishop was ready to resume. The delayed but triumphant Easter ceremony included thanksgiving for the safety of ship and crew.

Our friends argued about who should continue the storytelling. Stenio obviously knew a tremendous amount about Positano's history, and loved telling it. His eyes shone with enthusiasm as he remembered details he'd forgotten to mention. There was a slight problem, however, as we had language difficulties. Some of the others spoke good English, so we had many laughs in the telling and interpreting, particularly as they didn't always agree.

The ensuing centuries, we heard, saw a slow but inexorable decline. Wars with neighbouring states, feuds between nobles, a sequence of natural disasters, a plague epidemic, all these and more were to occur before the wheel of fortune turned again. But turn it did, and the seventeenth and eighteenth centuries heralded another period of prosperity. Once again, Positano became a successful trading centre. Ships travelled to the East carrying spices, silks, and precious woods. Splendid baroque villas were built.

"On our way home we'll show you the most magnificent of all," our picnic companions said. After the day's outing they escorted us to a marvellous *palazzo*, painted in the palest of pinks. This beautiful villa had been commissioned by Murat, a general in the French army. Murat and his wife Caroline, Napoleon's sister, had been appointed as viceroys to Naples. We walked into the foyer of the beautiful *palazzo Murat*, converted by the present owners for use as a hotel. Picking up a brochure, I admired sketches depicting the *palazzo* at a time when it served as a haven of peace and repose for Princess Caroline and her consort. The brochure also showed photographs of visiting chamber music ensembles which performed in the courtyard each summer. I could imagine how wonderful it would be to listen to music in such an evocative and enchanting atmosphere.

\*     \*     \*     \*     \*

A few days later, Stenio organised a dinner with the friends we'd met on our first evening. I was delighted to meet them again. And Peter was dying to tell us more about Positano.

"Stenio's told us quite a lot about the history of the place," we said. "We've got as far as the time of Murat."

"I'll take over from there," said Peter. He obviously knew a great deal of local history. "I'll start with the nineteenth century, when the period of prosperity ended with the coming of ocean-going steamships. Any town that lacked harbour facilities was at a disadvantage. Unable to compete as a port, Positano's fortunes declined, its people became poorer; life was hard. It was a time of mass emigration. Large areas of southern Italy were depressed. Work was almost impossible to find. Thousands of people left home, young men, families, sometimes whole communities. Many *Positanesi* joined the stream of emigrants; at one time more than half the population left for America."

"If you want to see evidence of this grim period," he went on, " Have a look at the district known as *la citta morta*, the dead city. That's where the results of this exodus are particularly noticeable. All the inhabitants of *la citta morta* left, many going to New York. Houses and gardens were abandoned, leaving the area desolate. A lot of it has been rebuilt, it's hard to imagine the semi-derelict conditions that existed here in the not so distant past. Happily, things have changed, and fortune now smiles again on this part of southern Italy."

Peter told us that after the First World War, a number of Russian and German artists came to live in Positano. Accustomed to the cold, to ice and snow, their delight at finding this little fishing village can be seen in their paintings. "You can imagine how they felt here," he said. "The Mediterranean sun was hot, the climate mild even in winter, the natural beauty an inspiration. And not only was the environment pleasing, the local people were welcoming and the cost of living low. It's no wonder these northern Europeans believed they had found paradise. I felt that way myself. Painters and writers have been regular visitors ever since."

"Give it a break," Carol yawned. She and Gino had had enough of listening to Peter. "The girls must be getting tired of your history lesson."

We assured her we were really interested in hearing all about their delightful little town. I certainly was, I'm always intrigued to learn the history of places I visit. But the waiter was hovering, waiting to take our order, so we spent some time deciding, or rather listening as the others ordered for us. They knew the specialties of each restaurant. And this was a *trattoria* noted for its seafood. I was happy to let them choose.

Over coffee Gino told us of the difficulties they had in coping with the ever-increasing numbers of tourists.

"The real boom in tourism started after World War II and it's never stopped. Tourist numbers keep growing at an amazing rate, giving us a whole series of unexpected problems. Our village had a population of about three thousand in the 1960s. Now it's regularly inundated with visitors. At the peak of the season we get a dramatic increase in numbers, in mid-August we sometimes have ten to twelve thousand people. The infrastructure is quite inadequate to handle such numbers." Gino made a face.

"The worst problem is the water supply. It's fine in winter, but can't possibly cope with the summer influx. They've imposed restrictions, introduced water rationing. Each area is allotted a quota at certain hours of the day."

"Tell me about it," said Carol. "You can't imagine what it's like," she went on, turning to us. "We fill saucepans and buckets, even the bath, in the short time our water's available. And it's not just the permanent residents, tourists suffer too."

"Another headache is the traffic." Stenio joined in the conversation, with Carol translating here and there. "Traffic control is a major problem. Parking's always been difficult. Finding a spot along the one and only Positano road is no mean feat at the best of times, but during the holiday season it's virtually impossible. I feel so sorry for visitors, happily driving through the town, blissfully unaware they'll find nowhere to stop. They follow the road winding through Positano, frustrated at every turn. All at once they discover, to their dismay, that they've come out at the other end. How disconcerting it must be, having planned a relaxing day at the beach, to suddenly arrive back at the main coastal highway."

"I feel sorry for them too," said Carol. "Even though I wish they'd stop coming and crowding the place. Long term parking's even more difficult" she said, warming to her theme. "Most of the houses and hotels aren't on the road, so finding a garage is a real problem for everyone, whether they're a tenant, a guest, or someone who lives here. There's a thriving business providing parking facilities, but permits to build large car parks are restricted by lack of available space."

"Everyone complains about how they manage the traffic," interrupted Gino. "But I've always felt secretly pleased that thousands of people can't park. At least it limits expansion. They can't spoil Positano too much."

26

"I couldn't agree more," said Stenio.  "We *Positanesi* criticise our city council and how they organise the traffic.  But we should give credit to the city fathers.  They've done all they can to keep Positano intact."

# SEA URCHINS

On one of our fishing excursions I was introduced to a local delicacy. *Ricci di mare,* sea-urchins, are highly prized as a luxury equivalent to oysters. Our friends had been diving for some time when one of the group surfaced in great excitement. Everyone crowded around, thrilled at his catch. When I saw what was causing all the fuss, I was singularly unimpressed. He stood clutching half a dozen small round objects covered with sharp, glistening spines. Menacing looking protuberances, brownish purple in colour, the spines moved slowly backwards and forwards in a continual motion.

During my days as a student I'd learned about sea-urchins. I remembered that they were classified as echinoderms, a phylum of marine animals that includes starfish, brittle stars and sea-cucumbers. Why this piece of information remained in my mind I can't imagine, it was certainly quite irrelevant to my life at the time. And yet, my first encounter with Mediterranean *ricci* triggered this unexpected response; facts crammed before a Zoology examination years ago and long forgotten, re-emerged from some hidden recess where they'd been stored.

At certain times during their life cycle, sea-urchins produce eggs. The mass of eggs, or roe, is highly coveted by local connoisseurs. Although collecting the prickly marine animals is difficult, it's just the beginning. Getting at the eggs is no easy matter; they are protected inside an ovoid membrane, which in turn is covered with dozens of threatening spines. Breaking the membrane and prying open the shell is quite a tricky operation, the sharp points can cause considerable damage. I noticed that many of our new friends had nasty lumps on their hands where a point had penetrated the skin. Apparently once the tip becomes embedded under the skin, it breaks off and can only be removed surgically. Despite this daunting prospect, the determination to savour sea-urchin antipasto seems to remain unaltered.

For a time I resisted all offers. I had absolutely no desire to eat any part of such a singularly unappealing species of marine life.

Eventually I realised my attitude was ungracious, and I felt I should at least taste a tiny morsel. Considering the difficulty involved in its preparation, the roe must be really special. Once I'd been persuaded to try the fleshy orange-yellow eggs, I understood my companions' enthusiasm. I learned to look forward to the succulent delicacy, with its intense aroma and distinct flavour. Eaten with lemon juice and fresh crisp bread, *ricci* taste a little like oysters, or perhaps caviar, with that tangy special flavour characteristic of the sea.

*     *     *     *     *

Summer in Positano is the period of *feste*. Each district has its own Church and patron saint, so that one celebration blends into the next. Almost every weekend brings a feast-day dedicated to one or other local saint. Usually the *festa* starts with a procession, the Madonna or saint is mounted on a stand decked with flowers and holy pictures and carried at shoulder height by six or eight men. The priest follows, next come altar boys in white cassocks, then young girls in pairs, 'Children of Mary', dressed in white with blue ribbons around their necks. Behind the children come the locals, whoever has the time and inclination takes part. Bringing up the rear is a brass band. The musicians play a mixture of Church music and well-known themes from Italian opera, usually stirring music by Verdi. The players wear dark suits. I'm sure they must feel uncomfortably hot, as the procession route is hilly and the weather extremely warm. Stalls selling food, sweets, ice cream, holy pictures, and a variety of assorted merchandise pop up here and there along the route. At night everyone awaits the grand finale. I loved the atmosphere of excitement, the air of hushed expectation. And then the joyful exclamations, the cheers as spectacular fireworks shoot up to illuminate the sky for miles around.

One of our friends at this time was an English girl called Diana, who by a strange coincidence, was also a biologist. She'd worked for five years in Africa, but then, wanting a complete change, had come to Positano as a nanny. Her employers, an American actor and his wife, had moved on and no longer required her services. But Diana stayed. Currently she was romantically involved with the owner of one of the beach restaurants, much to the horror of his mother. Mamma wanted her son to marry a local girl who'd help in the restaurant and produce lots of children. Whenever she saw Diana she swore at her. We couldn't follow the colourful language, but the meaning was crystal clear. "Get lost," she was saying. If there was anything at hand to throw, for example a chair, she threw it at her son's companion. Diana quickly learned to keep out of Mamma's way.

A memorable occasion was the feast of *San Michele*. Diana's boyfriend was called Michele, so of course a celebration was called for. Stenio and I were invited to a special dinner with many bottles of French champagne. Michele, who was very Latin in temperament, cried for joy.

"It's wonderful to be back in Positano," he kept repeating. "I spent all last year working at a restaurant in London, but I never got to understand the British. I never felt at home in England, everyone's so reserved. Now I'm just so happy." And he opened another bottle of French champagne.

*    *    *    *    *

It came as a shock to realise that three weeks had passed. We'd planned to spend a month in Italy, and that month was rapidly drawing to a close. Neither of us wanted to leave. Janet had no choice, she had to go back to work. But I had no such obligation, I'd completed my current research program and had as yet no further work commitment. And so, while Janet dutifully returned to London, I stayed on. I was having a wonderful time, I hadn't been so happy for years.

Stenio wanted me to stay. It was amazing, considering that we had no common language, how well we managed to communicate. Stenio had a sense of intuition which was uncanny, an ability to guess what people were thinking. He seemed to know what I was going to say long before I tried to find the words. He had a funny, quirky sense of humour and an infectious enthusiasm for life and people. And a fervent belief that Positano was *paradiso*. "Why would you want to leave me in *paradiso* and go back to cold old London," he kept saying. I didn't need much convincing.

With Janet gone, it was time to move out of the *pensione* and look for a different type of accommodation. I hoped to find a small flat or apartment, but this was not an available option. Instead, I discovered I could rent a room in an old house; an enormous room, which, as I had come to expect, opened onto a terrace with a magnificent view. The most striking feature was a floor of hand painted tiles - the tiles were very old, said to be from the seventeenth century. The whole house was in need of repair, I noticed large cracks in the walls, but the owner had renovated a few rooms.

My new home was perfect for a Mediterranean sojourn. The essentials were there - a bar refrigerator, basic cooking facilities, and a reasonable bathroom. Apart from such necessary features, my new abode had all the characteristics of another, older world. Diana moved into a similar room next to mine. This suited us both. Each morning we had breakfast together, then sat idly chatting while we waited to see what the day would bring.

*      *      *      *      *

Sometimes Stenio took me to visit little villages high up in the mountains. The only way to get there was on foot; we trudged up a pathway consisting of thousands of steps. These villages had remained isolated over the centuries; the influence of early Arab invasions could still be detected in the present-day communities, both in their features and their culture.

Directly above Positano, nestled in the mountains, is the village of Montepertuso. The little village is perched halfway up a rather odd-looking mountain. Just below the summit an enormous hole extends right through the mountain peak. It seems to have been punched out, from one side to the other, by a giant hand. In local dialect, *pertuso* signifies hole, hence the derivation of the name *Montepertuso*. A colourful legend is associated with this mountain and its strange hole. The village people enjoy their folklore, and delight in giving newcomers an account of how the hole came to be.

'One day', the story goes, 'the devil was pursuing the Madonna. She ran and ran, as fast as she could go, but the devil was right behind her. After a long, long chase, the Madonna became very tired, and Satan started to gain ground. He was catching up fast, almost within reach, when, suddenly, a hole miraculously opened in the cliff. The Madonna slipped through the opening, the devil was left behind. And that's how the village acquired its name'.

About twenty to thirty families make up the population of Montepertuso. These families have lived on the mountain for centuries. The surrounding countryside, rocky and barren, has not made their lives easy. Goods had to be brought up the mountain by mule, or on the backs of hardy men climbing up and down the innumerable steps. For years the villagers had pleaded with local government; a road up the mountain was badly needed.

But the luxury of a road was not available, and I always arrived looking hot and bothered. The Montepertusans, ever hospitable, invariably insisted we have a meal with them. For special occasions they sacrificed a few precious chickens from their flocks. Roasted on an open fire, accompanied by salads including every conceivable vegetable, these meals were very special. After dinner the local people improvised dances and songs around the fire. Sometimes the children were persuaded to dance for us.

Musical accompaniment was provided by the men. Among the musicians I recognized the now familiar face of the Positano postman. He was quite a character, a man who took his job very seriously. Determined to deliver each item of mail in person, he developed an uncanny ability to find his quarry. I had frequently been surprised to see our friendly postman appear with a letter addressed to me. Somehow he always managed to find me, handing over my mail at the beach, in a bar, or wherever I happened to be. His cheerful, weather-beaten face was always welcome. And here he was, playing the tambourine with great enthusiasm.

Another of the musicians played a strange instrument I'd never seen before. Known as a Jew's harp, it consisted of a small lute-shaped iron frame open at one end, in which a single flexible strip of steel vibrated. Holding the frame between his teeth, the player plucked at the strip with his finger, producing a rhythmic, resonant twang. This simple instrument, in Italian *scacciapensieri*, chase the worries away, has quite a history, having been known throughout Europe and Asia as far back as the twelfth century. It seems the name Jew's Harp is an anomaly; it's not a harp, nor has any evidence of its use by Jews been traced.

Nino, a virtuoso accordion player, completed the group. Not only did Nino play his accordion with infectious enjoyment, he also provided the vocal accompaniment. His slightly gravelly voice was well-suited to a type of music unlike anything I'd previously heard. Although the words were in local dialect, the singing, with its distinctly Arabic intonation, was reminiscent of the Middle East.

Among the characters who lived on the mountain, Concetta was one of the most intriguing. She was an old lady, exactly how old no-one could be sure. There were no records, and Concetta didn't know, nor did she care. She was always laughing, showing a missing front tooth and quite a few gaps elsewhere.

.      "I can exorcise devils," she told us, "I'll show you how I do it. Not today, though, I have to be feeling right."

Each time we asked her to demonstrate her skills, she was overcome by shyness. All she could do was giggle. So I never saw her perform an exorcism. Friendly and hospitable, Concetta always invited us to eat at her home. She proudly offered milk fresh from her cow, which was kept in a shed next to her house. I had a little trouble with the idea of drinking unpasteurised milk, but I couldn't hurt her feelings. Unfortunately Concetta spoke only dialect. My Italian was still pretty basic and my understanding of Neapolitan dialect non-existent, so everything had to be translated for my benefit. I regretted this, I would have enjoyed the opportunity to learn about the customs and traditions that had shaped Concetta's life.

A trip to Montepertuso was always a fascinating event. But you had to be feeling fit; it was an exhausting excursion. We never undertook the climb before late afternoon, when the sun had lost some of its heat. Once on our way, we were well rewarded. The scenery *en route* was spectacular, the higher we climbed, the more the view expanded. Over terraces and rocky tracks, past scraggy olive trees and abandoned, derelict stone houses. Finally we arrived at the village square, to watch the sun set over the mountain, transforming the rocky, arid terrain into a vivid blaze of crimson.

\*      \*      \*      \*      \*

One afternoon we climbed up two thousand, eight hundred steps to another mountain village. We were accompanied by a couple from Rome; Helen was Australian, her husband Marco Italian. I'd met them some years earlier, on my previous visit to Rome, and had come across them again in Positano, where they were spending a weeks holiday. We'd had several enjoyable evenings together and had become good friends.

Nocelle is a tiny village built into a cliff even higher than Montepertuso. The view of the mountain ranges is grander and more majestic, the rooftops of Positano more remote, and the little islands dotted in the sea blend into the faraway twin rocks of Capri, shadows outlined against a distant skyline. The heat haze of summer plays strange tricks, islands appear and disappear elusively on the still mirror-like surface of the Mediterranean.

The village comprises a tiny church with its characteristic steeple, a central *piazza*, a restaurant, and maybe a dozen houses. Friendly dogs sniff at approaching visitors, chickens wander across the path, children gaze in astonishment at strangers. Stenio was a regular visitor, and had long been a good friend to the village people, so we were given a warm welcome. Introduced to the villagers, many of whom came to take a peek at the unexpected visitors, we were complimented on our stamina and endurance. Nocelle was not on the agenda of the average tourist; visitors adventurous enough to undertake the marathon climb were rare.

It was time to order a well-deserved meal. We made our way to the restaurant, owned by a delightful family, and were conducted to a table on the panoramic balcony. The wife was a short, determined-looking woman with the deepest voice I've ever heard; her husband, tall and thin, had a wonderful smile which lit up his whole face. A serious and thoughtful man, he seldom had reason to smile. It can't have been easy to provide for a growing family. Several children emerged from the kitchen, shy as little fauns. A tiny girl carefully carried a heavy jug filled with home-brewed wine, her two brothers brought platters of food so large their hands could hardly hold them. Serious little faces concentrated on their allotted tasks.

One of the specialties of Nocelle is onion omelette, an omelette so delicious that my mouth waters whenever I think of it. Although I have the recipe and make it occasionally, the flavour is never as good. Part of the secret lies in the fat used to fry the onions. I don't have any *sugna*. Much used in this part of the world, *sugna* is a home-made lard. It's produced by melting down diced pork fat together with an onion to add flavour.

Pork was available only in winter; pigs were not slaughtered in summer. I imagine that, before the arrival of refrigeration, a fatty meat like pork may well have been a health hazard during the hot summer months. For generations, the women of the mountain villages had prepared enough *sugna* in winter to last throughout the year. Not only was it an essential cooking ingredient, they also spread it on bread, no doubt terribly bad for the cholesterol level. But what a delicious taste. And how the children loved it.

The *Nocellesi* produce a dried brown bread, rock hard, known as *biscotto*, biscuit. This rock-like bread is commonly soaked in water and eaten when soft. But there was a better method, I discovered. Stenio always ordered a salad of home grown tomatoes and dipped his *biscotto* in the salad dressing. Soaked in this mixture of local olive oil, vinegar, and masses of basil, it absorbed the aromas of Nocelle.

Fruit is served after each meal. Both green and red grapes are grown nearby; both are excellent. My favourite is a red grape, *uva fragola,* with a delicate taste reminiscent of strawberries. Peaches are fragrant and juicy; pears and persimmons, strawberries and berry fruits all have their season. No meal is complete without a strong espresso coffee.

After we'd eaten our fill and drunk our share of wine, we were feeling pleasantly relaxed and content with the world. Suddenly an unexpected storm blew up. It began to rain heavily, a veritable torrential downpour. The two thousand eight hundred steps resembled a waterfall, and it was soon apparent that we couldn't possibly go down that evening. We'd have to stay the night on the mountain. This caused consternation, the people of Nocelle were not equipped for overnight visitors. There were hurried whispered consultations. Finally a room was found, an enormous room containing four beds. The first, a double bed, was for our friends the married couple. Two single beds had been arranged side by side; one was exceptionally high, the other very low. They really were looking after us, *l'avvocato* and me.

Italians use titles as a matter of course. A schoolteacher is known as *professore,* a writer *scrittore,* a doctor *dottore,* in fact the term *dottore* refers to anyone with a university degree. So Stenio, a lawyer, was known as *l'avvocato.* People said "*Buon giorno avvocato",* or, since the locals spoke dialect, it was more likely to be "*Ciao avvocà.*"

*    *    *    *    *

To my surprise, Stenio loved inviting friends to dinner, he really enjoyed improvising and preparing. I was unused to men interested in cooking, but I soon discovered that food was a quintessential factor of Italian life, a favourite topic of conversation. They talked about it for hours on end; mouth-watering descriptions of what they'd eaten yesterday, what they might cook tomorrow, as well as the merits of the current meal. The men in particular seemed to derive enormous satisfaction from planning and cooking meals.

In the evenings we had little difficulty finding interesting dinner companions. We often had dinner with Carol and Gino. Sometimes in the evening they cooked spaghetti at home and invited us to join them, but generally we ate at one of the many restaurants. Carol had been living in Positano for about three months. She was good company. Having grown up in Hawaii she was a champion surfer, and told us lots of stories about the exotic life of Honolulu. Now she was happily ensconced in Positano with no apparent plans to leave.

What unusual people we met. There was Danielle, an actress and singer who'd grown up in Northern France, spent her youth in Paris, and later moved to Vienna, where she performed in operetta. I'd heard about her long before we met; it was said she embodied *la belle epoque*, that golden age of music, dance and fashion in pre-war Paris. Everybody talked about Danielle, everyone liked her. It was easy to see why, she was always laughing, and had a wonderful ability to communicate. When in the right mood, well dined and wined, Danielle could sometimes be prevailed upon to perform one of the songs from her repertoire. We loved to hear this echo from the past, recalling an era most of us knew only from the cinema.

We had German friends who were great hikers, travelling for miles into the surrounding countryside. They knew more about the local surroundings than did most *Positanesi*. Their annual holiday regularly coincided with Harry and Caroline, a couple from Tennessee now based in Paris. Harry was a writer, very serious and disciplined. Every morning he set his alarm for six o'clock. He got up immediately, and worked at his writing until eleven. The rest of the day was free.

"This was how Hemingway planned his days," Harry told us. "A routine good enough for Hemingway is good enough for me."

I'm terrified to move in the morning," Caroline whispered. "I might destroy his concentration." And she really meant it.

I felt sorry for her, having to creep around the house while Harry meditated on his latest novel. She was a delightful person, with a bubbling personality and wonderful sense of humour. When Harry was busy with his writing I sometimes played tennis with Caroline on the one and only tennis court in Positano. This suited us both, I'd been used to playing tennis regularly in Australia. We looked forward to our games together. We all got on well, Stenio and I often accompanied the two couples to surrounding places of interest.

Our evenings were multi-national. Dinner became associated with a mixture of people and languages, generally English, Italian and German, but other nationalities were included. I spoke a little German, but with lack of practice it had become rather halting. Now, in this new phase of my life, my German began to improve. The complications of switching from English to Italian or German in rapid succession, and of speaking the appropriate language at the correct moment made for considerable confusion, but also much hilarity.

Sometimes we were invited to cocktail parties given by one or other resident artist. Many of these artists held exhibitions during the year in Rome, Paris, or other large metropolis. But in summer, at the height of the tourist season, they had showings to display recent work and hopefully find buyers. These were international occasions, and I met fascinating people from all over the world. There were German art patrons, British connoisseurs, French writers, and American jet-setters. I wandered from group to group, practising my language skills and trying to appear as though I were part of the proceedings and had long been accustomed to this way of life. I'm not sure I always succeeded.

Among the artistic group at these gatherings I frequently encountered Gigi, a beautiful Swiss woman in her late thirties, and her partner, a twenty year old Russian painter. She was his patron and muse; I watched, fascinated, as she stood gazing at his paintings, then said with a sigh, "I can't believe you can create such beauty, how wonderful to have such a gift." She was right, of course, he did have great talent, and he obviously loved basking in her admiration. The young Russian was becoming well-known in the art world, and they had great plans. I felt concerned for Gigi, I hoped he wouldn't move on once he'd achieved success.

This milieu was a learning experience for me, a world I'd never experienced.

*     *     *     *     *

Stenio was the only lawyer in Positano. At that time, a lawyer was expected to combine the functions of priest, family counsellor, and financial adviser. People came to find him at all hours of the day or night, office hours were made to be ignored. Often while we were at the beach or having dinner in a restaurant, clients would arrive with their problems. Or they would stop him in the middle of the street and ask his advice. Since many local restaurant owners were his clients we were treated royally, the waiters had obviously been told to serve *l'avvocato* well.

His family had a dream house, partially rebuilt on ruins hundreds of years old; a villa with trees growing through the terrace, with courtyards and gardens, exotic trees and flowers. Urns and amphorae collected from ancient shipwrecks stood leaning against the remains of old stone walls. Builders had been restoring this villa for ten years, but I formed a distinct impression that no-one really wanted it finished. It was a sort of dream where they went in the evenings to sit on the terrace, admire the outlook and listen to music. On my first visit, as if by magic, the music of Beethoven played softly in the background, adding to the general air of unreality. Of course I realised that someone had carefully concealed a tape recorder, but somehow it seemed entirely appropriate. All I could say was *"Complimenti, l'idea è meravigliosa,"* the idea's great.

Although he had grown up in Positano, and loved the place with a passion, Stenio, was not a typical *Positanese*. With fair curly hair and light blue eyes he certainly didn't look like a southern Italian. In fact his mother had come from Poland. He didn't care about appearances; smart, elegant dressing was not his style; he was natural, suntanned and casual. But he did share the prevailing philosophy, the belief held by many, but not all *Positanesi*. In general terms this amounted to a rejection of the commonly accepted work ethic. "Why work oneself to death to make money?" was a comment I heard frequently. "There's more to life than work. There must be time for the good things; for reading, for listening to music, and above all, for enjoying the privilege of living in a place as beautiful as Positano."

*     *     *     *     *

I was looking tanned, fit, and healthy. This was a considerable change after a year spent in England, and contributed to my sense of well-being. Living in Italy is good for the ego; Italians like to flatter people and make a habit of telling them what they wish to hear. My Italian in those first months was probably atrocious, but whenever I went into a shop and said a few words someone would say, '*brava, signorina*', how clever you are, young lady. With such encouraging comments I couldn't help feeling a great success.

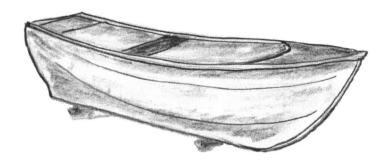

# FAMILY

Stenio's mother Rita (an Italianized version of her name) was a Polish dentist. She had studied and done her training in Poland. Having completed her course and graduated as a qualified dental practitioner, Rita felt she deserved a holiday. By a strange quirk of fate, her sister and brother-in-law, both industrial chemists, were working at a research institute in Naples. Making this her first stop, Rita arrived in sunny Italy. From Naples she visited Positano, loved the place, and proceeded to set up a dental practice. In those days the range of available dental equipment was limited; she possessed a hand drill and little else. Her arrival caused great consternation. The *Positanesi* had never seen a woman dentist, let alone visited one.

Rita spoke five languages, including Russian and French. Her linguistic skills did not include English, which she considered *bruttissima*, most unattractive, and flatly refused to learn. This aversion to English made things a little difficult for me, but we managed to communicate in German. She was a great talker, and as I understood German better than I spoke it, we got along reasonably well.

Her husband, Raffaele, was a painter, sculptor and dreamer. He was a most unusual and interesting person, quite unlike anyone I'd ever met. He loved nature and all things beautiful; his interests, however, did not extend to people. Raffaele would sit for hours in the courtyard of the beautiful unfinished house, gazing into space or meditating. He practised yoga, believed in Buddhism and reincarnation, played the violin - being self taught, his playing did not sound as he may have wished, but this didn't worry him at all. He also dabbled in prose and poetry, and had written works ranging from fairy tales to philosophy.

Raffaele was, I believe, a gifted and extremely versatile artist. His paintings, particularly the land and seascapes of Positano, are filled with light. As a young couple, Rita and Raffaele spent several years living in a tiny Calabrian village. Rita practised dentistry while Raffaele painted. During this period, he specialised in portraiture, creating striking charcoal sketches of peasant women. In later years, he preferred to indulge his love of nature, depicting exquisite flowers and birds in a range of media; water colours, oils, pastels, gouaches.

Although he continued to paint all his life, at some stage Raffaele decided to try his hand at sculpture. As with the paintings, his consuming passion was the portrayal of birds, animals and fish. Developing a highly specialised technique, his first step was to produce a model in wax. Next he made a mould from the wax model, then cast the sculpture in silver or bronze. To Raffaele, these castings were rough forms to be brought to life by etching, in meticulous detail, the individual features he wished to delineate. At times I looked on as he worked, admiring the skill and dedication with which he engraved incredibly fine lines until, under his touch, a tiny silver bird seemed ready to leave the studio and fly off into the real world.

When Raffaele wanted to sketch a certain animal, he would sit for hours, sometimes days, observing the creature and analysing its movements. Ideally, he preferred to study its activities in a natural environment. This was not always possible, however. An alternative was the Rome zoo, where he passed extended periods of time watching a particular animal; its habits, the way it held its head, how the muscles flexed. These meticulous observations served him well. So lifelike were Raffaele's creatures that they seemed to contain a latent energy, as if impatiently waiting to leap out of their confining metal body and come to life.

Raffaele was a striking-looking man with white hair, a small trim beard, and dark, expressive eyes. When working at home he wore old clothes, and usually thongs, but when he went to visit clients or sell his paintings, he dressed accordingly. Suitably attired in a black and white checked overcoat, a monocle suspended on a chain round his neck, a cane walking stick in hand, he was transformed. How distinguished and elegant he looked when he chose to make the effort.

Raffaele's indifference to, and lack of tolerance for anyone outside his immediate family led him to become something of a recluse. He flatly refused to participate in any form of social life. This caused untold complications, particularly in view of the fact that his wife was a sociable person who enjoyed entertaining. There were endless arguments which rarely led to a satisfactory conclusion. Within the family circle, however, he encouraged discussions on a wide range of topics, and mealtimes were animated and lively.

Every Sunday, Stenio's father and brother Elio set off at four in the morning to go fishing. In mid-afternoon, they invited us to a late luncheon lasting four hours or more. We were in for a long session of eating and drinking; I learned to expect a minimum of six courses, all based on the day's catch. The men prepared the fish, to the accompaniment of heated arguments about how to cook each particular species. Usually we started with *spaghetti alle vongole;* a succession of courses followed. Depending on its size and characteristics, the fish could be braised with tomatoes and herbs, dipped in flour and fried, cooked in wine, or grilled on an open fire. This culinary feast was accompanied by crusty fresh bread, home grown lettuce and rocket, and of course, plenty of wine.

The men considered seafood preparation their prerogative, but when it came to the normal evening meal, women were expected, as in most parts of the world, to do the cooking. Rita had a hard time satisfying her critical and discerning men. Having grown up in Poland, her culinary repertoire differed from the average Italian cuisine. Accustomed to criticism, she coped well with the comments her husband and sons invariably made. "There's not enough salt. Why do you cook with water instead of oil? Did you forget the garlic?" But she gave as good as she got.

"Do you really have to open another bottle? You had far too much last night." The subject of wine was always a cause for heated debate. Raffaele enjoyed his wine, being particularly partial to a glass or two of a good red with his dinner.

The dining room was pleasant and comfortable, the table and chairs bright yellow; the whitewashed walls, as might be expected in the home of an artist, well supplied with paintings. Rita had an endless range of white table cloths. These were, I soon discovered, a daily source of drama. As soon as we all gathered around the table, Raffaele started to pour wine. He handled the bottle with a flourish, regularly managing to spill a few drops with each glass.

"Look what you've done, Raffaele," Rita said crossly, grabbing the salt-cellar. Carefully and methodically, she rubbed salt into the stain spreading around each drop of red wine. He continued to eat and pour wine, she continued the salt treatment. Table talk was constantly interrupted, no matter what the topic of conversation. Since this situation occurred at every meal, it was accepted as part of the daily routine, a habit we all ignored. No-one even noticed the spotty tablecloth.

One memorable evening, as we were sitting down to a dinner of roast chicken, Rita noticed that the salt-cellar was nearly empty. Off she went to the kitchen to find a container of salt. Bringing it to the table, she started to refill the salt-cellar. All of a sudden, the top came off the container. Out flowed the salt; a stream of tiny white crystals accumulating to form a mound on the white tablecloth. Quick as a flash, Raffaele grabbed the bottle of red wine, and, with a satisfied gleam in his eye, poured a generous amount on top of the heap of salt.

*    *    *    *    *

To me, the family were warm and welcoming. They did all they could to make me feel at home, and showed great interest in my daily activities. Early in my stay, while I was still in the throes of making up my mind whether to stay or leave, I decided to buy a smart new outfit. Off I went in search of a suit. Heaven only knows why, Positano was such an informal place. After much thought, I determined to have a skirt and matching jacket made in pale cream corduroy, a fashionable fabric at the time. All the Bella family took an interest in these sartorial proceedings; the suit was duly ordered and made. It looked extremely smart. I proudly wore it next time I was invited to dinner. As luck would have it, on this particular evening, Rita had chosen to pick pomegranates from the tree in their

44

garden, and extract juice from the seeds. The pomegranate is reddish-purple in colour, and its juice is a vivid shade of purple. Of course, I managed to spill a few drops on my brand new pale cream skirt, producing a dramatic stain impossible to remove. What a performance; my soiled skirt caused a major drama. Suggestions and cleaning methods were made by all concerned. Eventually, after much discussion, the dressmaker was prevailed upon to change one panel of the skirt. The stained section was discarded. I don't believe I ever had the courage to wear the offending suit again.

*     *     *     *     *

It was hard to keep track of all the relatives of the Bella family. A few lived in Positano, others in towns along the Amalfi coast. An uncle had emigrated to America with his wife and family. Periodically Carmela, a maiden aunt who knew all about the family history, would appear. Carmela was very religious, and remembered everybody's name-day. A name-day represents the feast of the saint after whom the person is named. Many consider it more important than a birthday. I happened to be at lunch with Stenio's parents one day when Carmela arrived with an enormous cake. Everyone looked surprised, Carmela didn't often call in unexpectedly. "Why the cake?" asked Rita.

Carmela was shocked. "But today is the feast of San Raffaele. I can't believe I'm the only one in the whole family who remembers this day. It's so special for Raffaele." I gathered the same thing happened each year, but Carmela never became reconciled to Raffaele's indifference to his patron saint. Nor could she accept that his wife and children made no effort to celebrate.

Rita's sister, Sofia, who had been the first member of the Polish family to visit southern Italy, lived in Paris. She was a truly remarkable person. Having been a leader of the Communist party in Paris, she had a series of fascinating stories to tell, and an extremely interesting circle of friends. Her life had been tragic. During World War II, both she and her husband had been active in the French resistance. Her husband was captured and killed by the Germans. Shortly afterwards, their only daughter disappeared without trace

45

while skiing in Switzerland. Sofia had somehow come to terms with her life and was a charming, positive and interesting woman with a delightful sense of humour. I looked forward to her visits.

# DECISION

As the weeks passed I kept delaying my departure. One day blended smoothly into the next without any feelings of stress, or of the pressures that were part and parcel of the life I'd been leading. There was no routine, no deadlines to meet, no jobs that should have been completed yesterday. The major problems were deciding what to eat, where to swim, when to shower, what to wear. It took hours to make such decisions. There seemed to be something in the air which made it impossible to do anything, an immense effort was required to undertake the most simple task, like writing a letter or ironing a shirt. Even finding time for my few domestic chores was difficult.

Occasionally I did something active; one day I visited the Roman ruins at Pompeii, a drive of about two hours. Recovering from such a colossal effort took quite some time. I felt like one of the mythological Greeks who went to an exotic island and stayed on and on. Every day I changed my mind, one day I packed up to go, the next I decided to stay. Positano was like a drug, it seemed impossible to leave.

What was I doing here anyway? I'd grown up in Melbourne, studied Biological Science at Melbourne University, and started my career in Immunology at the Walter and Eliza Hall Institute. When, by a stroke of luck, I was offered a job at the National Institute for Medical Research at Mill Hill, London, I'd happily packed my bags and left for Europe, intending to do further study and gain experience in my chosen field.

This Italian holiday had come an appropriate moment. I'd been in London for over a year, and was fast approaching a moment of decision. I had several available options and was in a quandary, procrastinating, fully aware that I was at one of those crossroads that occur occasionally in life. It was extremely important that I make a wise choice.

I could go to New York; I'd been offered a position at Columbia University to continue working on my current project. I could stay in London. An English colleague had invited me to set up a tissue culture laboratory at a centre for biological research which was due to open shortly. I felt flattered to be asked, I knew there was great demand for places at this new institute. Finally, I could go home to Australia; my mother had been anxiously trying to persuade me to return for some time.

The institute where I worked was most prestigious. Peter Medawar, the director, was a Nobel prize winner, and his associates were highly regarded in the world of medical research. Young medical graduates and scientists came from many countries to spend a year or two with these luminaries. I appreciated the experience of being in such an intellectually stimulating environment, I'd learned a lot and met some exceptional people. However I was beginning to wonder whether this milieu was what I wanted, whether I was in fact suited to a scientific career. Was this the world for me? What did I want out of life? I started to ask myself a series of questions. When making a completely honest analysis of the situation, I had to admit that my Italian holiday had been in part a delaying tactic, an excuse to defer professional decision-making. Meeting Stenio had now added another dimension to the situation.

The world of research was becoming increasingly remote and unappealing. I didn't relish the thought of another year in London, while the idea of New York appeared vaguely threatening. Life in a big city held little attraction compared to the simple life to which I was becoming accustomed. I received word that a paper I'd submitted to an American Journal had been accepted for publication. The editors requested minor alterations. It proved amazingly difficult to sit down and concentrate on rewording a small part of a scientific paper. I spent days in Stenio's office with a typewriter in front of me before I managed to make the relatively minor adjustments required.

The days and weeks went by and in no time I found that summer had turned into autumn, the evenings were becoming cooler, and tourists were beginning to thin out. With less tourists around, the *Positanesi* made more fuss of Diana and me. I realized, however, that I couldn't stay on much longer without some definite plan. Stenio and I had long discussions.

"You can't leave now," he said. "There are so many beautiful places I have to show you. And friends I want you to meet." His enthusiasm was infectious. He kept talking about future events, all of which seemed to include me.

Should I stay or go? Did he really want me to stay? And for how long? What if I stayed for ever?

Trying to determine my immediate future, I resolved to go to Rome for a few days. Maybe it would be easier to think clearly if I got away from Stenio and Positano. I arrived in Rome without having made any arrangements, only to find that three international congresses had filled most of the hotels, and I had considerable trouble finding a room.

Fortunately, Helen and Marco came to my rescue. I stayed with them for a few days, telling them about my problems, my indecision, and indirectly asking their advice.

"Why do you consider spending time in Positano to be wasting your life?" said Helen. "You might equally well waste a year in New York. And I bet you wouldn't be as happy as you are now."

Marco couldn't understand my hesitation. He was in no doubt what he'd do.

"I don't like giving advice" he said. "But I can assure you that after a year in New York you'll feel five years older. But if you stay in Positano for a year you'll not only feel five years younger, you'll look it too."

"I feel so guilty doing nothing all day." I said doubtfully.

"For heaven's sake," Marco was exasperated. "Haven't you got any interests? Find something to do. Why don't you learn Sanskrit?"

Now I had the opportunity to get to know some of my distant cousins. Warm and welcoming, these new-found relatives were intrigued to hear that their recently discovered Australian cousin had become romantically involved with an Italian. Warning me about life in southern Italy, they cautioned. "Go back to Positano by all means, but be sure you go without any illusions."

And go back I did. Returning to Positano, I was welcomed by the locals like the prodigal son (or daughter). In a small town, where everyone knows his neighbour's business, my leaving and subsequent reappearance had been duly noted. For me this was one of the charms of Positano; I'd always lived in a big city, and the warmth and friendliness of a small Italian town was most appealing. And the people, warm and extroverted, made me feel part of an enormous family circle.

I started to toss around in my mind various available work possibilities should I decide to stay. Maybe I could:
- give private English lessons.
- teach English at the School for Tourism in nearby Amalfi - a school set up to train tourist guides and hotel staff.
- open a shop selling exotic things.
- work at a biological institute in Naples.
- open a laboratory to provide pathology tests.

As a start, I began giving English lessons to Stenio's brother Elio, and Italian lessons to Diana. My Italian had improved, and I was trying to extend my vocabulary and grammar. Stenio and I exchanged lessons, I tutored him in English; he returned the favour in Italian.

Although life in Positano seemed idyllic, there appeared, even in those early stages, small indications that someone accustomed to living in a modern city might find certain things irritating. For example, if I went to a bank to make the most simple inquiry, I was commonly confronted with a blank stare, or with confusing information. If I went to two banks and asked the same question, the odds on getting a similar answer in both were low.

And, having extolled the virtues of small town life, where everybody knew your business, I was beginning to realize that this situation was not always congenial.

A more immediate decision was required about my flat in London. Janet was waiting for me to return and I was still paying my share of the rent. I also had a car in Hampstead standing idly waiting. In early October I received a cable from my colleague in London asking when I was planning to start the tissue culture laboratory. This had been one of my career options. The telegram threw me into a state of panic. What should I do? Would I ever make up my mind?

What if I did decide to stay? Could I be happy here? It certainly was a wonderful, exhilarating place to live. But then I'd wake up wondering what I was thinking of. What was I doing in this southern Italian village, so small but so exotic? I'd always thought of myself as a sensible person, practical, pragmatic, not given to impulsive decisions. A city girl with a promising career. Yet here I was, seriously considering such a radical and dramatic change in lifestyle.

A few more weeks passed and I was still dithering. The weather was changing, autumn was fast advancing towards winter, and it became apparent that, with all my winter clothes in London, I might soon freeze to death. Stenio suggested I go to London and retrieve my belongings. His idea was to put the car on a train to Milan. He would meet me there and we could return together via Florence and Rome. Another scenario, perhaps more sensible, was that I go to London, sell the car, store my possessions, and return to Australia for a time to get my life into perspective.

My mother received frequent bulletins chronicling my current state of mind. She had been widowed at a relatively young age, and I was her only child. Therefore my decision was of more than academic interest to her, and she must have wondered, as she read her mail in Melbourne, Australia, whether I was slightly crazy. In retrospect I realize that she handled the situation very well, replying to my letters and trying to maintain a constructive attitude to

51

my constantly changing plans. At this stage I suggested (was it option IV or V?) that she come to Positano and spend Christmas with us.

By a strange coincidence, my parents had started their married life in Italy. My father, an engineer, had been working in Milan. My aunt had married her Italian professor and was also there. Of course, she invited her sister to visit. My mother was a keen skier; she loved the mountains, and Milan, with its proximity to famous ski resorts, was a perfect setting. She decided to stay and look for a job. And so my parents met, married, and spent several happy years in Milan. Their reminiscences, the recounting of episodes from that period of their lives, form part of my childhood recollections.

Having lived in Italy for an extended time, my mother spoke the language fluently. For all these reasons, I hoped the prospect of a Christmas visit might be quite attractive.

\*　　\*　　\*　　\*　　\*

Growing up in Positano gave rise, I discovered, to a number of characteristic phenomena. One of these was a single-minded enthusiasm; it seemed all *Positanesi* were in love with the place. They believed that their township was unique, that they were the luckiest people on earth; that it was barely possible to live elsewhere and still be happy. If, for reasons that were eminently sensible, they were obliged to spend time in another part of the world, their dream was always to come back as often and for as long as possible. If anyone were foolish enough to mention that there were other lovely resorts in the world, their comments were considered sacrilegious. I had visited the Croatian resort of Dubrovnik, an outstandingly beautiful place. I'll never forget the shock and horror when I once rashly remarked that Dubrovnik was perhaps the most beautiful place I'd ever seen.

Consequently, it was assumed that once my mother visited Positano, she'd think it was the most marvellous place imaginable. She'd surely agree that it would be absolutely fantastic for her only daughter to spend the rest of her life there. Stenio wrote to my mother.

'Even in winter Positano is warm and sunny, and everything here is simple and easy.'

*     *     *     *     *

In early November we made a series of momentous decisions that were to change both our lives dramatically. We decided to get married. And to live in Positano. All my soul searching, all my doubts about how and where to my pursue my career disappeared. Having come to this all important resolution, we were both very happy. I could now get my life back on track. My mother agreed to come to Italy to join me, meet my prospective husband, and spend the holiday season with us. Stenio and more particularly his mother were dying to meet her. I received a constant barrage of questions from my future mother-in-law.

"What's your mother like? Does she look like you; is she taller, shorter, fatter, thinner; is she intelligent, does she have a sense of humour?" The questions went on and on.

# LONDON TO POSITANO

The first step was to go to London and sort out the loose ends I'd left behind. In mid-November I set off for Naples airport, took a flight to London, and found myself in a different world. Signs directed passengers to the terminal; people stood politely in queues waiting to have their passports checked before lining up again for customs inspection. Outside, taxis waited in taxi ranks, the city bus service was clearly designated, a bus stood waiting at its specified stop. It all seemed ordered and easy, such a contrast to the frenetic activity and confusion of Naples.

A taxi took me to our Hampstead flat. Janet was pleased to see me and intrigued at my news. I gathered that my continued absence had been a source of considerable speculation over the previous months. I had to answer a barrage of questions, "Where will you live? Where are you getting married? And when? What does your family say? It was all quite exhausting, particularly as I had no answer to many of the questions.

The following day I visited the institute where I'd been working. My friends there were incredulous at my decision to live in Positano. One of my erstwhile colleagues offered his assessment. "You'll be bored in no time." I, of course, completely disregarded such critical evaluations. During my sojourn in London we'd often discussed the merits of living in a large city. Obviously, there were positive and negative aspects. On the plus side was the vast range of activities available at all times. Another fellow scientist maintained that he couldn't possibly live in a city of less than ten million people. Smaller cities just couldn't offer the choice of entertainment available in London; the first-class theatrical productions, the concerts, opera and ballet.

When we asked how often he went to a play or concert he evaded the question.

"I rarely go," he said. "But that's not the point. The point is I know it's there."

This, he believed, was essential to his well-being. Not everyone was so definite, but I realized that many of my colleagues shared his views to some extent.

I was not surprised, therefore, that my decision to settle down in a small Italian village was regarded as slightly eccentric, if not downright foolish. However, everyone wished me well, offered advice, and promised to visit when the opportunity presented itself.

During the preceding weeks I'd drawn up a list of things to do in London. Somehow this list kept getting longer rather than shorter. I was lucky to have a few good friends who were a tremendous help. I bought a trunk, took out car insurance, and started to pack my belongings and to purchase things that might not be readily available in my new home.

Janet offered to come with me to Italy. This was wonderful news. The daunting prospect of driving from England to Italy had been causing me considerable anguish. I was delighted to have her company; we would share the driving and do some sightseeing on the way. By a fortunate coincidence, Janet's boyfriend was already travelling in Europe. Everything began to fall into place. Tom wanted to join us in Milan, Stenio had arranged to meet me in Umbria. We adjusted our plans accordingly.

"Why don't we stop in Milan, pick up Tom, then go on together," said Janet.

"We could all meet in Assisi." I suggested.

"What a marvellous idea. I've always wanted to go there."

"Imagine the four of us in Assisi." Happily anticipating the joy of a few days in this most enchanting Italian town, we set about preparations for the journey.

\*       \*       \*       \*       \*

Leaving London in late November, we made our way through France to Switzerland, bypassing cities and small towns. After a long drive through beautiful countryside we arrived in Basel. We spent a delightful afternoon exploring; admiring the river, the lovely old buildings and elegant shops, and sampling Swiss food, particularly *rösti*, one of my favourites.

Next day we headed for Lucerne, stopping at the lake with its characteristic bridge, before driving off along the snowy roads. We put the car on a train to traverse a very long tunnel - an uncomfortable claustrophobic experience reminiscent of childhood visits to Luna Park. Emerging from the tunnel, we were pulled up by two grim-faced policemen and fined for some misdemeanour. Neither of us understood what we'd done wrong, but there was no point in arguing. We paid the fine and proceeded on our way.

Tired and dishevelled, we arrived at Chiasso, a small town on the Italian - Swiss border. We were examined by customs officers at the border post. They looked at us, two rather grubby, untidy looking girls in a dirty car containing one trunk, four suitcases, and a great deal of junk. It was easy to imagine what they were thinking. Why would two young women bring so much luggage into the country?

I told the inspectors I was going to be married in Italy. No-one believed this was a satisfactory explanation. And I had no way to prove it. They opened everything, and, not finding any smuggled goods - they missed the cigarettes and whisky I'd brought as presents - asked for the car registration. I happily handed over the documents I had with me, but to my dismay, after a prolonged examination, they made their pronouncement. "You can't enter Italy, you'll have to go back to Switzerland."

The car had been bought according to rules applying to Australian tourists in Europe. Apparently the international registration could not be renewed. For some reason, I was entitled to drive it in the United Kingdom but not elsewhere. I'd become attached to my car, a lime green Volkswagen station wagon with impressive international number plates. Initially, I'd been part of a

56

group who bought the car together, but as the others moved on, I progressively acquired their share. Now it looked as though this vehicle was going to complicate my already confused life.

I wept, I shouted in the best of Italian traditions - all in vain. By now a dozen or so officials had become involved; they declared their sympathy and patted me on the back, but clearly no-one was about to change the rules for my benefit. The car must remain in Switzerland. We could proceed by train with the trunk, the suitcases, and the rest of our belongings. This prospect was not only singularly unappealing; it would, in fact, be quite unmanageable.

At this point Janet and I decided to stage a sit-down strike. The customs officials were annoyed; first they attempted to reason with us, then they appealed to our better judgment. But we refused to be persuaded. We would not move. Finally a compromise was found. If we were prepared to pay a $400 deposit, we'd be allowed to proceed. They explained the new set of rules. I was entitled to drive the car for three months. After that, I could get my money back by marrying an Italian citizen, or by leaving the country. It all sounded rather odd, but we were not in a position to argue. We scraped together the required sum, and, much subdued, took the road to Milan.

Arriving in Milan, the next hurdle presented itself. We had difficulty finding a hotel room. In view of the battles we'd won, however, this was only a minor obstacle, and we eventually succeeded in finding accommodation on the outskirts of the city. I did have relatives in Milan, but I didn't feel I knew them well enough to ask their help. My aunt had died tragically many years earlier, and, although I would have loved to develop a closer relationship with my uncle, we had difficulty communicating. My Italian was at the stage where I could make myself understood, but the give and take of everyday conversation was beyond my linguistic capabilities. Nevertheless it was good to have an opportunity to renew my acquaintance with this kind, thoughtful and interesting man.

I met old friends of my parents who lived in Milan, and passed a pleasant few days visiting and sightseeing. The general reaction to my news that I was about to marry an Italian was one of pleasure, mixed with an element of doubt. Was it wise to commit myself to living in southern Italy? This was hardly surprising, given the lack of sympathy that prevails between the north and south.

In the meantime Janet had troubles of her own. Tom had been due to arrive at the Milan railway station at seven in the morning. She'd arranged to meet him there, and had got up at the crack of dawn, taken a tram and bus to the station, and waited on the platform. At the specified time, the train pulled in, the passengers disembarked, but there was no sign of Tom. Not knowing what to do, since there was absolutely no way of contacting him, Janet returned to the hotel, disappointed and upset. That afternoon, wandering disconsolately through *La Galleria*, the elegant arcade in central Milan, she heard her name called. To her amazement it was Tom. For reasons of his own, Tom had arrived at four in the afternoon. He was not at all surprised at their chance encounter; he'd never doubted they'd find each other.

\*        \*        \*        \*        \*

We expected Milan in early December to be cold and wet. But we hadn't expected the fog. I'd experienced thick fogs in London, and knew the difficulty of driving when the visibility is poor. There'd been occasions when I was aware that traffic, and more particularly, traffic lights, were right beside me, but I couldn't be sure of their exact location. This can be an extremely unnerving experience. But the fog here was far worse than anything I'd experienced in London.

Driving in Italian traffic is disconcerting at the best of times. Although I'm willing to concede that Italians are excellent drivers, to the uninitiated, there's a measure of excitement and unpredictability on the roads that's frightening. Motor scooters and small cars weave in and out between lines of traffic. Enormous trucks career along at great speed. Driving on three lane highways requires strong nerves. Cars on the inside lane tear along at the speed of light, while those on the outside proceed at a leisurely place. If you happen to be in the middle, vehicles from both sides pop up in front and behind as they overtake. With time and practice one learns the rules, but at first it's most intimidating.

I'd never driven on a freeway in heavy fog. I was about to have this new and unwelcome experience. When we left Milan we had no idea what we were heading into; no-one had warned us of the climatic hazards. There's something about driving on an *autostrada* when the visibility approaches zero, and you have no idea who's behind, in front, or at either side, which makes for an unforgettable experience. Janet, Tom and I set off, blithely unconscious of what was in store. Somehow we survived, more by good luck than anything else, and lived to tell the tale.

Finally, cold, miserable, and exhausted, we arrived in Assisi. What a wonder! I love Assisi, there's a feeling in this medieval town of something special, a vibrant, inspirational quality. You can understand why St. Francis, that most delightful of saints, chose to live here.

And Stenio was waiting to welcome us, looking very pleased with himself. You'd have thought he personally invented this enchanting place. So now there were four of us. Janet was still amazed at having miraculously found Tom, and we felt a sense of achievement at having reached our destination. After a shower and change of clothes I began to feel human again. There was still definitely room for improvement, after our adventures I looked and felt quite neglected. Next morning I decided to find a hairdresser. This caused untold teasing. "How could you, in such a beautiful place, waste a couple of hours having your hair done?" Undeterred, I set off and discovered a little salon. A friendly, capable girl did my hair, gave me a cup of strong coffee, and sent me off feeling a new person.

I was now ready to do justice to the mystical, inspirational town of Assisi. We visited the thirteenth century *Basilica di San Francesco,* an enormous complex which dominates the town and can be seen for miles around. Pushing open the heavy doors we were confronted with the wonderful frescoes of Giotto and Cimabue. I was fascinated by the twenty eight Giotto paintings depicting the life of St. Francis; scenes of the saint with his brown-robed monks giving his cloak to a poor man, meeting the Pope, being sent to heaven. My favourite shows St. Francis preaching to the birds, his expression kind and gentle.

Assisi is an architect's dream, a vision of splendid Renaissance buildings. And, of course, it's a great tourist centre. Fortunately at this time of year it was relatively uncrowded, and we could walk along the cobbled streets and hear our footsteps echo. What a thrill it was. We traced the route of countless pilgrims, competed with each other in searching out exquisite masterpieces, and felt free to indulge our imaginations in whatever fantasy we chose. The bells tolled, monks and nuns went about their business; the atmosphere of spirituality was almost tangible.

*     *     *     *     *

And now we were ready to move on. It was time to return to Positano, to make plans for our future together. We said goodbye to Janet and Tom, and headed south in my car with its dubious international number plates. As we drove slowly down through the centre of the Italian peninsula, we discussed the next steps in our somewhat complicated lives. There was much to do.

# SURROUNDINGS

As the weather became cooler, and the number of tourists started to diminish, we ventured further afield, undertaking sight-seeing activities of our own in nearby towns and cities. Certain areas were noted for their historic significance, others for their natural beauty. Most Italian cities have all of these features and more. About once a week we went exploring; there was never enough time to see all we wanted. Sometimes we went with friends, Carol and Gino often joined us, Diana and Michele also; sometimes we went on our own.

*    *    *    *    *

I'd always wanted to see 'the isle of Capri'. Noted for its natural beauty, the island has been extolled in song, filmed as a cinema setting, used as background in scores of books. Travel writers continually sing its praises. During the summer months, hydrofoil and ferry operators run shuttle services between Capri and Positano. As a result, all our visitors wanted to see this famous resort, with its elegant shops, excellent restaurants and spectacular scenery.

A day spent in Capri was always a pleasure. The island has been a renowned international resort for years, long before the advent of mass tourism. Luxurious old hotels, well known to travellers at the turn of the century, have been regularly modernized; several are still classified as five-star hotels. We usually went in only to admire; occasionally, when feeling extravagant, we ordered a drink or afternoon tea. Tea was served as in an English country manor. The table was beautifully set, with freshly laundered, stiffly starched tablecloth and napkins, silver tea service, dainty cups and saucers. There were cucumber sandwiches, cakes with cream, sugar cubes served with tongs, and cold milk in a silver jug. In Italy tea is customarily served with lemon; if you request tea with milk in a bar, the waiter will look surprised and probably bring hot milk frothed up in an espresso machine. Such a thing could never happen in an elegant Capri hotel! Since many distinguished tourists in earlier times were English, fashionable hotels acquired attributes expected by the English gentry, including the custom of serving tea with cold milk.

The island is quite large, with numerous beaches, best known are the *Marina Grande* and *Marina Piccola*. Everyone wants to sample the funicular rail; more conventional means of transport are available, but who wants a bus or taxi when they can take a funicular? The coastline is dotted with grottoes; the most famous, the blue grotto, is a tourist 'must'. In summer hundreds of people wait in line for small rowing boats that manoeuvre their way in and out of the grotto. The trip is not particularly comfortable; you have to almost lie down in the boat to get through the aperture in the rocks, but it's worth every minute. The phosphorescent blue of the sea reflected in the cave is unique and magical.

High up above the town is the village of Anacapri, reached by a scenic road which curves along the mountainous terrain. The surrounding land is quite heavily vegetated; in spring myrtle blooms and small wild flowers are dotted here and there. The road winds past splendid exotic villas overlooking the bay of Naples and the nearby islands of Ischia and Procida. Vesuvius and the cliffs of Sorrento form the background. We always visited the Roman ruins, where Caesar Augustus and later the Emperor Tiberius established their courts.

The beautiful house of Axel Munthe, made famous by his book, *The Story of San Michele*, was built on the site where, two thousand years ago, the palace of Tiberius had stood. Axel Munthe, a Swedish doctor, gives a vivid description of his life on the island in the early years of the twentieth century. He found Roman columns, fragmented statues, and slabs of coloured marble lying scattered on the ground. The Swedish doctor, a connoisseur and collector of artefacts from antiquity, was shocked to find that exquisite fluted marble columns and other priceless objects had been used as building materials, split to make garden steps, or simply thrown over the precipice by peasants wanting to plant vines.

Digging in the surrounding area, Munthe and his helpers uncovered sections of Roman walls, mosaic floors and carved columns. He incorporated some of these materials in the construction of his own villa, and decorated the courtyards with beautiful objects found during the excavations.

*     *     *     *     *

The fascinating city of Naples, also immortalized in poetry and song, is a place of contrasts. Its panoramic bay, with Vesuvius smouldering in the background, creates a profound impression - once seen, never forgotten. Neapolitans are justly proud of their city and its cultural heritage. Although we went there often, and I admired its beauty and tried to unravel its complicated history, I never really felt I really belonged. Perhaps I was intimidated by the sheer intensity of the place; the noise, congestion and frenzied atmosphere.

I'm sure the key prerequisite for a Neapolitan is adaptability, without it they couldn't possibly have survived. Stenio of course knew all the history: Greeks founded the city in the seventh century B.C, and *Neapoli* became one of the most important cities of *Magna Grecia,* the ancient Greek Empire.

"Later it was extended by the Romans," Stenio, my guide, explained. "They built grand patrician villas where they presumably luxuriated in splendour while slaves did all the work."

"After that came a series of conquerors," he went on. "Byzantine, Norman, French, and Spanish. The city has been occupied so many times, and dominated by so many foreign rulers. Each invader left an imprint in the art and architecture that gives the city so much character."

Whenever we visited Naples we walked for miles, stopping at magnificent monuments, guidebook in hand, then moving on to the next point of interest, until I felt utterly confused. So much to see, and such a sprawling city. I never really managed to find my way around, and despite days spent crisscrossing the city, I saw only a fraction of its splendours. I'm sure you could live in Naples all your life and still have trouble classifying its treasures.

Neapolitans are exuberant, charming, and full of fun. Over the years, I acquired friends who lived in some of the lovely, elegant districts. Whenever we could, we had lunch at a marvellous restaurant on the harbour which, I was told, had inspired the nostalgic song *Santa Lucia*. Three groups of musicians competed for the attention of diners, each group playing its own repertoire with great vivacity. Little boys dived for coins thrown in the water by patrons who looked on while they dined in comfort.

According to Stenio, Naples and Neapolitans have been much maligned. The city is often categorized as a place full of bandits waiting to grab the money of the unwary traveller. Tourists are warned to hold their handbags tightly, and to wear money belts. "People exaggerate," he insisted. But he did admit that the region is home to the Camorra, a local form of the Mafia. The famous outdoor market has stalls where every conceivable object can be bought or sold; antiques, electrical equipment, second-hand goods, sheets and towels marked 'Made in USA'. The area buzzes with a heterogeneous mix of people; here even Stenio advised me not to let my wallet out of sight.

The word *scippare* was coined to describe a technique of bag-snatching developed almost as an art form. The procedure can be roughly described as follows: two young men, sitting one behind the other on a motor scooter, ride up beside an unsuspecting tourist. The man in front grabs the handle of the tourist's bag at the exact moment that his accomplice accelerates, whereupon the owner promptly lets the bag drop, and the riders speed off. This hazardous problem was not exclusive to Naples, it was also endemic in Rome. I can testify to this personally as my mother was twice *scippata*. On both occasions she managed to hold on to her handbag, determined not to be robbed, or as she put it, made a fool of. The result was not pleasing, once she was pulled along the road clutching the handle of her bag. Her knees were torn, her stockings in shreds, but her satisfaction at having outwitted the *scippatori* was enormous.

\*      \*      \*      \*      \*

Whenever we had visitors, a drive along the Amalfi coast was obligatory. We headed south, showing our guests some of the most spectacular scenery imaginable. Our first stop was the little church of San Pietro, behind which, partly hidden from view, the glamorous luxury hotel of the same name has been hewn out of the surrounding rock. The secluded entrance is off the beaten track. I always enjoyed the look on our visitors' faces when, walking around the church, they were suddenly confronted by an elevator. It looked remarkably out of place. We pressed a button, took a short ride between walls of rock, and exited to find ourselves in an elegant hotel lobby.

Here we were greeted by our friend Salvatore, the manager. Salvatore's uncle, Carlino Cinque, a local hotelier with imaginative ideas, started the hotel in 1962. His original plan had been to build a small villa underneath the ancient chapel. Eight years later, his ideas had expanded and the result was the stunning Hotel San Pietro. Salvatore was extremely proud of his uncle, and rightly so. Carlino was an inspirational genius; his hotel, built into the cliffs below the tiny chapel, has achieved international fame.

The building is tucked into a precipice, with reception areas and guest accommodation contained in a series of overlapping ledges. Landscaped gardens cascade down terraces built into the sloping hill; plants and vines drape walls and ceilings. We took a second elevator down two hundred and seventy five feet to arrive at a seaside tennis court and private beach. If we had the time and inclination, we stopped for a drink or lunch. It was a joy just to sit and admire the panorama.

Our guests were always reluctant to leave, but eventually we moved on. I encouraged them to look at the view as we passed gorges and drove around hair-pin curves, remembering how terrified I'd been on my first encounter with the Amalfi drive. We passed through the village of Praiano, enjoying its own tourist boom as travellers flocked to the area. On towards Amalfi the road continued its picturesque way, becoming narrower as it proceeded south. Large stretches were cut through the mountain; our car seemed dwarfed between perpendicular cliff-faces. Suddenly we emerged to confront a wonderful seascape, or a little fishing village whose cottages faced out to sea. Villages with romantic sounding names, Atrani, Furore, Conca dei Marini, Vettica. We drove over bridges spanning rivers or deep valleys far below. The roads are a marvel of modern engineering.

Each village has its own particular charm and attraction. For example, Conca dei Marini is famous for its *grotta di Smeraldo,* emerald grotto, comparable to the blue grotto of Capri. Giant stalagmites, stalactites, and alabaster-like rocks glow in a strange luminous emerald light, creating an eerie feeling of unreality.

*       *       *       *       *

We came to the city of Amalfi. Anchored in the harbour are graceful yachts, fishing boats, and ferries taking tourists around the coast.

I first visited Amalfi at the time of the annual festival of the four Maritime republics, a colourful pageant commemorating the city's ancient splendour. In the Middle Ages, Amalfi was a leading commercial and naval power, rivalling Pisa and Genoa. Its powerful fleets controlled the seas. Amalfi was a dominant force in Mediterranean commerce, trading in Alexandria, Tunis and Constantinople; its leaders, known as Doges, controlled large areas adjoining the Dukedom of Naples.

The festival is spectacular. Four boats compete in a historical regatta, designed to recall battles fought long ago. A procession follows - a fascinating parade along the waterfront, where local enthusiasts don the regalia and traditional costumes of the ancient Republic. The day culminates in a breathtaking display of fireworks. In this part of the world, I soon discovered, every festival ends in dramatic fireworks.

I came to know Amalfi well. Its magnificent ninth-century cathedral dominates the main square. The rich, multicoloured facade is beautiful, inlaid with mosaics representing scenes from the life of Christ. Surrounding the cathedral is a network of alleys and covered passages. I liked to walk behind the chalk-white city walls, to look through the long narrow slits and imagine how soldiers had once crouched behind these openings ready to protect their city and repulse invaders. There's a wonderful arsenal, an impressive fortress, and a series of Saracen towers. The historic Capuchin monastery has been converted into an elegant hotel. In the harbour square stands a monument dedicated to Flavio Gioia, the reputed inventor of the compass, who was to cause endless problems when we came to build our house.

Local people proudly tell visitors about *La Tabula Almaphitana,* the oldest existing maritime code. Widely accepted by neighbouring powers from the 900s to the 1500s, this maritime charter dealt with the relationship between trader and carrier, and between captain and crew, spelling out the rights of seamen. "You can see it's still highly relevant in this century; every day we read reports of crises in industrial relations," say the locals.

Behind the *Duomo,* a narrow path climbs through citrus groves, scattered cottages, and tiny waterfalls to reach *la Valle dei Mulini.* We visited this valley to see ancient paper mills, said to be the oldest in Europe, where *carta a mano,* hand-made paper, is still produced today.

Amalfi's lemons, large, juicy, and fragrant, are cultivated on pergolas; in winter they're covered to protect from wind and hail. Limoncello, a lemon-based liqueur typical of the area, is popular in the Amalfi coast towns, and is now sold worldwide.

*     *     *     *     *

Most beautiful of all is Ravello. Wagner lived there, Greta Garbo and Jacqueline Onassis were regular visitors. The American writer, Gore Vidal, is a well known member of an expatriate community who have made Ravello their home.

Situated in the hills above Amalfi, Ravello perches on a cliff jutting over the immense Gulf of Salerno. To get there, we had to drive up a narrow winding precipitous road. On either side are terraced gardens; every inch of land is cultivated. There are olive trees, grape-vines, vegetables in season. Flowering plants grow in sensuous profusion.

Each summer, a German orchestral group gave concerts in the gardens of the famed Villa Rufolo. In late afternoon, as the heat of the day was slowly evaporating, we took our seats on the hilltop. We sat beneath the clouds, listening to music. The sound effects in that setting were awesome. The cliff sloped down to the sea. Far away in the distance, a few boats rocked at anchor. We watched the sun set slowly in a haze of red, orange and yellow, to the accompaniment of Dvorak's New World Symphony. What a magic evening. I wished it could go on forever.

The Cathedral is a Byzantine masterpiece, the pulpit a marvel of golden mosaic, supported by six inlaid spiral columns each standing on the back of a stone lion. Villas Rufolo and Cimbrone are famed for their magnificent gardens.

We often took visitors to share this special place. Although Ravello is a famous tourist resort, we never had the feeling of being crowded or overcome by hordes of people. There are of course the inevitable shops selling local goods, but that's part of the fun. Local merchandise includes exotic, brightly decorated pottery and ceramics. Much of the production comes from nearby Vietri, and the temptation to acquire is hard to resist. We heard the same conversation over and over again, particularly among our married friends. Invariably it was the wife who insisted. "I just have to buy that darling little vase, or jug, or platter," while the husband, knowing he'd have to carry the bags, tried in vain to dissuade her. "You can see it's heavy and fragile. You know we don't have room in the suitcase." The wife usually won the argument, and I have no doubt, given the superb ceramics of Vietri, that the shops of Ravello will continue to prosper.

# MARRIAGE

Having made the momentous decision to get married, it would have been reasonable to expect the next step to be simple. Not so, however. When we started to think about it, and to discuss the logistics of our wedding, we realized we were confronting a minefield. Most of my friends lived in Melbourne, and naturally enough, that's where they married. Often the marriage was celebrated in the parish church or the chapel of their old school. Despite childhood dreams of a beautiful wedding, all in white, my aspirations had changed over the years. My mother was happy to come to Italy, I had no close relatives in Australia, and although I would have dearly loved to have my friends with me at the marriage ceremony, the idea of going to Australia was never a serious consideration. It was too difficult, and would create endless complications.

A wedding in Positano, however, posed a different set of problems. Stenio had lived in Positano all his life and knew everyone in town. And, in the time I'd spent there, I'd also got to know many local people. So the possibility of having a small and private function in Positano was fraught with difficulty, and the likelihood of offending a large number of people. I was not at all enthusiastic at the idea of having a big wedding without any of my old friends. Stenio, and indeed the entire Bella family, shuddered at the thought of a large, formal Italian marriage. So what were we to do?

We had endless discussions, looking at various options from every point of view, until Stenio got fed up. "Why do we have to have a wedding at all," he said, "why don't we just go to the *Municipio* and have a civil service? Then we can tell everyone we're married."

"But my mother's coming specially from Australia," I'd reply.

"All right, she can come too."

"What about your mother?"

"She won't mind, she doesn't like formal events."

"Don't you believe it, she may say that but she'd be mortally wounded if she were not included."

The discussions went on and on.

After much soul searching, ceaseless debates, suggestions and hypothetical solutions, we decided to head south. We consulted an atlas, looked at lots of brochures, and finally discovered a little village called Maratea nestled in the mountains. We had both heard of Maratea, a beautiful and remote village in the region of Basilicata. Situated between Campania and Calabria, this area had not yet been discovered by tourists. It seemed an ideal solution; by marrying in a place where we knew no-one, we could have a private wedding without causing offence. And so we decided to go there. We would invite only our parents to celebrate the event with us. With considerable difficulty, we found the names of the relevant authorities in Maratea, and wrote to inform them of our intention.

The next hurdle was to procure the necessary documents. Satisfying the requirements of officialdom was not easy. I'd learned that anything you want to do in Italy requires an inordinate amount of red tape, and marriage was no exception. Strangely enough, it proved much simpler to obtain the relevant documents from Australia than it was to get the required papers from the Italian authorities. I went to the Australian Embassy in Rome, explained what I wished to do, and in a relatively short time, received the requested documents. Despite the fact that Stenio had lived most of his life in Italy, he faced a continuous chain of problems. Wherever he went there was some complication: the office was closed, the person who handled the files was on holidays, there had been a fire and documents were lost. The delays were endless. I began to wonder if there was some sinister motive behind all these stories, but I soon discovered that such delays were normal.

Eventually, after weeks of frustration, we succeeded in obtaining all that was needed. We were ready to tie the knot. My mother arrived, my mother and father-in-law made their arrangements. We packed our bags and set off, all in one car. The trip was not too long, everyone was in good spirits, happily anticipating the future. We drove up into the mountains. Higher and higher we went, as the road climbed steeply up to *Monte San Biagio*. Finally we found what we were looking for; a large signpost indicated we were about to arrive in Maratea. What a magnificent setting. We had chosen well.

Maratea is a delightful place, a mountain village with an impressive view of the surrounding countryside. Above the town, at the summit of the cliff, stands a colossal towering statue of Christ, arms outstretched, welcoming all who come to visit. The cliff drops away to reveal a spectacular coastline, a twenty kilometre stretch of rocky mountains which jut out over the sea.

We found the local priest and the mayor. Although we had written to them quite some time earlier, our arrival was apparently quite unexpected.

"Did you receive our letter?" we asked. No-one seemed to know.

"But it's all arranged," said Stenio. "We're getting married here tomorrow. I have the documentation in my briefcase."

This news was received with considerable excitement and some suspicion. The people of Maratea could not comprehend why two strangers, one of whom was not even Italian, should have chosen their little village for a marriage ceremony.

"Why on earth have you come all the way to Maratea to get married?" asked the mayor. "We've never heard of such a thing." I could understand his bewilderment, it was hard to explain why we'd chosen to behave in such an unusual way.

"We were looking for somewhere special and different," said Stenio. "We'd heard this is a charming village; we wanted to find a place where no-one knew us. Maratea seemed a perfect solution." This way of thinking is quite bizarre to the average Italian, for whom the large family network is an important factor of life. Surely a marriage is an occasion for celebration, for inviting the whole town. The mayor and his entourage never managed to understand our strange decision, but, after we'd found the local bar and offered them a few drinks, they decided that we were just *un po' pazzi,* a little crazy. We weren't doing anything wrong, so they might as well enjoy this unexpected event. After talking together for a while we became friends; they were flattered at our choice. If we wished to be eccentric and conduct our lives in this odd manner, why should they care.

It was a great occasion for the whole village. Everyone came to meet us, crowding the little church to participate in our wedding. We were surrounded by well-wishers, who prepared a wonderful feast and even managed to produce a bottle of French champagne.

\*       \*       \*       \*       \*

"I'd like to propose a toast to *la bella Signora Bella,*" said the mayor.

And so it began. Until that moment, I hadn't even thought about the embarrassment the name Bella would bring. Of course I knew that *bella* means beautiful. Everyone knows that. And it had, I admit, struck me that it was rather a strange surname. But not until I actually acquired the name by marriage did the reality sink in.

Whenever I was introduced, someone would say,

"*Ecco la bella Signora Bella.*" Here's the beautiful Signora Bella.

Another variation was, "*Bella di nome, bella di fatto.*" Beautiful in name, beautiful in fact.

It didn't matter who I met, whether they were young or old, rich or poor. The response to my name invariably took the form of a pun. This seemed to be as automatic as it was predictable. Occasionally, I'd meet someone who didn't make the obvious comment. Maybe it didn't occur to them, maybe they thought it was too much of a cliché'. Whatever the reason, I really appreciated their restraint. I felt like hugging them.

It was even worse when I had to introduce myself. When confronted with people you hadn't met, it was customary to shake hands and announce your surname. How embarrassing to take an extended hand and reply with the word *bella*. I always imagined people were looking at me and thinking, "Poor thing, does she really think she's so beautiful?"

At least it won't matter when I'm speaking English, I consoled myself. But I wasn't to be let off so easily. Because in English, Bella is not uncommon as a Christian name. Consequently, when I presented myself as Bella, I'd be asked "And what's your surname?" The last straw occurred one day when I was introduced to a pleasant-looking couple as Susi Bella. For some reason, they assumed the whole thing was a Christian name. "And the surname?" they enquired.

# SETTLING DOWN IN POSITANO

We spent our honeymoon in Calabria and Sicily, discovering some of the incredible riches to be found in that part of the world. Returning to Positano, we rented a small apartment. Here we would live temporarily, while preparing to build our future home. Our plan was to renovate and extend a part of the dream house which the Bella family had already started to restore.

*     *     *     *     *

Over the years we had a steady stream of visitors. Some were Italian, many were Australian. The first question was always, "How do we get to Positano?" This was not easy. "Isn't there a train?" people asked. "Or a regular bus service." There were no trains, but coaches servicing the Amalfi drive did stop at Positano. Alternative transport was available, in fact there were several possible combinations, all extremely time consuming. Its relative inaccessibility was one of the charms of the place, had it been easy to reach we would no doubt have been inundated with beach lovers on day trips. While we residents were reasonably content with this state of affairs, I was well aware that it didn't compensate guests for their inconvenience.

I spent so much time explaining how to get to Positano that I developed a circular letter providing detailed information. I hesitated to enclose timetables as official times kept changing.

"You can take a train to Naples," my instructions specified. "Then transfer to a nearby station and board the little train known as *la circumvesuviana*. As the name indicates, this railway follows a circuitous route around the base of Mt. Vesuvius to Sorrento, stopping at a few small towns. You might find the trip interesting, but it's slow, and you still have to get a bus or taxi from Sorrento. Another alternative is to fly to Naples, again you need some form of transport to Positano. You can do as I did and travel by ferry from Naples or Sorrento. Or you can rent a car and drive yourself."

Coming south along the Amalfi road by whatever means from Rome, Naples, or Sorrento, the point of entry to Positano is known as *La Chiesa Nuova,* the new church. Many Italian towns and villages have a *Chiesa Nuova* - sometimes these churches are hundreds of years old, but at a certain point each was newly built, and the name has remained unchanged.

"If you come by car," I told prospective visitors, "watch out for the Positano sign, then drive on slowly until you come to *la Chiesa Nuova.* This is where you leave the main highway. Make a right hand turn, and you'll find yourself on the local road heading into town. Continue until you get to Fornillo. You won't have any trouble finding it, there's a clearly marked sign. Leave your car in the public carpark and ring me. There's a telephone booth nearby, or you can ask any of the local shopkeepers to give me a call. I'll come and meet you."

"If you come by coach, tell the driver to let you off at Positano. Collect your luggage, cross the road and wait for the local bus. If you're feeling fit, you might prefer to walk down the hundreds of steps. It's a long walk, but you'd probably enjoy it. We can pick up your luggage later."

When possible, I went to meet friends at the bus stop. How often I stood there waiting, watching the tourists mill about and recalling my own introduction to Positano; the keen anticipation and my sense of frustration at the interminable delays. Perhaps it all contributed to the pleasure of arrival, I couldn't help thinking. Certainly there had to be a feeling of satisfaction at having overcome a challenge.

Gathering together my visitors, I rejoined the local traffic. The short drive was always a great success. "How fantastic." I heard on all sides. The road, cut into the side of the mountain, gently winds its way down, past gateways leading to secluded villas, past restaurants, shops and small hotels. At each curve I noticed my passengers looking around in wonder at the landscape ahead. Even after years of familiarity, I never ceased to feel a thrill of excitement, a sense of expectancy at each twist and turn along the route.

About half way down we stopped at a *piazzetta*, a small square, where the surrounding rock-face curves to form a natural grotto. Here stands a majestic Madonna, resplendent in blue and white robes. This is the grotto of Fornillo, and at this point, in order to reach our house, we had to leave the road. Placing the car in my parking spot, we set off again, carrying the luggage. From here it was all on foot.

The sector surrounding the grotto is known as Fornillo, and, as always in this part of the world, the route consists of narrow alleyways and flights of steps interspersed with tiny *piazzette*. It was not easy to give directions to newcomers. I preferred to meet my visitors. They could find their own way as far as the grotto of the Madonna, then I was happy to accompany them on the last circuitous stage.

We headed off along a narrow lane of twists and turns, down steps, walkways, and more steps, past the delightful little stone church dedicated to *Santa Caterina,* the patron saint of Fornillo. Doorways led into small cottages; arched entrances on either side displayed names of nearby *pensioni*. We greeted tourists going in and out, and porters carrying packages. Half-hidden behind high walls were villas with whitewashed facades, surrounded by silver-grey olive trees and dark green citrus, heavy with fruit. On either side a profusion of foliage and brilliant trumpet-shaped flowers, red, purple and orange, tumbled over stone walls. The path meandered on and on. From time to time I glanced around at my visitors. I couldn't help smiling to myself as I saw the looks on their faces.

"Where on earth is she taking us? We'll never get there." It was easy to imagine what they were thinking.

"Don't worry," I promised. "In a few seconds you'll be well rewarded."

And so they were. For eventually we reached the last steep flight of steps leading to the Bella property. Down we went, and found ourselves in front of an imposing portico. Amazing as it might seem, this was our front entrance.

"Here we are at last," I announced dramatically. We could finally stop and draw breath.

"We'll never ever find it again," was the usual comment.

But although it was easy to get lost, the homing instinct must be strong. Despite the confusing number of lanes which branch off and disappear in all directions, our guests invariably managed to find their way back. Only on rare occasions did we get a phone call from some unfortunate traveller who'd become hopelessly disoriented.

*     *     *     *     *

The first time I saw the arched stone entrance framing the wonderful heavy oak doors, I fell in love with this ancient house. I wanted to move in immediately. Plants pushed their way through gaps in the wall to embellish the imposing overhead arch. I stopped for a long moment to absorb the atmosphere; the impressive recessed entrance suffused with the perfume of jasmine, the enormous weathered double doors. Reverently I touched these doors, they were old, very old, and solid. The massive doors were hinged to their door-jambs by three pairs of interlocking iron rings, rusty with age.

At the centre of the arch was a crest belonging to who knows what ancient family. Unfortunately no one could tell us the significance of the emblem, so skillfully carved into the stone by some early master craftsman. The abandoned, neglected portico evoked an image of past glory. Who had owned this house, I wondered. The walls still standing were hundreds of years old. What techniques had been used at the time the building was first erected? I was to learn, as our construction project progressed, that many of the methods had not changed much in the intervening period.

Pushing the heavy doors open, we found ourselves in a ruined antechamber. Stepping inside, we entered an enormous room

77

which echoed with ancient memories. How overwhelming it was; the almost tangible feeling of past generations who'd lived in this place. Above was a high domed ceiling, beyond, an archway opened into a small alcove. This alcove, I was told, had served as an oven for baking bread. I determined that, if it were at all possible, this spot should again be used for the same purpose.

A doorway led into an adjoining room, similar in size. Here the stone walls were a foot thick and in remarkably good condition. In accordance with Arab custom, all the rooms had vaulted ceilings. Over the years, the cupola had fallen in, giving rise to an extraordinary effect. Looking up, we saw a circle open to the sky, overgrown with a profusion of plants, forming a fantastic overhead garden. Was it an illusion? Weeds, wildflowers, and tiny shrubs grew luxuriantly above the ruined walls, tendrils of creepers trailed down. Lizards scuttled back and forth in the heat of the day, to be replaced in the evening by more slowly moving geckos. I felt as though I were standing on my head, why was the garden above and not below? "This can't be real." I said to anyone who might be listening. "I knew you'd love it." Stenio smiled at me.

I stopped to examine my surroundings. The slope of the land was so steep that, looking out to sea, I had the impression we were suspended over a precipice. Terraced to cope with the incline, the site was on three levels. I'd never seen anything like it. The ruins of a villa hundreds of years old, the surrounding trees and gardens; how absolutely stunning. And the view! In the distance, across the blue-green Mediterranean, the stippled village of Praiano sparkled in the sunlight.

"We can't possibly rebuild these ruins," I said to Stenio.

"Why not?"

"It would be a crime, it's all so beautiful. What if we add on to these incredible walls and destroy the whole effect. The building's so rich in history, it makes me want to know the people who lived here."

78

Anyone who has grown up in Europe has a different perspective. Over the centuries, Italy has been inhabited by countless generations. To carry my argument to its logical conclusion, Italians would be expected to gaze in admiration at the abandoned homes of their ancestors. They might learn a lot about the past, but they'd have nowhere to live.

So I was not surprised at Stenio's reaction to my doubts. "How ridiculous," he said. "Of course we must restore the house. I promise we'll change as little as possible. We'll rebuild according to the original concept."

He was right of course. We could hardly use the rooms in their present condition. And I wanted a modern kitchen and bathroom. I understood his logic, but I never really felt comfortable about it. I felt responsible for a loss, the loss of a wonderful, romantic environment.

*     *     *     *     *

When I was first introduced to this property, certain sections had already been restored under the supervision of Raffaele, and according to his demanding standards.

A garden courtyard divided the building into two sections. At its centre, in a square garden bed of white standard roses, was a Greek statue, a bust of Psyche. Splendid Psyche, sculpted in white marble, stood on a stone pedestal surveying the ornamental garden around her. At the rear of the courtyard was a decorative wall two stories high. Skilled stonemasons had meticulously scalloped the upper edge of this feature wall, and carved out a recessed alcove at its base.

On a white marble bench in this central alcove, Raffaele sat for hours, meditating and perhaps planning his next painting. Iron lacework doors opened on either side to reveal a small cocktail cabinet. Occasionally I was allowed to sit on Raffaele's cool marble bench, and, like him, gaze out to sea. I could take a glass and select my preferred drink from the wall niche. And in the evening, should I wish to read, I could switch on the lamp which hung above, suspended in a filigree cage of wrought iron.

Several rooms had already been restored. One, a bedroom which ultimately became ours, was on the second floor. It was dazzling; a light-filled spacious room with bright-yellow floor-tiles, whitewashed walls and a high domed ceiling. An edging in warm pink marble framed the doors and recessed double windows overlooking the craggy hillside. Opening shutters on the arched french doors, I beheld the superb ocean vista which by now I'd come to expect.

On the opposite side of the courtyard, a carved wrought iron grille separated two adjoining rooms. Here all was a pale blue-grey: tiles, walls, and iron work. Double doors opened to a balcony enclosed by an iron railing, painted to match.

The elegantly refurbished sections were surrounded by broken stone walls in various states of disrepair. The general outline of the original building was clearly defined; gaps in the walls indicated the earlier location of rooms and stairs, windows and doorways.

*     *     *     *     *

We were determined to restore the house according to the original plan. The Arabic concept was one of flowing lines, cupolas, arches, and recessed niches. We would adhere faithfully to the existing design as far as possible. The locally trained craftsmen were in complete agreement. Like us, they were anxious to preserve the characteristics of the old building. So it seemed we were about to embark on a happy, harmonious project. I was really excited at the prospect.

We were fortunate to have my father-in-law as architect. He had long dreamed of recreating the abandoned villa. Being an artist, he could of course visualize the finished product. I have the greatest admiration for anyone with this ability, which I lack completely. Until I see a completed project before my eyes, I am quite incapable of imagining how it will look. This has frequently caused me problems. And I was well aware that the next year was going to be a time for decisions.

The first step was to find a builder. Giovanni, one of the local craftsmen, had been recommended. We met with him and were favourably impressed. Next we had to convince Raffaele that Giovanni was the right man for the job. After much discussion and on-site planning, we signed a contract. To my knowledge, there were never any architectural drawings. Raffaele, however, knew exactly what was required. It was all in his mind, and who were we to argue. He had planned every detail of this house for years. And he obviously understood how each feature should be incorporated, the completed rooms were testimony to his conception. I never understood what criterion he'd used in deciding which rooms to restore, or why. To me it seemed strange to start with the upstairs rooms. Since the lower floors hadn't been cleared, nor the stairways fixed, we risked breaking a leg clambering to reach the beautiful renovations. Not to mention the logic of luxurious bedrooms with no bathroom facilities!

He certainly had to contend with all sorts of unforeseen difficulties. When he started the process of restoration, the owners of the villa directly above tried to prevent him building at the second floor level. It was not difficult to understand their distress at the prospect of losing an unimpeded ocean view. To achieve their ends, and preserve their vista, they resorted to a devious stratagem. The plot centred around Flavio Gioia, reputed inventor of the compass. Although the people of Amalfi claimed him as their own, and had erected a statue in his honour, their assertion was hotly disputed by the *Positanesi*. According to folk-lore, the local hero had grown up in Positano, supposedly in the Fornillo area. Our city fathers had affirmed their right to this famous ancestor by affixing a memorial plaque to the historic bell tower.

This controversial hero became the pretext used by our neighbours to present an objection to the Municipal Council. They contested Raffaelle's right to a building permit on the following grounds:

81

- the property had been the home of Flavio Gioia.
- he was born on the actual site where we planned to build.
- the area should be preserved as a national monument.

Their lawyers initiated proceedings to prevent construction on this so-called 'sacred site'. Eventually they lost their case, but the drawn out litigation succeeded in delaying the building. Not to mention needless headaches and expense.

A further problem was the inaccessible position. Although the isolation and wonderful panorama it afforded was part of its charm, there was no denying the difficulty in transporting materials on-site. For someone like me, accustomed to living in a modern city, the problems appeared insurmountable. Building materials, bricks, stones, tiles and whatever else was needed had to be carried down thousands of steps. Workmen, baskets on their shoulders, made endless trips with each delivery. Large, bulky household items had to be transported; we needed a bath, a refrigerator, a washing machine, all posing enormous logistical problems. Whenever we were about to choose an awkwardly-shaped appliance, I would say, "We can't buy this, they'll never be able to get it down the narrow steps and tight corners." But everyone, sales staff, builders, and my husband said, *"Non ti preoccupare"*, don't worry. The local tradesmen were accustomed to such problems. To someone like me, used to having a delivery truck arrive at the door, it seemed impossible. Fortunately, I was wrong.

*     *     *     *     *

The idea was to divide the property into two parts; we would have one side, the Bella family, the other. I had my reservations about such proximity with my parents-in-law, but this sort of arrangement was reasonably common. We planned to reconstruct our part of the complex immediately; they would complete their section at a later date.

We spent many happy hours drawing up plans. Our house would consist of the original entrance hall, a large dining room, and a sitting room from which a staircase would lead up to three bedrooms, each with its own balcony. A terrace overlooking the lower garden was to extend out in front. I was thrilled with our planned kitchen. As I had hoped, it was to be in the alcove behind the dining room. To ensure adequate light, we decided to create an open living area with an enormous archway opening to the kitchen. This seemed an ideal solution, not only would the opening provide sunlight, it would add to the architectural harmony.

.

Raffaele designed decorative niches, wrought iron grilles, and vents shaped like half moon crescents. Many of these features had been incorporated in the original house.

*       *       *       *       *

I thought the walled garden courtyard linking the two sections of the house was absolutely perfect. The back and side walls formed three sides of a square. In front was a low stone border, interrupted at regular intervals by garden beds. Multicoloured roses grew in the flowerbeds. Ground-covering plants and herbs carpeted the courtyard in green profusion, creating the impression of a manicured English lawn. Walkways surrounded the garden, while Psyche reigned supreme in her contemplation of sea and sky.

Stone steps led to the lower terrace, which, apart from a few trees, was a wilderness. In contrast, the upper level had been cultivated with lemon trees, oranges and mandarins, and a fruit to which I was now introduced, the feijoa, native to South America. Other unfamiliar fruits grew here; I had never before encountered *nespole*, loquats, or *cachi*, persimmons. Michele the gardener planted vegetables; we picked our own beans, pumpkins, zucchini, potatoes, and occasionally lettuces - if we got to them before the snails. Rather less to my taste was the fact that Raffaele and his sons liked to have fresh honey, and to this end had installed several beehives in this upper garden. I failed to see the joy in having bees swarming around whenever I went to collect lemons. I fought and lost the battle to get rid of the bees.

*       *       *       *       *

The actual construction process was about to begin. We were in for an exciting and demanding time. Building a home is stressful at the best of times, but in Positano there were extra pressures, quite a combination of them. We were restoring a pre-existing edifice; we were dealing with tradesmen who had their own ideas. I learned that many if not most Italian artisans are convinced of their own artistic ability and resent being given instructions. To be more precise, they agree wholeheartedly with whatever you say, and take absolutely no notice. Why should they upset you by arguing, when they fully intend to do as they see fit?

Added to this were the logistics of delivery, plus the fact that we had to go to a nearby town or city, either Sorrento, Naples, or Salerno to look for tiles, bathroom fittings, kitchen cabinets and electrical goods. Would we use gas or electricity for cooking? If gas, it would have to be bottled, and I could foresee regular crises finding someone to deliver the heavy cylinders. Electricity presented another quandary, discovered early in my stay. The electricity supply was erratic; when the wind blew strongly, or an electrical storm occurred, the power was likely to go off, leaving us frantically searching for candles. We wanted to install central heating, and Stenio started looking at various options. Decisions, decisions - it was not going to be easy.

I had never before been involved in planning a home, and knew little about the everyday demands of housekeeping. I'd always taken such things for granted. Although I had great faith in the artistic abilities of Raffaele, I soon realised that he was not remotely interested in what I considered necessities of life in a modern society. Fortunately my mother visited us frequently, and her advice on practical matters was a great help. Life in Positano was conducted according to time-honoured custom, few of the advances of modern science had made their mark. I often felt like a pioneer.

*       *       *       *       *

Now began an exciting time. We set out early in the morning to find articles for the new house. Often we went to Salerno, passing through Amalfi and the small villages along the Amalfi coast; a trip involving hazardous driving on the narrow road. In winter, traffic was less of a worry than during the summer season, but there were other problems. In this hilly terrain, where much of the land had been terraced, landslides often occurred after heavy rain. As a result, large parts of the road would be closed; sometimes we had to go miles out of our way to detour through mountain roads. Eventually earth moving equipment was brought in and the roads repaired, but this was regarded as a matter of no great urgency. *Domani,* tomorrow, was a word I came to know well.

Among our first purchases were fittings for the kitchen and bathroom. Anyone who has ever built a house knows what a nightmare this entails, but the incredible range of goods available in Italian showrooms magnified the task. Choosing tiles in Italy is a daunting prospect; I have never seen such variety. We'd agreed to use marble floor tiles in the sitting and dining rooms. How confusing it was, marble tiles were displayed in a staggering collection of shapes and colours. I loved them all. Eventually we chose a large square tile with variegated pieces inset randomly. For the terrace we selected travertine; rectangular tiles to be laid in a herringbone pattern.

Upstairs the colour had already been decided, we agreed to pave the adjoining areas in the same bright-yellow as the existing bedroom. But the bathroom? Warehouse after warehouse had a never-ending array; an infinite variety of colours, patterns, and sizes. What to choose? At long last we settled on pale pink with a delicate white design. It would match well with the marble of the stairs, a warm sandy-pink. We were both delighted with our choice.

As for bathroom fittings, the possible options were enough to cause a nervous breakdown. The same applied to the kitchen. On the *autostrada* to Naples several *supermercati dei mobili*, furniture supermarkets, offered a wide selection of household goods. These roadside centres catered to a variety of customers. Elegant designer furniture stood side by side with articles in incredibly bad taste. We visited dozens of showrooms and finally made our selection, choosing kitchen cabinets in a neutral colour and pleasing design. We breathed a sigh of relief - the first steps had been taken.

Little did we know that each time a delivery was due, frantic phone calls would announce that whatever we'd selected had suddenly become unavailable. I learned many new skills during that time. One was the art of compromise. There was no point in getting upset or losing my temper; this proved counter-productive, somehow we had to solve each crisis as it occurred.

*     *     *     *     *

In Minori, a small town between Amalfi and Salerno, we came across an *antiquario*, antique dealer, who gradually became part of our lives. His shop was full to overflowing with an extraordinary collection of objects. Plaster saints, dressed in elaborate costumes and enclosed in glass cases, were displayed on shelves next to second-hand electrical goods and incomplete sets of cutlery. Crockery, some delicate, some garish, was arranged haphazardly. When we had the time and persistence to sort through several large rooms behind the shop, we discovered wonderful hidden treasures. Here we found our fireplace, with its mantelpiece of exquisitely carved marble. We searched for hours among motley bric-a-brac for the surrounds, finally managing to find all the pieces. After our stone mason fitted them together, a process akin to solving a jigsaw puzzle, we were rewarded with a decorative work of art which gave us infinite pleasure.

We became good friends with Carmine, the owner of this intriguing shop, and over the years we always stopped *en route* to Salerno. It was worth while, in time we collected marvellous antique furniture, Sicilian oil burners, copper pots, and an endless variety of ornaments. On each visit we searched for items of interest, but negotiations on price with Carmine were a source of constant surprise. He was quite inconsistent, at times asking an enormous sum for an object of no apparent value, while on another occasion he'd happily exchange a priceless antique for an old radio.

Carol introduced me to a weekly outdoor market in a small village called Piano di Sorrento.

"About once a month they have stalls selling American sheets and towels. Don't ask how such high quality products get here," she said. "It's better not to ask too many questions."

Maybe they were seconds, but I accumulated an excellent supply of household linen and never once found defects. Not only linen was sold; there were plates, pots and pans, gadgets, paintings. You never knew what you might find. It was a great atmosphere, hectic and exuberant. We enjoyed these shopping trips, how can anyone avoid buying and collecting in Italy?

Vietri, between Amalfi and Salerno, was the place for ceramics. Pottery old and new, classical and modern, often individually worked and hand-painted, was produced and displayed. Ceramic factories, where artisans practise their craft much as their predecessors had done in the fifteenth century, compete for local and international trade. One factory we visited was housed in a building one block long and five stories high.

We walked along street after street of shops, some tiny, others quite large. Shopkeepers competed in selling tableware together with an endless range of platters, bowls, jugs and urns, all in the glowing bright colours for which Italian pottery is justifiably renowned. Shelves were stacked with tea and coffee cups, walls lined with clocks and art works. I accumulated a wonderful supply of *ceramica;* a tall, beautifully shaped jug in vivid tomato red, turquoise pieces with an abstract theme, a set of oven proof casserole dishes decorated in a floral pattern, so lovely that I hate to use them - what if they break! A jug and matching bowls painted with green and yellow lemons bring the Italian sun into the darkest room. As wedding presents we were given an extensive range of locally produced majolica, including *a* hand-painted dinner set. Unfortunately ceramics have a habit of breaking, and my Vietri pottery is no exception. I realise I over-react whenever a piece is broken. Stenio always laughed at me. "It's not a tragedy," he said, "worse things can happen."

87

I acquired a collection of ceramic donkeys. A popular local product, usually green or grey, they come in all sizes. Some have a cart attached, some have a rider or carry a load, others are sold in sets of increasing size. Whatever the format, they always have cheeky faces and long drooping ears.

# MARIETTA

One of the best things about life in Positano was Marietta. Marietta became an essential part of our life. She was a font of sensible advice, with a practical solution for every problem, and a cheerful smiling face to welcome us whenever we walked into the house.

For the first year of our marriage, we rented a small, unpretentious house with a tiny courtyard and no view. Much of my time was taken up with our building project. During this period we had a constant stream of visitors; old friends from Australia, more recent acquaintances from England (Janet and Tom sometimes came for long weekends), fellow travellers I'd met in Europe. I loved entertaining friends and introducing them to my lifestyle. I was always busy, but my activities rarely involved any form of housekeeping. We went out for meals rather than invite guests home.

All this was about to change now, as our new home neared completion. I was beginning to realise that I had very little idea how to run a house. I'd have had much to learn wherever we'd chosen to live, but organising daily life in southern Italy was more complicated than elsewhere. There were language problems, and a completely unknown set of rules governing the minutiae of everyday life. It was customary to have someone to help in the house; to organise the shopping, cooking and cleaning. But Marietta was much more than that. She became an integral part of the family. We relied on her to look after us, to arrange the details of every day events, and to cope with the many hassles that confronted us on a regular basis. Although I never admitted it, I was aware that, in the most subtle way, she actually ran the household.

Marietta was the eldest daughter in a large family. Several of her brothers and sisters had emigrated to England or America, but Marietta had always been the daughter on whom her mother depended. As the parents grew older she became the mainstay of her family. When I first knew Marietta, she was in her late thirties, with dark hair, a round happy face, and twinkling brown eyes. She spoke dialect with her fellow *Positanesi*, but we always talked Italian. Although she had a pronounced Neapolitan accent, as did most locals, neither of us were aware that dialect words occasionally slipped into her Italian. I must have picked up the odd word that formed part of her vocabulary, because I'd find, when talking to friends from Rome or northern Italy, that they sometimes looked puzzled and asked, "what does that mean?" I was surprised, convinced I'd been speaking perfect Italian. Apparently I'd absorbed certain Neapolitan expressions, unfamiliar to them, but part of my daily conversation with Marietta.

Marietta had firm ideas about the social order of Positano and where I fitted in. She made it clear in no uncertain terms that her status was at stake if I mixed with people she considered unsuitable. She usually answered the phone; if I replied to a call a head would unfailingly appear around the corner to ask, "C*hi era*?" who was it? If the caller was to her liking she nodded her head in approval, but a frown indicated that the person on the other end of the phone did not accord with her sense of protocol. "Signora," she objected. "Why do you want to spend time with those people, you won't enjoy their company?" Having grown up in Australia, I was unaccustomed to the pecking order that was still very much part of the European social system.

Each morning Marietta arrived early, staying until late afternoon. We started the day by discussing what we'd eat at lunchtime, the midday meal was a major event. Having agreed on the menu, I made out a shopping list. Marietta put considerable thought into the ingredients needed, she enjoyed cooking and loved to be complimented. Producing appetising meals was a source of satisfaction and pride to her. After lengthy discussions, I set off to order the day's requirements at the local shop. Sometimes I returned with *le spese*, but more often a delivery boy was sent.

The local store was known as Palatone, although this was not the name of the family who owned it. It was a nickname, I never discovered whether the word had any significance, nor how it had been acquired. Several brothers, all known by the same name, operated grocery stores in different parts of the village. People went every day to buy food; going to the nearest Palatone was a way of life for the *Positanesi*, and in fact for anyone who lived in town. Groceries, wine, detergents and non-perishable goods were always in stock, but cheese, *prosciutto, mortadella, salami,* and dairy products had to be fresh. Fruit and vegetables were available only in season; cold storage was not even considered. So people went to Palatone to examine the day's merchandise, to see what was in store and what looked good. They lingered for hours, ostensibly to select with care each piece of fruit, to check the canteloupe or water melon, to deliberate about the choice of vegetables. But it was also a meeting place, especially for the women. Shopping was interspersed with enquiries about family and friends, discussions of the latest gossip, exchange of daily news. The visit to the store served not only to buy provisions; it was a social event, a part of the culture.

Greeting my fellow shoppers, I carefully sorted through the colourful display, then, catching the eye of the shopkeeper, gave my order. In due course it would be delivered. Our local store was always well stocked. It was run by a husband and wife team who worked twelve hours a day, seven days a week. Their four children helped after school and on weekends. Friendly, helpful, and tolerant of foreigners like myself who sometimes made mistakes in ordering, or whose questions might be difficult to comprehend, they tried to oblige, going out of their way to procure items like breakfast cereal, Liptons or Twinings tea, or other goods outside their normal range.

I had problems with the milk, which rarely tasted as I believed it should. For some reason, fresh pasteurized milk was delivered at unexpected hours of the day, and, since it needed to be refrigerated immediately on arrival, considerable ingenuity was required on my part. I'm sure the Palatone family considered me quite obsessive on the subject. I was known as '*la signora australiana*', or '*la signora dell' avvocato*'. I can imagine their comments about this difficult *signora* whenever I made a fuss about *il latte fresco*, fresh milk.

Cream was not sold at the store; it had to be bought at the *latteria*, dairy. The fact that it was unpasteurized created a dilemma for me with my background in microbiology, particularly as I loved

91

dessert with cream. Sometimes I compromised with my conscience, only to be punished when the forbidden cream didn't taste as fresh as I might have wished.

But the milk and cream were exceptions. In general, fresh produce in Positano was excellent. Fruit and vegetables were outstandingly good. Never have I tasted more luscious peaches, nor such sweet and juicy tomatoes. It was a pleasure to browse among *la frutta e verdure,* everything looked so appetising; red, green and yellow peppers, artichokes, glossy purple eggplants, melons in a variety of colours, shapes and sizes, clusters of grapes; a profusion of perfumes and colours to tempt the senses. Marietta's shopping list usually included a few items from the vast assortment of available herbs. Italian cooks have devised methods to turn the most bland and uninteresting components into delicious dishes. I still had to discover the traditional way of using each ingredient. I had much to learn.

*     *     *     *     *

Meat was obtained at the *macelleria,* butcher's shop. If I wanted to be sure of an excellent dinner, I bought chicken. Fresh supplies were delivered each day from the surrounding district, and were among the best poultry I've eaten anywhere. I never had a failure with chicken, whether roasted, boiled, cooked *alla cacciatora,* or served as salad, I was invariably pleased with the result.

Pork, available only in the winter months, was also good. I'd always loved roast pork, particularly the crisp browned skin known as crackling. I told Salvatore, our local butcher, how we roast pork in Australia. I described the process; first we ask the butcher to make incisions in the skin, then, before putting the meat in the oven we rub oil or salt - people argue over the relative merits of each - over the surface. After the required time in the oven we produce tender meat with a crisp and crackly crust. Salvatore looked perplexed. "You couldn't use such a method here, *Signora,*" was his reaction. After he showed me a side of pork hanging in his cold room, I understood why. Pigs are killed at a heavier body weight than is customary in Australia, so that, at the time of slaughter, a considerable amount of fat has been deposited. I could see the difficulty of roasting a piece of pork with all this fat attached; it was not a pleasing prospect. Besides, there was no problem in finding a use for the fat, *sugna*, lard was a staple item in local households. But Salvatore, out of the kindness of his heart, devised a way for me to have my crackling. When I bought pork he cut the rind off a selected piece of meat, removed most of the fat, then reattached the skin, tying it on firmly with string. This was seen as another peculiarity of *la signora australiana*, but I appreciated his effort to please me.

Lamb was sold once a year at *Pasqua*, Easter, and was different, both in appearance and taste, to that which I'd previously known. We always enjoyed our Easter *agnello*. I bought a side of lamb and roasted it in one piece, lightly flavoured with garlic and rosemary. This was just enough to feed a family of four, and was delicious. As for lamb chops, a staple of every Australian home, they were so tiny I could hardly find them.

But beef and veal, unfortunately, were not good. The butcher had a supply of so-called *vitellone*, which can be translated either as old veal or young beef. "What's for dinner today," he'd ask the customer. "Schnitzel, casserole, what would you like?" He then set the mechanical slicer to whatever thickness he deemed appropriate, and cut the *vitellone* accordingly. I had trouble with this system. Stenio knew I loved a juicy steak. Occasionally he tried, at considerable expense, to give me a treat; asking Salvatore, or one of the other local butchers, to provide us with the best fillet steak for a special dinner. It was invariably a disappointment, we chewed away on a tough old piece of meat, pretending it was wonderful. Most of the restaurants provided good beef; they must have received their supplies elsewhere. Certainly in other parts of Italy the meat was excellent, *bistecca alla fiorentina*, florentine steak, is justly famous.

Over the years, Salvatore and I became good friends, but my first encounter with him was extremely embarrassing. Unsure of what to order, I solved the problem by saying, "Please can I buy some meat?" The Italian word for meat is *carne*, and the letter 'r' must be pronounced. It must in fact be trilled, an effect which is achieved, according to my textbook 'by flipping the tip of the tongue against the gum of the upper front teeth'. I never really succeeded in mastering this sound, difficult for anyone accustomed to speaking English. Unfortunately for me, in Italian *cane* means dog, so my friend the butcher and others in the shop were amazed. They understood, "Please can I buy some dog?" This became the standard joke; whenever Salvatore saw me coming he would say, "Would you like some dog today?"

*     *     *     *     *

Marietta was an excellent cook. I always looked forward to her midday meal. We had tasty pasta dishes with a variety of sauces, home made *gnocchi*, healthy vegetable soups. Pot roast *girello* was among her specialties. A piece of yearling beef - which she always selected personally - was larded with bacon and garlic, then braised in a sauce of grated vegetables, wine and stock. I liked to serve this meat and delicate gravy with mashed potato.

Other favourites were *minestrone, risotto, pizza*, stuffed artichokes, stuffed tomatoes. Whatever we desired, Marietta produced. I have many of her recipes, but it was difficult to elicit details. Her cooking had been learned by experience, not from recipes; it was a little of this, a dash of that. When I asked how much pasta, bread, parsley, or other ingredient she used, she replied with a laugh, "*Ma Signora, non lo so, quello che ci vuole.*" I don't know, Signora, whatever's needed. So I took notes as she cooked, trying to estimate quantities.

One of her outstanding preparations was *parmigiana di finocchio*. Using fennel instead of eggplant, she produced a delicious variation of the typical local dish, *parmigiana di melanzane*. I don't know whether Marietta personally invented the recipe, I've certainly never come across this particular combination elsewhere. The following is an extract from my notebook.

'Cut each fennel bulb into about six pieces and cook in boiling water *al dente,* underdone. Drain, roll in flour and fry in oil.

94

Arrange fennel slices at the base of a greased casserole dish, top with freshly prepared tomato sauce, sliced mozzarella and grated parmesan.
Repeat ingredients in alternate layers and bake in moderate oven for about 20 minutes.'

The evening meal in Italy is, at least in theory, a light repast. Somehow we had trouble with that concept. I'd been used to a light lunch and substantial dinner. Stenio had been accustomed to the opposite. So, in our early years together, we tended to eat two sizeable meals each day. In time, we realised this was not wise. But we never really sorted out a sensible arrangement until we had children.

*    *    *    *    *

Entertaining was a way of life in Positano. Sometimes we had house guests, often we invited friends to dinner. On these occasions, Marietta usually prepared the first course before she left for the day. Her repertoire included a variety of pasta dishes which could be prepared some hours earlier and placed in the oven when required. I didn't always admit, when my guests complimented me on the excellent dinner, that it had not been all my own work. Sometimes I did, depending on the mood of the moment. Since Stenio enjoyed food and loved cooking, he often suggested a particular fish or chicken specialty as main course, and was more than happy to do the cooking. Dessert consisted of fresh fruit. Why would anyone bother to serve a complicated sweet in summer, when fresh fruit was so good? It's easy to see why I thoroughly enjoyed giving dinner parties. Having said all that, I hasten to add that I also enjoy preparing for special occasions. I sometimes surprised our guests by serving a non-Italian, even an Australian dinner.

I discovered during my first few weeks in Italy that food forms an essential feature of the local culture. Food preparation, a favourite topic of conversation among both men and women, is of paramount importance. There are endless discussions about what to eat, how it should be cooked, what ingredients to add. I never ceased to be amazed that dinner guests could spend a whole evening in intricate debate about various aspects, not only of the meal they were currently eating, but of previous culinary experiences. They might recall and analyse in minute detail last week's luncheon, or a memorable reception months ago. Alternatively, everyone would offer suggestions for a *festa* planned at some future date; the menu, how best to cook the fish or meat, whether pasta or soup was more appropriate, what wines to serve. All this while consuming, and obviously enjoying, an excellent meal prepared with considerable care by their host.

One balmy summer evening we invited friends from Rome to join us for dinner. After drinks and *antipasto* we started on the first course, butterfly pasta with a smoked salmon sauce. This was a specialty, and I waited for the usual compliments.

"This pasta's excellent, how did you prepare the sauce?" asked Aldo.

Before I could answer he went on, "Have you tried it with rice, *risotto al salmone affumicato*. I made a similar *salsa* last week, but I used *vongole*, clams, and served it with *tagliatelle*." At this point I was lost for words. Not that it mattered, he didn't expect a reply.

Subsequent discussion about the relative merits of thick, thin, short or long pasta was interrupted by Pietro, who said sensibly, "I wouldn't change it, why alter a successful recipe?"

Then Elena started. She'd invited friends for the following weekend and decided to buy *pesce spada*, swordfish, which was in season at the moment. The conversation moved to swordfish. Elena liked it marinated and grilled.

"Absolutely not." Aldo's wife was adamant. "We had swordfish last week. I cooked it with tomatoes, capers and olives."

"*Troppo buono,*" too good, agreed Aldo, fingers to lips in an indicative gesture.

Conversations like this could go on for hours.

# THE NEW ARRIVAL

During the time the house was being built I became pregnant. Although I was thrilled to be expecting a baby, I was a little nervous at the prospect. We were confronted with an immediate problem; where should this exciting event, the birth of our first baby, take place? There were five doctors in Positano, but no hospital. We started to make inquiries; where should we go to find a good obstetrician and a well-equipped maternity hospital? Everyone I asked was delighted to give advice, but of course, opinions varied, rarely did two individuals agree. We asked Italian friends. Some said, "Go to Rome or Milan, don't have your first baby in Naples." This seemed a good idea, I would certainly feel more comfortable in either of these cities, but we had to be practical. Carol had introduced me to other foreign girls who'd married into the local community; maybe they could help. I called to visit several friends who'd recently had babies, and asked their opinion. I listened as they recounted their experiences, and gathered all sorts of information - which clinic they preferred, their feelings about the quality of nursing, their reaction to one or other obstetrician. But this only added to my confusion.

Eventually we made the first decision. The sensible solution was to have the baby in Naples. At least it was reasonably accessible. Having agreed on the city, we had to select a clinic. There was general consensus that the best available option was a hospital known as the International, whose director was a highly regarded Swiss doctor. Several women recommended this doctor and the facilities he provided. So I rang the *ospedale internazionale* and made an appointment.

Going to Naples was always an adventure. We set off well in advance of the required time, allowing about two hours to reach the outskirts of the city. Then we had to find our way through chaotic traffic to our destination. No doubt for Neapolitans, hectic traffic is a routine of daily life, but for the uninitiated, it can present a distinct problem. Since Stenio knew his way around the city, we coped reasonably well, and arrived at the hospital without too much delay. We were delighted to find ourselves in a beautiful part of Naples; the position was spectacular, overlooking the city and bay. I would come to know this outlook extremely well, much better than I might have wished.

We were greeted by a receptionist, shown to a waiting room, and invited to sit and wait. After what seemed an interminable delay, we were ushered into an elegant consulting room. Dr. Gerhard, the Swiss doctor, was all that I had expected; distinguished, perfectly groomed, and absolutely charming. After examining me, he was most reassuring. "Don't worry," he said. "We'll look after you well. I'm sure you'll be happy here. I can't foresee any problems." He suggested that I come for a second check-up at a later date. The baby was due towards the end of May.

We returned home reasonably content with our choice. I had plenty to do. As well as the continual decision making as our house neared completion, I now had to start thinking about the requirements of a brand-new baby. My mother was due to arrive soon, and I knew she'd be happy to help.

Italians adore babies, and love to surround them with beautiful things. Everywhere we went we found an astonishing number of shops selling exquisite outfits for newborn infants. Plus a bewildering variety of prams, pushers, bassinets, cradles and other neonatal equipment. I thoroughly enjoyed our shopping trips, and came home each time with bulky packages, keeping *i facchini*, the porters, busy carrying parcels and boxes to our new home. One or two *facchini* could usually be found waiting at the grotto of Fornillo, chatting to passers-by until someone called for their assistance.

*     *     *     *     *

As summer approached, the number of tourists increased. They arrived in taxis, in cars and passenger coaches, on motor bikes, or by whatever form of transportation they could find. As the narrow curving roads of the Amalfi coast became clogged, there were more and more reports of traffic jams. Visitors were caught in a series of mix-ups and delayed for long periods. Guests arrived at inconvenient times to find their hosts had started dinner without them, or even worse, had finished their meal. Others found that, through no fault of their own, they'd missed some carefully planned event, causing embarrassment to all concerned. I started to worry that, when the time came for my baby to arrive, I might be trapped in such horrendous traffic. I imagined nightmarish situations where I was forced to give birth by the side of the road, or in some tiny village. How could I be sure of getting to the hospital in time?

By late May, I was looking quite large and beginning to feel apprehensive. One morning I woke with a strange uncomfortable sensation. Perhaps this was the beginning of the long awaited labour pains? I had the impression that something momentous was about to occur. So, with my mother and Stenio, we set off. We were well prepared, suitcases packed and ready; everything had been planned in advance. Our friend Mimi the taxi driver had been expecting a call, and had promised to provide us with immediate transport. He assured us that if he were unable to come personally, he would send a replacement. As luck would have it, Mimi was available. I was delighted he could accompany us, his was a reassuring presence. We had acquired a small nucleus of people who could be relied upon in moments of crisis. They adopted us as their responsibility, and were always happy to help at a moment's notice. Mimi was one of these marvellous people.

As expected, the roads were packed, both *en route* to Naples and in the city itself. Mimi calmly and competently navigated his way through the chaos. Arriving at the *ospedale internazionale,* we waited to see the doctor. A receptionist informed us that Dr. Gerhard was not available that morning. His assistant had been called, however, and would be with us at any moment. So we waited for this unknown doctor to appear. The assistant turned out to be a young French doctor who had grown up in Morocco. He'd arrived only recently and was busy settling in; his wife and two children had moved into a nearby apartment. He examined me carefully, then appeared lost in thought. Eventually, he gave his considered opinion.

"It could be some time," he told us. "Maybe one or two days, maybe more, before you can expect to go into labour. But in view of the long trip from Positano, and the risk of traffic delays, I think you'd be better off not to return home. Why don't you stay nearby for a day or two?"

I needed no persuading. Directly opposite was an extremely elegant hotel. It was one of the better hotels in Naples, and was priced accordingly. We booked in for a few nights, and I was happy to spend the following days enjoying the luxurious room with its large balcony. A funicular rail led down to the city centre, and we went each morning to look at museums, art galleries or shops. We had lunch in good restaurants and saw a few films. With my mother I visited elegant shops of household decor. It was novel to have time to browse, instead of having to hurry back in the evening for the long return trip to Positano. I acquired a sofa for our sitting room, and sundry accessories. I was particularly thrilled with my new Spanish style lampshades of blown glass set in a wrought-iron frame.

I was quite enjoying this life. After the third day, with no sign of anything happening, I returned to the hospital to consult the senior specialist. He agreed with his assistant. "Don't worry, the baby will arrive at any minute," he assured me. Stenio had commitments in Positano, so he left, promising to return at the first sign of activity. My mother and I stayed on.

We made friends with several of our fellow residents, in particular an American woman who, like us, had chosen to stay at this hotel because of its proximity to the international hospital. She and her husband had been on a cruise when he suddenly became ill and had to be rushed to hospital. After visiting him each morning, she was at a loss at how to fill in the rest of the day. Each morning she greeted me with, "How's little cornflake today?" or "Any sign of Debbie?" For some reason Debbie had been proposed as a possible name. As the days went by we waited, speculating about which of us would leave Naples first.

We were now in early June, and the world was tense at the sudden outbreak of war in the Middle East, the Six Day war between

100

Israel and her Arab neighbours. Our hotel was filled with Americans expelled from Arab countries. I spent my evenings reclining on a *chaise longue* in one of the beautifully appointed reception rooms. Together with my fellow guests, I sat glued to the television awaiting each news bulletin as Israel battled for its existence.

Eventually, after two weeks, Adriana decided to enter this world. There was a final irony. After the long wait, it happened that, on this of all nights, a minor landslide had occurred in the area where the hospital was located. The young doctor's apartment was slightly damaged. As a result, he was frantically busy moving his family into temporary accommodation. He was not remotely interested in my imminent need for him. The senior doctor was, for some unexplained reason, again unavailable. And so we were left to the tender mercies of a very young and very nervous nurse. There was no sign of a trained midwife, or indeed of any qualified medical practitioner. Stenio was told to put on gumboots - the reason for this remained another mystery - and come to the theatre to assist the young nurse. Fortunately, it was an easy birth and all went well. I hate to think what would have happened had there been complications. On paying the hotel bill, we realised that Adriana was undoubtedly one of the most expensive babies to have been born for quite some time.

But she was a happy baby and gave us much joy. A first baby is very special, and we were delighted and proud to return home with our perfect little daughter.

*       *       *       *       *

I was determined not to return to the rented house. This new and exciting phase of our life must begin in our new home. Having begged and bullied the workmen to the best of my ability, I had almost, but not quite, achieved my goal. The essential elements of the building were now in place, but many minor details were still to be completed. Would the *operai,* workmen, ever finish the job? I began to have serious doubts. We must have had the world's slowest painters, they'd started in January and were still adding the final touches.

Giovanni proved a friend. "I understand the *Signora* perfectly," he said. "Even if we have to work long hours, we'll have the house at a point where you can move in. You'll be able to come home with your new baby, I promise."

And so, despite the fact that everything was not quite ready, we moved in as soon as I came out of hospital. Stenio had arranged that Marietta would come each day as soon as we took up residence in Via Fornillo. Thus the arrival of Marietta coincided with the arrival of Adriana in our lives. We came home to a spotless house. My mother-in-law had prepared dinner and was waiting expectantly, tremendously excited to see her first grandchild.

If I had little idea of how to manage a house, I was completely unprepared for coping with a newborn baby. In Australia young mothers were encouraged to go each week to their local health centre. How I envied them! Marietta, who had helped her mother raise a large family, became my substitute health centre and mothercraft nurse, advising on each new dilemma. She had an enormous fund of practical common sense, and her presence was a great relief to me. I have always been a worrier at the best of times, and this was not an easy situation. A nearly finished house in a small village, a particularly tiny baby - hardly a prospect to inspire confidence.

Fortunately my mother had rented a house nearby, and, thrilled with her new granddaughter, was happy to help whenever possible. She had a friend, Mizzi staying with her. Mizzi had worked for many years as a trained nurse, and was full of advice for the new mother. So I had quite a choice, I could seek counsel from Marietta, my mother, my mother-in-law or Mizzi. And, of course, there was Dr. Spock. I consulted Dr. Spock daily. His book on child care, with its sensible suggestions on how to cope with every day problems, became my bible.

\*      \*      \*      \*      \*

When we started building, one of our first tasks had been to lodge an application for the installation of a telephone. Having a phone in the house was high on our list of priorities. As soon as we received a building permit from the local council, we made sure that all the necessary papers were completed immediately. But, despite frequent requests to the relevant authorities, the phone was not connected when we took up occupancy. Most of our immediate neighbours were not permanent residents, coming from time to time for brief holidays, so the houses near us were frequently unoccupied. Although I was slightly uneasy at the prospect of being so isolated, I refused to wait any longer. It could take months before the bureaucracy decided to connect telephones in our area. We would just have to manage.

When the baby was a few weeks old, Janet and Tom came to stay. I was delighted, they were good company, and we'd been looking forward to their visit. Janet and Tom were lavish with their compliments. We all like to be flattered, and I was no exception, deriving great pleasure from their admiration. "What a fantastic house," Tom would say. "Aren't you lucky? Imagine living in this beautiful environment." Or "Isn't Adriana a perfect baby, so pretty?"

One evening I was giving Adriana her daily bath while Janet looked on. Mizzi had taught me how to bath the baby. Her method was quite tricky, as it involved turning the tiny infant around. This ensured a perfect result, there was no doubt that at least once each day I'd have a thoroughly clean child, but it was a slightly hazardous operation. At first I was nervous, but I'd been using this method every day, and had become quite relaxed about it.

We were chatting, while I proudly demonstrated how skilled I'd become in coping with the demands of motherhood. As we talked, I turned the baby over, holding her by the shoulders. Suddenly Janet said, "Why's she thrashing round like that?" I looked in horror to see that my little baby had become quite distressed and was blue in the face. "What happened? Is she all right? Do you think she swallowed some bath water?" We were both talking at once, convinced Adriana was about to drown. "Call a doctor, quick," said Janet in alarm. I suddenly realised that, not having a phone, I was not in a position to call anyone. What were we to do? "You stay there," said Janet. "I'll go and get help." Neither of us even considered the fact that, not speaking a word of Italian, she'd have little hope of explaining the situation.

So Janet ran down the stairs, out the front door and up to the road, calling as she ran, "*Bambina Bella*, blue, blue!" Who knows what the passers-by thought. All I know was that, in record time, I heard a commotion outside. People were running down the steps to our house. Soon they were banging on the front door - a door-knocker had yet to be installed. It wasn't long before Stenio and Tom appeared, together with Mizzi and my mother. Then my mother-in-law rushed in. Friends arrived, one after another. So much for life in a small town! Word gets around quickly. By the time all this help arrived, the crisis was over. As I discovered, babies are much more resilient than we imagine. Most manage to survive and thrive in spite of their mother's mistakes. From that date, however, I never used the Mizzi method to bath a child.

*    *    *    *    *

Despite the occasional crisis, life was good. Builders and tradesmen added final touches to the house. At times I thought we'd have *operai* in our home forever. But gradually we found that fewer workmen were arriving each morning. Much to my relief, technicians at last connected the phone. I could now communicate with the rest of the world. The plumber, after many return visits, managed to remedy a few of the more obvious defects that had occurred during installation.

Just as we were congratulating ourselves on a job well done, Giuseppe the painter reappeared with two assistants and set to work. For some reason he wanted to repaint every room. Cans of paint were everywhere, the smell of freshly painted walls pervaded the whole house. After three days, Giuseppe stormed up the stairs to my room, overcome with fury.

"I refuse to be treated like this, *Signora*," he announced. "I'm leaving."

"*Perche*?" why? I cried in anguish. Without giving me the opportunity to reason with him, he packed his materials, gathered his assistants, and off they went. We never discovered what had happened to cause such offense. And so we had to start again; find another painter, match the colours he'd used, and wait until the new team was available.

I had already learned that Italian tradesmen tell you what you want to hear. Why make a client unhappy if they can avoid it? So when I rang the plumber, electrician, or painter, they listened politely, expressed their disappointment at my inconvenience, and promised to fix the problem immediately. "When will you come?" I'd ask. "*Domani*" was invariably the reply. It didn't take long to learn that, although the literal translation of *domani* is tomorrow, in these circumstances it was more likely to mean next week, next month, or 'when I get around to it'. I've never been very patient when confronted with a household item in need of repair, and I didn't find it easy to cope with the system prevailing in my adopted country. But there was no point in getting upset or angry when an expected tradesman failed to appear. Nothing would change, he'd still come exactly when it suited him. There was not a thing I could do.

# AUSTRALIA

Christmas in Australia. What a wonderful idea! Despite the charmed life I was leading, there were moments of nostalgia. Never had I been so busy. Never had I met people from such a variety of countries. Summer, with its hectic round of social engagements, was exciting. Each morning I wondered what new and stimulating experiences the day would bring. But I still missed Australia, and the close friends I'd known for most of my life. Coming home after a busy day, I often wished I could ring one of my old friends for a chat, or maybe just drop in to say hello. I loved receiving letters from home. It seemed that my departure from the norm, from the way of life accepted by most of my contemporaries, had caused much discussion among friends in Melbourne. My exotic new life style had, I gathered, become a topic for dinner party conversation.

At odd moments, I used to imagine dialogues taking place over a dinner table on the other side of the world. Relaxing at the beach in a comfortable deck-chair, a sudden reminder of childhood beach holidays could set me off. Before I knew it, I was embarking on a flight of fantasy. There I sat, lost in reverie and quite oblivious to my surroundings, until a voice in the background interrupted my chain of thought. *"Che stai pensando?"* What are you thinking about? With an embarrassed laugh, I reluctantly came back to the real world.

During my early days in Italy, keeping up with the language was often a struggle. At times I found myself floundering in the midst of an animated discussion, as my companions, warming to their theme, began to talk so rapidly that I completely lost the thread of their argument. At that point, I usually gave up. It was so much easier to switch off, to let my mind wander. I stopped listening and started to daydream; conjuring up a more diverting, and certainly more comprehensible discourse in far-away Melbourne.

These fictitious conversations were always about me. In my flights of fancy, someone would say enviously, "Isn't Susi lucky to be living such a glamorous life in that beautiful, famous resort?" or

106

"Who would have imagined she'd settle down in a fascinating Italian town? How fabulous!" But then, suddenly, I'd stop and wonder. Maybe I was completely wrong. What if their perceptions were quite the opposite. Perhaps people were saying, "She must be crazy, fancy choosing to live in a tiny, remote Italian village." I definitely preferred the first version! Reflecting on these hypothetical discussions thousands of miles away, I told myself that it was a great experience to live in such a special place, and that I was indeed fortunate. Yet now and then I felt unsure. Had I made the right choice? If only it were possible to combine my two worlds.

When the opportunity to visit Melbourne presented itself, I was thrilled. I had long wanted to show Stenio the city where I'd grown up, to introduce him to people who had played an important role in my life. Hopefully, he would gain a better understanding of my background, so different from his own. I was really looking forward to seeing friends from the past, telling them about my exciting new life, and catching up with events in their world. How satisfying to show off a new husband and baby!

But these anticipated pleasures were not the principal reason for our visit. Whenever I mentioned our prospective trip, someone would tell me we were crazy to undertake such a marathon project with a tiny baby. I had no doubt they were right, obviously this was not the ideal moment for an extended voyage. There had to be a better reason, a more pressing justification for our decision to travel half way around the world. And indeed there was.

When I left home several years earlier, my intention had been to work for a year or two, acquire research experience, and hopefully combine this pursuit with holidays in Europe. I'd always longed to travel widely, to discover places I knew only from books. But I'd always planned to return to Australia, never for one moment had I imagined I was leaving for good. Now that events had taken a completely unexpected turn and my life had entered a radically different phase, I needed to sort out the many loose ends I'd left behind. I couldn't keep relying on other people to manage for me. I must learn to be responsible for my own affairs.

107

There were a number of business problems to be resolved. My mother had left a few weeks earlier, flying home to attend to the complexities of unfinished transactions. Since I was an only child she had relied on me since my father's death, and I felt an obligation to be with her, to assist in putting our family affairs in order. I realised, of course, that I was complicating her life enormously. It would be unreasonable and inconsiderate to opt out of my responsibilities, leaving her to cope alone with all her worries, plus the consequences of my actions. I hadn't anticipated the complications resulting from my decision to change countries.

Then there were all my belongings; how had I ever managed to accumulate so many things? There were boxes and trunks to be retrieved out of storage. I was tempted to throw everything out, but I knew I'd regret such an impulsive act. Each individual carton would have to be opened, while I agonized over what was worth keeping, what to discard or give away. Then everything would have to be repacked. I'd have to find a carrier and organize transport. Not a job to look forward to, but one that had to be done!

I was well aware of the bureaucratic requirements confronting me. I knew I'd find a mountain of documents to sign and forms to fill in. No doubt I'd spend hours standing in queues. Why was it all so complicated, both the Australian and the Italian governments seemed determined to make life difficult. But I had no choice, each detail must be in order before I was entitled to become a resident of another country.

My mother naturally wanted to spend part of the year with me, her only daughter, and my new family. Now it was her turn to make decisions. Should she sell her home in Australia, and perhaps buy a property in Positano? She could use this as a base, invite friends to stay, and spend time travelling in Europe. Since my mother was originally from Europe, the prospect of returning to live on that continent did not displease her. Certainly I'd caused an upheaval in her life that she could well have done without. How much easier it would have been if I'd married the boy next door. However, all this activity was exhilarating, we made plans which were constantly changing, and I admired her cheerful enthusiasm and cooperation.

*     *     *     *     *

In November, we left Positano with Adriana, just five months old. Despite some misgivings about the wisdom of globe trotting with a small child, I felt very excited.  I needn't have worried, I soon discovered that travel with a baby is easy, infinitely preferable to a long flight with a toddler.  Babies eat and sleep; they have no desire to go wandering.  The flight attendants were helpful; we were given seats with considerable space for a cot, kindly provided by the airline.  Although Stenio and I felt tired on arrival, Adriana was in fine form.

It had been a very long trip.  We arrived in Rome to be told that our flight had been delayed, and that all passengers should board a bus waiting to transport them to a city hotel for an overnight stay. In other circumstances I would have been thrilled at the opportunity of luxuriating in a first class Roman hotel, but not at that particular moment.  The complications of procuring a cot, baby food, milk, and nappies somewhat spoiled the occasion.  We did take the opportunity to ring Helen and Marco, suggesting they join us for a drink in our glamorous hotel.  They'd travelled with young children and could give us useful tips.  Our enforced stay turned out to be surprisingly enjoyable.  But when, twenty four hours later, the identical situation recurred in Sydney, and we were obliged to make another overnight stop, we were not amused.  Although I had friends living in Sydney, I was in no mood for a reunion, or for introducing my new husband. All we wanted was a comfortable bed and some sleep.

We arrived in Melbourne to be met by my mother and friends.  How strange to hear everyone speaking with an Australian accent.  Although relatively few years had passed since I'd left Australia, so much had happened in the intervening period that I felt I'd been absent for a long, long time.  The drive from the airport into the city was an odd experience.  Familiar signs advertised brands I'd forgotten, posters displayed products I knew well but had never seen in Europe.  As we passed through shopping centres, I felt an illogical sense of surprise to find everything written in English, street names, signposts, traffic notices. All of a sudden I found myself translating what I saw into Italian. Despite my weariness I began to laugh. Everyone looked at me. "Don't ask me to explain," I said. "I'm thoroughly confused myself."

Rows of houses on quarter acre blocks lined streets radiating out from major thoroughfares. Carefully tended gardens surrounded homes of brick, brick veneer, or timber. The style varied according to the fashion prevailing at the time of construction, but all were solidly built and in good condition. It couldn't have been more different from Positano. I wondered what Stenio was thinking.

I'd become accustomed to small, easily manoeuvrable automobiles like the baby Fiat, to motor scooters weaving their way in and out between cars, to the pandemonium on Italy's congested roads. Here the roads were wide, the traffic controlled, the cars, including the Holden, imprinted on my memory as 'Australia's own car', large and shiny. Characteristic green and yellow trams rattled along as they always had, occupying the central part of major roads. Everything looked neat and tidy. My overwhelming impression was one of order. The colours, the vegetation, even the blue of the sky were characteristically Australian. How good it was to be back in an environment I knew so well, everything seemed exactly as I remembered. I felt at home.

But these initial observations proved superficial, I soon discovered that all was not really as before. I'd been away more than twelve years, and Melbourne had changed during my absence. The city sky line had altered, high rise buildings had sprung up, new developments appeared. Small motor vehicles did exist, in fact they were quite common. I could see the effects of large scale migration from Europe; the influx of diverse ethnic groups had added a new dimension. It was amazing to hear foreign languages spoken, to find restaurants serving delicacies from many countries. Profound changes were taking place in a society which had been relatively homogeneous. But on that first day I was struck by similarities with the past, reviving nostalgic childhood memories. No doubt I saw what I was looking for, ignoring anything that didn't fit in with my preconceived ideas.

We were taken to a comfortable home where wonderful friends offered us hospitality. "You're welcome to stay as long as you like," said my friend Anna. "Take your time, relax, have a rest before you start looking for accommodation." We gratefully accepted her offer and stayed for several days. I happily rediscovered the Australian life style. Our hosts were helpful and friendly, everything was done with a minimum of fuss and bother. Meals were simple but good; breakfast, in particular was a joy. What a variety of cereals there were, I was tempted to take a photograph to show Palatone. In the past I'd laughed at Australians who took vegemite to Europe, now I was surprised at the pleasure a jar of this local product could arouse. Our hosts offered us cooked breakfast, but we were more than happy with cereal, toast, and freshly brewed tea, none of which were easy to obtain in Positano.

Lunch consisted of sandwiches. Even though I'd grown up taking a cut lunch to school and subsequently to work, I'd forgotten such local customs. What would happen, I wondered, if I were occasionally to suggest sandwiches for lunch in Italy? The idea might amount to sacrilege. I made a mental resolution that, at an appropriate time, I'd attempt to introduce this unprecedented concept. It was worth a try.

At dinner time, most families sat down to a roast or grill; why bother with complicated dishes when the meat was good and inexpensive? I proudly showed Stenio that steak really can be tender, unlike our disappointing experiences in southern Italy. Stenio was so enthusiastic about the barbecue that he bought a small portable model and took it back home. Whenever we had guests he proudly demonstrated this typically Australian product. "See how they grill meat in Australia. It's a great idea, simple, practical and effective."

\*　　　\*　　　\*　　　\*　　　\*

Our visit to Melbourne was an enormous success. Australians in general, and my friends in particular, are extremely hospitable. We stayed for several months, and enjoyed ourselves immensely. It was indeed a wonderful holiday. Our main problem was how to fit in all the invitations we received. My diary was full, it was hard to find a free evening; there were dinner parties and barbecues, weekends in the country or at the beach. Stenio was most impressed by his visits to farms in country Victoria, discovering a landscape quite unlike anything he'd ever experienced. Having grown up in a densely populated part of the world, the sense of space, the vast areas available as farmland came as a revelation. One of the highlights of this period were days spent at the races, again a totally unfamiliar spectacle. Thoroughbred horses in all their elegant splendour, the colorful outfits of the jockeys, the picnic lunches - how he relished giving detailed descriptions of these events to his friends. "You should go to Australia, see how good life is there," he told them. Although Stenio's English was rather sketchy, no-one seemed to mind. He loved everything about his visit. I did, too, I felt so happy to be among old friends.

We were interviewed by local journalists who produced articles with titles like 'local girl lives romantic life in Italian beach resort'. There ensued a brief moment of glory, photographs and stories appeared in the daily papers and the Women's Weekly. Our fame didn't last long; we were displaced from centre stage by an extraordinary event.

Just before Christmas, the Australian Prime Minister, Harold Holt, disappeared while swimming at an ocean beach, an area known for its treacherous currents. "How could such a thing could happen?" we asked. "How can you just lose a Prime Minister? Shouldn't a nation's leader be surrounded by bodyguards?" There were a few suggestions of foul play. I wondered whether the European papers had discussed this event, and what their comments might be. Having regularly watched the news coverage provided by Italian television, its detailed analysis of world events, I used to reflect that Australia, so interesting to me, was never mentioned. Journalists dissected in fine detail the various aspects of happenings in Europe, America, Asia, and Africa, but rarely Australia. Surely the disappearance of a Prime Minister would rate a comment.

*    *    *    *    *

We rented an attractive house. Friends were generous, lending me all the baby equipment I could possibly need. We hired a car; it was impossible to circulate in Melbourne without one. As the weeks went by I caught up with Melbourne news. I visited friends and met their children, most of whom had been born during my absence. Shopping at supermarkets was a new experience; I had to learn a whole new system. Here it was not customary to shop every day; there was no Palatone equivalent, and of course no Marietta. I adapted my housekeeping routine to suit the local rules.

Christmas was approaching and I planned to make the most of it. We'd have a traditional Christmas dinner - roast turkey with cranberry sauce, baked ham, roast vegetables, plum pudding and brandy sauce. It's amazing how such customs assume enormous importance when they're unavailable. I realised we were conforming to a tradition instituted in Europe, where December comes in winter, rather than at a time which can be exceedingly hot. Even so, a hot Christmas dinner had become, in my mind, a symbol of what was right. How I enjoyed this very special meal, remembering our hazardous roast dinners in Positano.

Next day was Boxing Day. Following another Melbourne tradition, we packed a picnic lunch, loaded the car with beach umbrella, folding chairs, towels, sunburn creams, everything that could possibly be required for a day of sea and sun. We joined a long line of cars, and proceeded to spend half the day waiting and sweltering in a hot car. Stenio thought we were crazy, and said so repeatedly.

"At least the drivers don't sound their horns non-stop," I said. "See how polite Australian drivers are."

I can't believe we're doing this," he replied. "We can walk to the beach in Positano. Why on earth should we go through this ordeal? Who cares whether the drivers are polite or not?"

I had to admit he was right. Not every Australian custom is perfect.

*　　*　　*　　*　　*

Despite superficial differences, I realised that the pattern of daily life is remarkably similar wherever you live. In a few aspects, however, I noticed a distinct disparity between my contemporaries in the two countries. Certain priorities varied. For example, there was a striking difference in their attitudes to family planning. Most of my Australian friends, particularly those who were Catholic, had at least four children, some had five, six or even seven. In Italy, on the other hand, I was continually listening to pronouncements on what constituted the ideal unit. The consensus was for a nuclear family of mother, father, and two children. Some argued that one child was adequate. When I had temerity to ask whether anyone had ever considered the possibility of having three or more children, I met with a stunned silence. Not one lone voice could be heard in favour of a large family.

Italian women with professional qualifications were determined to pursue their careers, making whatever arrangements they could for child-care. Often grandparents were called upon to mind children, or just to baby-sit. In Australia, by contrast, most of my friends were quite relaxed about their professional lives. They seemed content to devote themselves to bringing up their families while the children were young, hoping to go back to work at a later date. This divergence in outlook among women of similar educational backgrounds became a topic for endless discussions. Perhaps the relative economic security in Australia was a factor? Since this was a time of large scale immigration and full employment, women had few financial worries; presumably their husbands would continue to bring home a good income. Why hurry back to work, why not wait until the children were at school? The demand for trained people was such that women were assured of finding work in their chosen field if and when they desired to rejoin the work force. In Italy, on the other hand, jobs were scarce. University graduates, including doctors and lawyers, often struggled to make a living. Did this explain the difference in attitudes?

Introducing such debates on my return to Italy, I was firmly disabused. "You must be crazy, you haven't understood us at all," my friends said. "The difference in economic climate may be a factor. But you've really missed the point. Why on earth do you imagine we've done years of study to obtain a qualification, only to give it all up? Why should we stay home to change nappies?" My friend Mirella, an archaeologist, was adamant. "I adore my children, and love to spend time with them. But I infinitely prefer to continue my research, to use my intellectual abilities, and see the children at my leisure. Even if all my salary goes to pay for someone to look after them. That way we're all happy."

*    *    *    *

From the moment I left the maternity hospital with my new baby, I'd thought with envy of young mothers in Australia. Whenever they had a problem, even a tiny niggling worry, they could go to their nearest health centre and all would be resolved. How lucky they were. I, a born worrier, didn't have this option. I often felt confused and unsure. Was I giving Adriana the right milk, was it enough, why wasn't she putting on more weight, why did she cry? Now that we were in Australia I, too, could seek expert advice. I could hardly wait. All my problems would be solved!

One of my first priorities, therefore, was a visit to the local health centre. Early one morning we set off. Dressed in a pretty Italian outfit, Adriana looked fresh, tidy and quite adorable. Arriving at the health centre, we entered a large waiting room to join a group of young mothers. They all knew each other and were chatting happily. The babies looked plump and placid, I was sure they ate all the food they were given, cried at the right time, and did everything perfectly.

The visit started badly. Adriana, although small for her age, was extremely active. First she grabbed everything within reach, pulling rugs from under the babies on either side, while their mothers looked at me in dismay. Next she tried to leap off my lap, banging her head on a nearby chair. The sister came out of her office saying, "Don't tell me the noise I just heard was a child hitting its head. You'd better take her home and keep her in a darkened room in case of concussion." I ignored that, but by now I was feeling decidedly hassled and inadequate.

Eventually it was our turn. I filled in the necessary forms, and we were ushered in to meet the sister. I introduced myself, explaining that, although I was Australian, I'd been living in Italy and was here on a temporary visit. I told her how delighted I was to have this opportunity to seek her advice. We discussed what food Adriana should be eating, what her weight should be, her nutritional requirements. We soon discovered that, by the standards of the health care nurse, I was doing most things wrong. We came to the need for fresh fruit. I mentioned a particular gadget popular in Italy; a glass apple grater which produces a mashed apple pulp much loved by small children. Whereupon the sister said in an icy tone, "Why don't you go back to Italy if you think everything there's so marvellous?"

So much for my long-awaited visit to a health centre. I had so looked forward to this opportunity, and it turned out disastrously. I went home feeling depressed, was I a complete failure as a mother? But perhaps I'd needed this experience. Maybe it was not such a misfortune to be without access to the child care system. Who needs a steady dose of discouragement and disapproval?

I had not anticipated the fact that a baby's biological clock ticks on, regardless of its migration from northern to southern hemisphere. Adriana was not remotely interested to know that we had changed from night to day, or that she should now alter her cycle of four-hourly feeds. She was bright and chirpy at night, wanting to sleep during the day. After my recent negative experience, I was certainly not inclined to ask advice at the health centre. So we continued to have a cheerful baby waking at all the wrong hours. By

116

the time she'd become accustomed to our new time table, we were almost due to return and reverse the situation.

She did cope extremely well with all the demands made on her. Not only had she been required to adapt her routine to suit our convenience, she also had to put up with being shown off to all my friends. Added to this was the indignity of being subjected to a series of vaccinations, triple antigen injections, oral Sabin vaccine, and anything else that was available. She tolerated these impositions cheerfully, smiling and gurgling happily, and giving us a great deal of enjoyment.

*     *     *     *     *

Like all good things, our Australian holiday came to an end. It had been a positive experience, a happy time for us both. On the flight between my two worlds, returning from the new to the old, I was full of conflicting emotions. I couldn't make up my mind whether I was sad to be leaving, or happy at the prospect of returning to my new home. There was an element of both.

Expatriates face a number of problems, among which is a feeling of ambivalence, of belonging in two places, which can be quite disturbing. I've discussed this quandary with others who've lived in more than one country. It can be an enriching experience, an opportunity to appreciate the good points of two societies. But you always miss something, there's the old longing for what's familiar. I was a typical example. Although I loved my life in Positano, and would not have considered changing it, I missed the relaxed Australian way of life, and of course, my friends. How confusing to feel at home in two quite different worlds. Where did I really belong?

Living in Europe was wonderful. How stimulating it was to wander through the historic centre of an ancient city, to discover relics of the past, to admire Renaissance splendours, to sit beside a fountain knowing that people have sat on a particular stone step for centuries. But I'd forgotten the exhilaration that Australia, with its vast unoccupied areas, could bring. In a matter of hours, I could

117

drive out of the city into wide open countryside, into a landscape of bushland dominated by grey-green eucalypts or gum trees. What a thrill it was to stand on a vast expanse of white sand at a deserted beach, with no visible sign of life in any direction. Wherever I went in Europe, whether to the coast, the mountains or just walking in the countryside, there was never a moment's solitude. There were always houses, passers-by, people working in the fields. In the past I'd never been conscious of these issues. But now I became aware of a selfish irritation that someone else invariably chose to share some beautiful vista at any particular moment. Once or twice I asked my Italian companions, "Do you ever feel hemmed in? How can you bear to be constantly surrounded by people?" But they looked at me in astonishment, no doubt confirmed in their belief that foreigners are a bit odd.

*       *       *       *       *

My musings on whether I was a well-adapted expatriate were cut short. We were about to land in Singapore. The stewards gathered around, advising us how best to organise our stop. Should I leave all the paraphernalia, the bottles, baby food and nappies on board, or should I take a supply in case of delay? Having come to some logical conclusion, we proceeded to disembark. We were taken to a transit lounge, and sat down to wait. And wait. The scheduled stop was about an hour. This fitted reasonably well with my feeding timetable, allowing an afternoon sleep for our over-excited baby. We waited. An hour passed, then another. Nobody offered any explanation. Looking at my watch I was shocked to find we'd been on the ground more than five hours. We'd been provided with a meal and a few drinks, but no explanation.

Eventually a loudspeaker crackled, there was to be an announcement. A disembodied voice came through the microphone, "Ladies and gentlemen, this is your captain speaking. We've been advised that a bomb was placed on board. A comprehensive search has been carried out, and we're quite convinced there is no bomb. As additional security, we've delayed the flight until after our scheduled time of arrival in Calcutta. I'm convinced the plane is safe; there's absolutely no danger. We are, however, obliged to

118

communicate this warning to you. We will proceed to Rome as planned, but each passenger must make his own decision. You are free to decide whether you wish to continue on this flight, or prefer to wait for a later plane."

What a nightmare! My first inclination was to stay in Singapore. But we were now informed that very little accommodation was available. Apparently a series of conferences were in progress, and all the better hotels were fully booked. The few hotels with vacant rooms were not recommended for European travellers. What should we do? The captain, seeing our distress, came over to our table. "I wouldn't worry too much," he said reassuringly. "I'm sure it's all a hoax. We've waited for the deadline to pass. If there'd really been a bomb on board, it would have exploded by now." He seemed confident, obviously he believed we were safe. Was he right? There was little time to ponder as the plane was about to leave. We decided to proceed.

Boarding the plane I felt extremely nervous; was it fair to a tiny baby to take a chance we'd all be blown up? Engines roared, the plane took off, we were airborne. Nothing untoward occurred. I had to go into the staff quarters to warm a bottle. To my dismay, I saw a stewardess frantically searching among bags and clothing. Was she looking for a bomb? Obviously she didn't feel calm. I returned to my seat, put Adriana in her cot, and strapped on my seat belt. The same stewardess appeared at my side, "I wouldn't put the baby in the cot," she said, "I'd advise you to hold her firmly in your arms". Hardly designed to inspire confidence.

It must have been one of the worst days I ever experienced, strapped into my seat, waiting and wondering. I was never convinced the danger was over, at every noise I imagined our last moment had come. But even this interminable journey finally ended. We'd made the right choice! The plane had not exploded. We were all still alive.

*     *     *     *     *

It was lovely to be home, even if the new house was, as ever, still awaiting completion. I woke to the sound of the sea, to the ebb and flow of the tide as waves gently rose and fell on the beach below. We had breakfast on the terrace, the outlook as beautiful as I'd remembered. Salmon-pink buds were opening on the bougainvillea I'd planted in an enormous lichen-covered amphora; once used to store oil or wine, it now stood in a protected corner. I sipped my freshly roasted coffee, enjoying its heady, fragrant aroma. But I couldn't sit on in a daydream, basking in the warm sun and admiring the view. I was not a tourist enjoying a Mediterranean holiday. I had a home, a family, responsibilities.

Marietta was thrilled to see us and full of compliments. "*Come state bene*," how well you look, she said. "How the baby has grown." I went to Palatone to restock my depleted kitchen. He and his family were happy to see us. "*Bentornata Signora*," welcome back, everyone said. Walking into town we were enthusiastically welcomed by all the *Positanesi* we passed. It was good to catch up with friends. The phone rang, people called, wanting to hear about our trip. "Had we enjoyed our time in Australia; were we happy to be back?" I felt I'd come home. Maybe I did belong here after all. Stenio spent the following weeks telling all and sundry about his wonderful holiday in Australia. As time went on his stories became larger than life.

# A VILLA WITH HAND PAINTED TILES

My mother arrived a few months later, and immediately started house hunting.

"I've finally come to a decision," she told us. "After you left, I started to think seriously about how I should plan my life. Where do I really want to live? After days and nights of soul searching, I've come to the conclusion that the sensible thing is to make Positano my base. I don't want to live here permanently, but I'll be able to come and go as I please. I can travel in Europe, perhaps spend a few months each year in Australia, then come back and enjoy life here with you. Hopefully, once I'm established in a place of my own, I'll be able to invite guests."

Her many friends enthusiastically encouraged the idea of buying a house in Positano. Who wouldn't be delighted at such a prospect? It seemed a perfect situation for all concerned, she'd buy a house, they'd be welcome to visit, everyone would be happy.

Her friend Di became a frequent visitor. " Aren't I lucky you decided to live in Italy?" Di said to me each time she arrived. "Who would have imagined that Hella would end up buying a house here. When we travelled together in the past, we got really tired of living in hotels. We often said, 'Wouldn't it be great if someone invited us to stay in a private home.' Now we have the ideal set-up. I love coming to stay, Hella enjoys the company, and we have a marvellous opportunity to explore surrounding places. Or we can go on extended trips." They did all these things. Di would come from Australia, stay a week or two in Positano, and off they'd go; to Austria, France, Spain, or wherever took their fancy.

\*        \*        \*        \*        \*

It was early spring, the days were becoming fine, people started to prepare for the summer season. Having made her decision, my mother was anxious to implement her new lifestyle as soon as possible. There was no local equivalent to an estate agent as we understood the term. Stenio had, in the past, acted as intermediary in buying and selling real estate. Now he began to make enquiries about properties for sale. Looking for a house can be a disappointing and frustrating experience, and no-one expected my mother's quest for a Positano home to be easy. We looked at two or three places. The first sounded promising; it had obviously once been splendid, but was now in a distressing state of disrepair. The idea of becoming involved in refurbishing another house, when we had not yet completed our own restoration, was singularly unappealing. Another had a wonderful view, and had been renovated to a most exacting standard. Unfortunately the asking price was so wildly extravagant it wasn't worth considering.

News went around the village that *la Signora, la mamma della moglie dell'avvocato*, the mother of the lawyer's wife, was looking to buy a house. Our phone started to ring as prospective vendors called. People stopped us in the street offering property that had belonged to their family for as long as they could remember. Everyone was sure they could provide exactly what we wanted. Some had places half way up the mountain, others suggested abandoned cottages that hadn't been lived in for years. Stenio looked at a few, my mother at others. It was all quite discouraging. Maybe it would be wiser to rent?

When we heard that a neighbouring house was on the market, we were not particularly hopeful. Certainly the location would be extremely convenient, it was worth a look. From the unimposing facade, no-one could possibly have imagined that a lovely old villa, comprising four levels, was hidden behind an unspectacular entrance. Nor that my mother would be lucky enough to find a delightful place only two doors from us. By a remarkable coincidence, the owner had decided to sell just at a time appropriate to our needs.

I'd never been inside this house, in fact I was hardly aware of its existence. On the few occasions I'd explored the extended area of Fornillo, continuing along the narrow lane behind our home, I'd obviously passed by without really noticing. This was easy to do; it was effectively hidden from view. A small unpretentious green door at the centre of a whitewashed wall constituted the only accessible entrance. The facade was deceptive, revealing little of what was inside. Had I thought about it at all, I'd have assumed the self-effacing doorway led into a small cottage.

No doubt I'd also seen the front many times; it was visible from the beach below, or from a boat approaching the coastline. I'd often looked up at the group of typical Mediterranean houses facing out to sea. But despite my familiarity with the area, I'd never taken particular notice of the Fornillo houses. Clustered on the side of the mountain, in keeping with and blending into their surroundings, they presented a harmonious whole. It seemed strange that I'd never stopped to wonder who owned or lived in each individual home. I hadn't the faintest idea what to expect.

Concettina had the key. She acted as caretaker; her role was to open the house every now and then, check that everything was in order, and cope with unforeseen problems. On the rare occasions that the owner, a Signora Scarlatti, came to spend a few days at her seaside villa, Concettina scrubbed and cleaned until even the brass doorknobs were shining. She would proudly open the door with a flourish, then stand by expectantly, waiting for *la padrona* to comment on her handiwork. *Casa Scarlatti* was not her only responsibility; she had a key to several neighbouring houses and was extremely conscientious in carrying out her duties as *guardiana*.

Concettina was one of the local characters. With her bright and cheerful personality, she knew everyone. On my daily trip to Palatone, I invariably passed her somewhere along the way, deeply immersed in animated conversation. It was hardly surprising, therefore, that she was a source of local news, always first to hear what was happening. Concettina realised before we did that my mother would want to see the neighboring villa.

"I suppose your mother-in-law will want to look at *casa Scarlatti*," she suggested, passing Stenio in the street.

"Well yes, she may well be interested," he replied. "I'll speak to her, and let you know if she'd like to inspect the house. Can we can borrow the key?"

"No, no, *la Signora* would never forgive me if I didn't show you around personally." Concettina certainly intended to be involved, why should she be left out? Who knew what might eventuate? Next time our paths crossed she discussed the matter with me. I detected a certain lack of enthusiasm at the prospect of change, from her point of view there was little to be gained. The present situation suited her perfectly; she was devoted to *la padrona* and took pride in keeping the villa in order. However, Concettina was extremely practical, and, having, however reluctantly, anticipated a possible outcome of my mother's house hunting, she preferred to be in charge. It seemed that Tuesday was to be the day for our inspection. Concettina had a precise schedule, Tuesday, villa Scarlatti, Wednesday, *casa* Albertina, Thursday house of the *Contessa*.

On the following Tuesday we set off at the appointed time, knocked at the narrow green door, and waited. Eventually Concettina appeared, out of breath from hurrying up the stairs. She was dressed in her best Sunday outfit; today she was *la padrona di casa*, lady of the house. "*Benvenuti*," welcome, she said, ushering us into a small foyer. We found ourselves on the upper floor of a charming old home. On one side the entrance hall led into a rudimentary kitchen, on the other was a bedroom, spacious, whitewashed, full of light. Concettina opened a yellow door to reveal a spotlessly clean bathroom, tiled in a pattern of yellow and green flowers. Stepping onto the balcony, we looked down on a series of terraced gardens. A little of the magic of the place began to make itself felt. It was a lovely sunny day, we couldn't have chosen a better time.

A narrow marble stairway led down to the next level. Like everything else in this house, the staircase was full of surprises. Tiny candle-like lamps in filigree holders illuminated small niches on either side. Originally designed to hold candles, they'd been adapted to twentieth century needs with electric light fittings. Daylight filtered in through a recessed arched window; an ancient black Sicilian oil lamp stood on the marble window ledge. Set into the walls were glazed hand-painted tiles, brilliantly decorated with primitive designs. Some artisan in bygone days had depicted rural scenes: women in long skirts balancing urns on their heads, *contadini*, peasants, working in the fields, donkeys carrying their load. In groups of four or six, these brightly coloured works of art provided a foretaste of the wonderful ceramic paving yet to come. I could sense my mother's mounting excitement. Maybe this was the home she'd been looking for, the answer to her prayers.

Like our house, the building had been constructed according to the concepts of Moorish architecture. Many prominent features were similar; massive whitewashed walls, domed ceilings and wall niches, arched doors and windows. A giant archway divided the spacious living room, *il soggiorno,* into two parts. In one corner was a fireplace. The *pavimento* of this enormous area was a sea of emerald-green striated tiles interrupted by feature tiles with rustic motifs similar to those we'd just admired. Naively executed in vivid colours against a white background, men and women carried their tools of trade: stepladders, baskets, pitchers and bowls; stylized goats and donkeys watched the activity. Another series portrayed the signs of the Zodiac. I could see my mother trying to look non-committal, knowing that Concettina was studying her reaction. Her observations would no doubt be promptly reported back to the owner.

Opening wooden-shuttered doors, we found ourselves in a courtyard paved with irregularly placed stones. Built into the vine-covered wall at the far side was a grey stone bench. A coral tree covered in crimson pea-shaped flowers overhung the patio, its leaves and flowers, strewn on the ground, formed a bright carpet of red and green. Blue and white hydrangeas filled the flower beds. The outlook was similar to ours; the coastline seen from a slightly different angle, Praiano just visible in the distance. Beyond, as far as the eye could see, was ocean.

Steps led down to a first terrace and on to a second lower level. The garden was a tangled profusion of plants and creepers, of climbing roses, wisteria, bougainvillea and vines. Two wonderfully healthy peach trees, one white, the other yellow, caused us to exclaim with delight. Imagine having your own luscious home grown peaches. We turned to go back. The overhanging mountain loomed large above the house. We took our leave of Concettina with carefully neutral remarks.

"What should I tell the Signora?" she asked.

"We'll let you know," Stenio replied.

,

There was no doubt the place was extremely large and in need of considerable renovation; our close inspection had revealed areas that had been badly neglected. "You realise if you buy this house you'll have problems," Stenio warned. "You'll have to spend months waiting for tradesmen, coping with delays, fighting a never-ending battle." We hadn't heard what price the Signora was asking. Would it be exorbitant?

As the days went by my mother began to show signs of stress resulting from wanting this place so badly. She was sure it would provide her with the perfect solution. But would the dollar go up or down relative to the *lira*? Would the Signora take the view that now, with a buyer in sight, the time was right to raise the price? We heard all sorts of rumours. 'The house had been on the market for years, but no-one wanted it.' 'There'd been a series of interested purchasers, but the Signora could never make up her mind.' Stenio decided to phone the owner direct. She agreed to come and discuss the situation during the following week. We anxiously awaited her arrival.

\*     \*     \*     \*     \*

Signora Scarlatti was a fascinating woman, elegant, sophisticated and charming. She lived in Milan, but I felt certain she'd be equally at home anywhere in Europe. Attractive and perfectly groomed, with white hair tied softly back, enormous green eyes and a smiling face, the Signora was dressed in the smart, casual style typical of *la Milanese*. She gave the impression that nothing could possibly disturb her perfect poise. I never ceased to admire such Italian ladies, their innate sense of style, their instinctive ability to put on a cotton shirt and jeans, throw a pullover around their shoulders, and

126

look as though they'd just stepped out of the pages of a fashion magazine. It seemed unfair that some people should be born with this indefinable quality, never to be acquired by those less fortunate. I observed them enviously, resigned to a future where I would forever lack this skill.

In addition to owning this delightful villa, Signora Scarlatti had other impressive attributes. An excellent *raconteur,* she told us a little about her life as wife of an Italian diplomat. She and her husband had been stationed in several international cities, spending considerable periods in Asia and America, as well as Europe. I hoped there would be future opportunities to hear tales of the past; our present situation could hardly be described as a social occasion. We had more pressing matters to discuss. We sat on the terrace while Concettina brought freshly brewed coffee in dainty cups. As we sipped our coffee, the Signora related the story of her villa. It had quite a long history. I was intrigued to learn that in recent times it had been owned by the Roman film director, Vittorio De Sica.

To our amazement, some of the beautiful antique furniture was to be included in the sale. Whoever bought this house would acquire some incredible pieces. There was a sixteenth century *cassapanca*, chest, a heavy oak table, two wonderful *comodini*, bedside tables, a delicately-crafted inlaid writing desk. We couldn't believe the Signora would leave these marvellous things behind, didn't she treasure them? Perhaps the antiques were of little importance to her, maybe she had nowhere to put them. Or did she have such a quantity of valuable possessions that a few more or less didn't matter? We were certainly not about to enquire. She might change her mind.

My mother was thrilled to have found her lovely villa. Despite the obvious limitations, she refused to admit it was less than ideal. "Can't you see what a glorious place this has been," she kept saying. "Just look at those hand-painted tiles, at the wonderful domed ceilings. Imagine me living in a house that belonged to Vittorio De Sica. And who knows what other interesting people have lived here. I'd love to find out more about the local history. Don't try to discourage me, I just adore everything about it."

We had many discussions about the wisdom of making this acquisition, but in fact, from the moment my mother saw the house, the sale was a foregone conclusion.

"I just love it," she repeated. "I'll enjoy every minute of doing it up. It's going to be the best thing I've ever done. You'll see."

Since she really wanted to buy the villa, and was more than happy to restore the kitchen, bathrooms, and whatever else needed fixing, we saw no reason to dissuade her.

The final agreement was drawn up; now the contract had to be signed. We all set off to visit *il notaio*, the notary. In Italy, all purchases above a certain figure have to be legally processed by a *notaio*. Until then, my mother had never had a recognised surname, or at least one acknowledged by the *Positanesi*. She was known as *la suocera dell' avvocato*, *la mamma della moglie di Stenio* or just *la Signora Elena*. She seemed undisturbed by this fact, but I felt it was unfair that her existence should be defined only by her role as mother or mother-in-law, particularly as she had a decidedly strong personality. To make matters worse, her Christian name varied according to where she happened to be living. Having been christened Helena and known as Hella, she became Helen in Australia, then Elena in Italy. In addition, official documents in Italy list a woman first by her maiden name, the married name comes second. She certainly had every reason to be confused.

The contract signed, we opened a bottle of French champagne. "Auguri," congratulations, we all said. It was a happy occasion. In fact, my mother derived great enjoyment from her acquisition. She really loved that house, and spent the following years refurbishing one section at a time. At first she decided to have the living quarters upstairs; to renovate the bedroom, bathroom and kitchen, and use the downstairs area for entertaining. Having carried out these alterations to her satisfaction, she suddenly changed her mind.

"I really think I should do up the downstairs kitchen," she told us with great enthusiasm one morning. The next day she was even more enthusiastic. It became a way of life, figuring out how to redecorate her lovely home. Usually after a few days or weeks, she'd reconsider, deciding it was all too hard, but sometimes she actually proceeded. Certainly, this villa became a source of much joy to her, and, indeed, to us all.

# LA TRAMONTANA

The wind was blowing. *La tramontana, the* dreaded wind from the north. It blew, day and night, for days on end. Would it never stop? It whistled through the tree tops, wild gusts brought down giant trees that had seemed solidly rooted in the landscape. Doors and windows rattled so much we thought our whole house might be torn apart. We were effectively imprisoned, forced to stay at home, since the narrow lanes around us had become wind tunnels. Should we risk going out? Sneaking tentatively out the door we saw papers, leaves, twigs and all sorts of unidentified matter swirling around. More alarming were large branches from nearby trees, shards of broken glass, even heavy objects lifted up by gusts of wind. Better to stay inside, it couldn't last for ever. When, after two and a half days, the wind finally calmed enough for us to venture out of doors, we crept out cautiously to explore the damage. Our garden looked bedraggled, covered in detritus. Outside, the steps and nearby lanes were almost blocked by debris; it was hard to find room to walk. We discovered that the front number plate had blown off our car and disappeared. We searched the car park and notified the police. Since the car still had international registration, the missing plate was soon recovered. The *tramontana* had taken it to the other side of town, but our licence number was easy to track down. Next day there was a knock at the door. "I recognised *la targa dell' avvocato,*" said Giacomo, the bootmaker.

Growing up in Melbourne, I'd become accustomed to dramatic changes in the weather. Melbourne is reputed to have four seasons in one day. I'd learned to be prepared, to take an umbrella on sunny spring mornings, and never to go out, even on a heatwave, without a jacket. Above all, I'd learned never to trust the weather forecast. Meteorologists were understandably Melbourne's most maligned professional class. Summer temperatures were unpredictable. It was common to find, having planned a barbecue in advance, that a sudden unexpected cool change upset everything. Instead of a fine summer evening it might rain, or the temperature could drop by twenty degrees. Even on a morning of brilliant sunshine, we had absolutely no assurance that the evening would be fine.   So often it happened that, just as dinner was cooked and everything carefully prepared, the balmy weather evaporated, a storm erupted, and we were forced to flee helter-skelter, clutching the remains of our beautifully set table.   In we all trooped with our barbecued steaks and sausages, carrying bowls of salad, jugs and glasses, spilling wine as we hurried indoors.

Positano was not like this, I'd been told.   The climate was completely predictable.   Summer arrived, the temperature was the same each day, we could eat out on the terrace in the evening, there were no unexpected changes.   Once the weather became warm, it was customary to put our winter clothes away, fold up the blankets, remove the doonas and rugs.   I was surprised to discover that floor coverings, including highly prized Persian carpets, were carefully rolled up and stored in mothballs during the summer months.   This was a custom prevalent throughout Italy, and I had to admit it was quite logical.   What a pleasure it was on a hot day to enter a room and feel a cool marble floor, or a pavement of ceramic tiles under my feet, instead of walking on woollen carpet.   And of course we felt completely secure in the knowledge that none of these things, warm clothes, rugs or quilts, would be needed until the following November.   I happily accepted this situation, believing I now lived in an ideal climate.

These illusions were rudely shattered.   It was not so simple.   In fact the weather was not always clement.   There were the winds.   The *scirocco* in summer was most unpleasant, a scorching wind from the south-east.   When the s*cirocco* blew its effect was dramatic.   Hot, humid and debilitating, it set nerves jangling so that everyone was on edge.   The nicest people became bad-tempered; it was not a good time.   Then the devastating *tramontana* occurred once or twice a year, leaving considerable damage in its wake.

Even   the   perfect   summer   occasionally   brought disappointment.   One memorable, never to be forgotten year it actually rained at the height of summer, on the fifteenth of August, *Ferragosto*.   This mid-summer day, the feast of the Assumption, was the high point of the season and a public holiday.   I'd learned never to go out, and certainly to avoid the shops on *Ferragosto*, because the whole of Italy seemed to come to Positano. On this particular occasion, not only did it rain, it poured; rain teemed down as if it would never stop. What consternation this caused. *"Non è possibile"*, I heard on all sides. Such a thing had never happened. What could it mean? There was chaos; picnic lunches had to be eaten under cover, the restaurants couldn't cope. The road was choked as disappointed holiday makers returned to their cars, angrily tooting their horns and arguing with each other.

*      *      *      *      *      *

Life in Positano was defined by the seasons. Summer was the time of peak activity, the time when tourists came, businesses thrived, people worked hard, often day and night. It was a time of glamour, of exuberant social life, of entertainment. Visitors arrived on luxury yachts, by car, bus or boat; they came from all over the world. The place was alive, it buzzed with activity.

*L'autunno,* autumn, was a beautiful season; the days lovely and sunny, the evenings cool and pleasant. The autumn months were spent cleaning up, counting the gains and losses, catching up on sleep after summer's exhausting pace. The mad rush was over. There were still tourists, but now you could walk calmly and peacefully without seeing hordes of people day and night. I advised friends planning a visit to come, if possible, in late September or early October. Restaurants and shops were still open, but now the shopkeepers and restaurateurs were relaxed. They finally had time to be friendly and helpful.

As winter approached we became accustomed to hearing the roar of the sea, and to frequent squally storms. Sometimes the rain brought particles of red dust, leaving windows stained with red spots, and stinging the eyes of passers by. *"Sabbia dalla Sahara"*, said the *Positanesi*, sand from the Sahara. Wherever the red dust came from, whether it had been blown from the African desert or originated elsewhere, the effect was not pleasant.

Winter was brief but intense.  The mountain tops above Montepertuso and Nocelle were covered in snow.  On very rare occasions it actually snowed in Positano, but this was most unusual. Although our house was equipped with central heating, there were invariably problems associated with obtaining fuel.  We needed a constant supply of *nafta,* diesel oil.  Owing to the location of our house, oil had to be transported in plastic jerrycans.  We ordered fifty or sixty containers at a time.  To make this delivery, the oil company either had to send three or four men to carry the twenty-litre jerrycans down the hundreds of steps, or employ local porters.  Since the whole procedure was inconvenient, time-consuming and expensive, the suppliers were less than enthusiastic about coming. This posed a continuing problem.

Stenio had to exercise great diplomatic skill in solving our recurring predicament.

"If we order a consignment too far in advance, we won't have anywhere to put it," he said whenever the subject came up. "You know we never have enough storage space."

"But if we wait till the last moment, we risk being without fuel in the middle of winter."  I preferred to have *nafta* available, whatever the storage difficulties.  Once during a really cold spell we ran out of fuel.  To my dismay, almost two weeks passed before we managed to obtain a fresh delivery.  First, we had to contact the supplier, who rarely answered the phone.  Next we discovered that the road was blocked; a severe rock-fall had rendered the principal highway impassable.  So the fuel truck couldn't reach us until the road had been repaired.  The city council had to be alerted and persuaded that this repair was urgent, and that its scarce resources should be allocated forthwith.  "Why should fixing the road be given priority over other projects?" they asked.  What a nightmare!  How could an apparently simple matter become so complicated?  Stenio had become philosophical about such difficulties, but I was unable to achieve his equanimity.  Particularly when it meant living in a freezing house.  I certainly had no desire to repeat this experience. Once was enough!

Winter was quiet, the streets empty, the town semi-deserted. The tempo of life fell back into the slow rhythm of bygone days. As the majority of hotels, *trattorie,* shops and boutiques closed for several months, a large proportion of people were temporarily unemployed. Many *Positanesi* took their own holidays during this slack period, going to visit other parts of the country, or savouring life in one of the big cities.

The local lifestyle underwent a radical change. Women tended to stay at home while their husbands went each day to the nearest bar. On cold days the smoke-filled bars were crowded with men playing cards. The most popular game, known as *scopa* or *scopone,* had long been played in this area. Two, three or four people contested each round, using specially designed, brightly coloured cards. I learned to play *scopa,* a game quite different to any card game I'd previously known. It required a little skill, a lot of luck - the lucky suit is gold, the lucky number seven - and the appropriate pack of cards.

To me, this period of tranquillity had a number of positive aspects. I was aware of a sense of well-being, a lack of tension among the locals. People stood around in the streets and *piazze* chatting and laughing; their air of determined purpose apparently vanished with the first chill wind. Shopkeepers were free to talk. Husbands and wives had time to communicate. Children, many of whom had been obliged to work in the family business during summer, returned to school. After school and on weekends they were free to play; to kick a football at the beach, ride a bicycle down the road, eat pizza or *gelato* in a local bar. In the absence of tourists, they enjoyed the pleasures of village life. Families could at last have meals together. Winter was a time for the family and community; for the resumption of traditional village activities, for enjoyment of the extended family.

Spring, *primavera,* with its promise of new life, was a delight. Spring brought cheerful smiling faces and a vigorous new phase of activity. People repaired and painted boats for the approaching period of active commerce. Hotels, restaurants and shops were given a coat of paint, renovations and extensions in anticipation of the tourist season kept tradesmen busy. Dressmakers and tailors designed clothes, reams of fabric were ordered and delivered, sewing machines whirred. The annual cycle recommenced.

Although we were not personally involved in the tourist trade, our lives also followed the annual cycle. It could not be otherwise, we were part of the town. We mixed with a wide range of people, from art dealers to *contadini*. This was one of the pleasures of Positano, this mixture of personalities and nationalities which formed part of my daily life and varied according to the time of year.

*     *     *     *     *

For me, summer was a time of fun. I learned not to make plans too far in advance, it was better to improvise. Old friends or interesting new acquaintances appeared unexpectedly, the phone rang with a familiar message, "I'm here for twenty four hours and I'd love to see you." We were invited to parties and dinners, friends came to stay, we went swimming.

It was a time to renew acquaintance with annual visitors who'd become our friends. The German walkers appeared, maps marked out with interesting excursions. I was happy when Caroline and Harry, our Tennessee friends arrived; I looked forward to playing tennis with Virginia. Danielle and other 'regulars', writers, painters, and musicians turned up, staying for indefinite periods. One day they were here, the next, they'd gone.

We often went on fishing trips, as we'd done when I first arrived. Spearfishing was a favourite pastime. The champion fisherman was known as Dodo, a nickname which seemed to suit him. Since Dodo and his fellow enthusiasts invariably caught more fish than we could possibly eat, we were offered first choice. Having selected whatever took our fancy, we could afford to be generous, giving the rest to friends and neighbours.

As time went on, Dodo's remarkable ability became legendary. Stories and photographs were circulated, news of his prowess spread, while the reported size, weight and number of his trophies kept growing in proportion to his reputation. His unerring ability to catch deep-sea fish, in particular the highly-prized bass, was amazing. The white, firm-fleshed *cernia* was becoming increasingly difficult to find in the heavily fished Mediterranean waters. Somehow, Dodo regularly managed to come up with this sought-after specialty.

Returning home after our fishing trips, we frequently found a group of people eagerly waiting as our boat docked. There they stood, friends and complete strangers, hoping to buy fresh fish or seafood. Whatever quantity our master fisher was prepared to sell, he always found a buyer. If the highly-regarded *cernia* was available, word spread fast. Local restaurateurs were generally among the expectant crowd; every restaurant wished to provide its clientele with this delicacy; discerning diners were prepared to pay exorbitant prices for such a treat. On a few occasions I was lucky enough to be invited to a gourmet meal of deep-sea bass, prepared in one of the top restaurants. It was a memorable culinary experience.

I was surprised to learn that Dodo was a lawyer. He lived in a small provincial town near Naples, and spent his professional life working in the large and successful legal practice started by his father. But his real love was spearfishing, and he could undoubtedly have earned a good living from his hobby. He talked about giving up the law and working as a full-time fisherman, but maybe, had his hobby become a regular job, it would have given him less joy. In any case, Dodo felt a sense of obligation towards his father. *"Papa* would be devastated if I were not prepared to take over his business," he often said. "Imagine what he'd say if I told him I want to be a *pescatore* instead of an *avvocato.'*

I don't know if I ever heard Dodo's real name. He had studied law at Naples University together with Elio, my brother-in-law. Since that time he'd regularly visited the Bella family in

Positano. Among the best dinners at their home were occasions when Dodo, after a day at sea with Stenio and his father or brother, cooked a prize fish. Not only was he good at catching fish, he knew exactly how to prepare each species. He used our house as a base, and we looked forward to his visits, and to the subsequent evening meal.

*     *     *     *     *

Summer was also a time for glamorous social occasions. Regularly occurring events became milestones on the annual calendar. The 29th of June is the feast of Saints Peter and Paul, *Pietro e Paolo*. On this day each year, a *festa* was held at the hotel San Pietro. This was an occasion not to be missed, a celebration to end all celebrations. The first priority was to be included in the list of invited guests, and all sorts of stratagems were devised to fulfil this condition.

In preparation for the annual *festa*, teams of workmen were employed to ensure that the grounds and gardens were at their best. And they were truly magnificent. Guests gathered for drinks in the garden, champagne flowed, the ladies were beautifully dressed; diamonds, emeralds and rubies glittered. It was an occasion for grand display. When the doors opened to reveal the buffet dinner, there were gasps of admiration. It was stunning to behold; long tables laden with every delicacy imaginable; lobsters arranged on their shells, roast pheasant, rare beef, seafood of every variety. Steaming bowls of pasta in an endless combination of sauces were carried in by a succession of waiters; decorative salads added a bright splash of colour. And the desserts! Profiteroles, meringues, exotic fruits, *marrons glaces*. An army of chefs must have laboured for days on end.

At a given signal the crowd closed in on the heavily laden tables as though this would be their last meal. I never ceased to be amazed at the spectacle of well-dressed people fighting over food. By the time we reached the table there was never any lobster or pheasant left. "See who gets the most lobster," Stenio whispered as

137

we watched, fascinated. Elegant ladies and their partners struggled away from the banquet, balancing plates overflowing with delicacies.

The evening concluded with a dramatic display of fireworks, a scene to remember. Clusters of coloured lights dramatically shot up sky-high, dropping slowly back to sea in a shower of sparkling gold.

\*     \*     \*     \*     \*

The film director, Franco Zeffirelli, had a beautiful property just out of town, not far from San Pietro. Perched on the side of a cliff, hidden from view, the entrance was a concealed driveway which turned steeply down from the Amalfi road. With typical artistic flair, Zeffirelli had restored three adjoining villas, all looking out to *i faraglioni*, the rocky spies of Capri. In summer Franco came with a select number of guests to spend a few weeks relaxing and sunning themselves on flower-filled terraces. We often saw visitors from *Tre Ville* at one or other of the local *trattorie*. A constant parade of famous people were among their number, Gregory Peck, Rudolf Nureyev, Elizabeth Taylor, Placido Domingo, to name but a few.

It was suggested to Zeffirelli that he organise a summer festival in Positano, and he agreed with enthusiasm. The idea appealed to him and to all of us; he was considered one of the most original and creative of Italian directors. The festival proved a great success. Among the events was a performance given by the Italian ballerina Carla Fracci. On a giant stage erected on the beach, *la* Fracci performed excerpts from the romantic *Les Sylphides*. The vision of this great ballerina in white tulle dancing at the water's edge was magic. Another attraction, perhaps less successful, was an evening of Shakespeare. Zeffirelli presented "Macbeth' in three languages, Act I in English, Act II in Italian, and Act III in German. The rationale was that most of the audience would understand at least one act. Unfortunately, few could follow the whole play. Certainly, the idea was original, but I don't know whether it was ever repeated.

138

Each year in early September a series of chamber music concerts were given in the courtyard of *Palazzo* Murat. The lovely baroque building provided a wonderful backdrop, chairs were placed in the garden, and the atmosphere lent itself to an appreciation of music. The musicians came from many countries. The flute player made an annual visit from Argentina, the cellist was Yugoslav, the pianist an Italian friend from Rome. I looked forward to these performances as one of the highlights of the summer season.

We attended as many events as possible. It was not difficult, we had no need of a car; everything was within walking distance. Sometimes we had dinner with Diana at Michele's restaurant. Part of the entertainment consisted of people watching. Dressed in the height of fashion, a parade of elegant ladies strolled by with husbands, fiancès, or partners. I recognised many of the outfits, those which had been bought locally.

For the smart *Signora*, a significant part of each beach holiday was devoted to shopping. The boutiques of Positano had a wide range of fashionable resort wear, I met women who came from Rome and Milan in late spring to stock up on beach clothes for the following summer. Walking past the shops day after day Diana and I became expert window shoppers, well informed about what was in vogue. Italian women are incredibly fashion conscious. One week everyone was wearing mauve: mauve skirts, shirts, shorts, sandals, handbags. A few weeks later, after I'd bought a pair of mauve shorts and matching top, I noticed with dismay that the colour had disappeared from sight, everyone was now wearing white. I never quite managed to learn the rules, but since I was considered a local, the boutique owners gave me good discounts.

Buying clothes was never a problem. Positano had many dressmakers, some worked in boutiques, others were self employed. In time, I acquired a *sarta*, a dressmaker of my own. Did I need to have clothes made? Of course not. Wasn't I living in a recognised fashion centre where people came to buy their summer outfits? I could buy at a discount. But I adhered to the local custom. Everyone went to their *sarta*, it was a status symbol, after all

Positano fashion consisted of beachwear. This might be all right in summer, but how could I look chic when I went to Rome?

Sandal making was another local skill. I became friends with Beppe, a master shoemaker who had perfected the technique of providing made-to-measure sandals in record time. His barrow was located in front of a row of boutiques near the *spiaggia grande*. The required components were displayed on either side of his work bench, leather soles on one stand, heel-pieces on the next. Most colourful was the mountain of leather straps; black and white, red and green, silver, gold, every shade imaginable; some were furnished with metal studs, others with sparkling beads. Thick, thin, single straps or multiples intertwined and knotted, an unending variety of combinations was provided for his customers' choice.

Beppe would grin at me as I passed, revealing a mouthful of tacks held between his teeth. Whether any were ever swallowed I don't know, he certainly seemed to be testing providence. People lined up beside his stand, spending hours deciding which configuration would best suit their needs. Once they made a decision, Beppe assembled the parts in a matter of minutes, checked the size and fit, and said goodbye to one satisfied client before moving on to the next. I was a regular customer, over the years I acquired quite a range; flat-heeled for the beach, others for sophisticated occasions. My favourite was a high-heeled clog, extremely comfortable and smart, though perhaps not ideal for negotiating the steps of Positano.

\*       \*       \*       \*       \*

Often, after a day at the beach, we decided to have a quiet meal at home. This was so easy, given the fresh ingredients available. What could be better? Stopping at Palatone on my way home, I bought fresh mozzarella, black olives, locally grown tomatoes, and anything else that took my fancy. With our home grown basil and the virgin olive oil provided by Stenio's clients, in no time we had a refreshing *insalata caprese*. For starters a little *antipasto*, a few slices of *prosciutto*, a loaf of bread, a glass of wine. And of course, there was mouth-watering fruit to follow; peaches, a slice of watermelon, figs from our garden. There was no need to cook, this was surely the best dinner imaginable.

After dinner, the custom was to wander down to the local bar. Here we invariably found friends seated at outdoor tables, usually Trudi and Peter were there, sometimes Caroline and Harry, or Carol and Gino. Relaxed and content, they sat sipping coffee or campari soda. The bar we frequented overlooked the waterfront, we watched tourists coming and going to restaurants and night-spots below. Music wafted up as bands warmed up for another busy night. In the background fishing boats bobbed up and down. Among the groups who moved from one bar to the next, I often saw familiar faces. It was a perennial topic for conversation.

"I'm sure I saw that woman in the hot pink top last year." said Trudi.

"You always think you've seen everyone before," Peter was impatient. "But you can never remember their names or where you met them."

"Well I agree with Trudi, I remember seeing that woman year after year." I couldn't help adding a few comments.

We played guessing games as we analysed passers-by. Had we met that couple previously, what were they doing in Positano, were they enjoying themselves? What a mixture, cosmopolitan, exotic, some rich and famous, others aspiring to join their ranks. Sometimes I thought I recognised a face only to discover the person was a well-known public figure; there were painters and writers, film stars and captains of industry. It was embarrassing to approach a complete stranger, then suddenly realise that the feeling familiarity was a result of media exposure. We didn't meet all the celebrities, but it was fun to watch the promenade, to speculate about the pecking order. Who was trying to meet whom? "You keep romanticising the people in these *passeggiate*. They're probably just

ordinary tourists with no pretensions, enjoying their holidays."
Stenio laughed at us.

*     *     *     *     *

How fortunate I was. I enjoyed the long carefree days of swimming and sunbathing, the trips around the islands in our little boat. Entertaining at home was also a pleasure. Having consulted Marietta in the morning and decided the menu, I came home to find the table beautifully prepared on the terrace. Marietta had produced one of her dinner party specials, a pasta dish, a *parmigiana di melanzana,* or maybe *crepes al formaggio*. I prepared whatever else seemed appropriate, then sat down to a relaxed dinner with friends.

And of course we were invited to visit surrounding villas - a constant source of interest. I loved to speculate about the villas I passed each day; were they as old as ours, who had built them, who owned them now? So I was thrilled when I had an opportunity to satisfy my curiosity. Fortunately no-one minded if I roamed from room to room, in fact most of our hosts were delighted to show me around. I was quite naive, exclaiming enthusiastically at various items, an antique table, a lovely painting, an ancient map of Italy. "Where did you find this wonderful map?" I'd say. "How did you know it would fit so perfectly on this wall?" I became known as the Australian who asked questions. But I realized that my sophisticated Italian hosts were secretly flattered at my admiration.

Most of the buildings had been tastefully restored. I wandered through the rooms admiring wonderful antique pieces or elegant modern styles. Occasionally I was disappointed; a few villas seemed all wrong, inappropriately furnished by some trendy, highly-priced interior decorator. But usually I came home full of enthusiasm, inspired to visit our friend Carmine in Minori. Perhaps he'd acquired some special piece since my last visit. I always hoped to find a lost treasure; Carmine's warehouse was full of surprises. And every now and then I was lucky.

*     *     *     *     *

The summer days went on and on, seemingly for ever. But the joys of our glamorous life began to wane; we were reaching a point of saturation. As autumn approached I began to look forward to a period of rest. How wonderful it would be to have some free time. I had a list of books to read, places to visit, things to do. I hoped to improve my Italian, study Italian history and literature, do some shopping, spend a few weeks in Rome. Peace and quiet, no visitors, no social life. I couldn't wait. But somehow, despite a genuine longing for time to myself, I had problems adjusting. I was caught up in a collective feeling, a sort of mass psychosis that affected *Positanesi* at summer's end. The official signal that the summer season was over, that winter was approaching and life was about to enter a new phase came from an unexpected quarter.

Every morning during the high season, a ferry filled with passengers left for Capri, to return in late afternoon. New arrivals came down the gangplank, tourists returned from a day of sightseeing, hotel staff waited to meet intending guests. In later years *aliscafi*, hydrofoils, made the return trip several times each day. Towards the end of September, the passenger boats made their last crossing for the season.

This event followed a prescribed ritual. The ferry blew a farewell salute on its siren, a long, low wail which echoed over land and sea. What a sad moment this was, a moment filled with emotion. When I heard the mournful, piercing blast, I was overcome by a sense of sadness and despondency. I felt completely miserable. I couldn't help myself.

I wasn't the only one. The dirge like sound produced a similar devastating effect on us all. Maybe it was hypnotic, why should all Positano become gloomy and miserable at the sound of this last salute to summer? No-one really believed that life was over, that from now on we would sit around with long faces month after month. Afterwards we laughed about this strange power of suggestion, the overwhelming feeling it created, and our absurd inability to resist. Why should I react in such an exaggerated

143

manner? What caused this sense of impending doom? But the following year it happened again. And again.

As each season merged into the next, we moved from one world to another. Each had its own charm and character, and the regular transition became an essential part of life. But the moment of change was always accompanied by a degree of trauma, both personal and collective; a momentary reluctance to accept the inevitable.

# VICO EQUENSE

Marietta believed I was far too active.

Why don't you ever have a siesta after lunch, Signora?" She would stop in the middle of cleaning the kitchen or preparing the dinner, to look up disapprovingly as I was about to go out the front door.

"None of the people I've worked for in the past have ever been so energetic," she'd say. "You'll be exhausted if you don't slow down."

But there was always so much to do. There were visitors, dinners, shopping trips. And I loved going on outings to nearby places of interest. There was never enough time to do all I wanted.

When I discovered I was pregnant again, I realised I would now have to obey Marietta, at least for the next few months. There was no doubt that, once I consulted a doctor, I'd be advised to slow down and take things easy. The principal question was where to find a reliable obstetrician. After my somewhat traumatic experience at the International Hospital in Naples, I was determined to find an alternative. There must be an easier way to have a baby.

We'd heard good reports of a clinic in Vico Equense, a small town not far from Sorrento. The clinic had been established a few years earlier by a Doctor Guida, an obstetrician who'd spent ten years working in the United States. It was certainly closer than Naples, and friends assured us that the doctor and his staff were well regarded by colleagues and patients alike.

Vico Equense is situated on a promontory overlooking the Sorrento peninsula. We regularly passed through on our way to Naples, but, despite spectacular views over the bay that I always admired, I'd never been tempted to stop there. Its only claim to fame, as far as I was concerned, was a *pizzeria* noted for selling *pizza al metro*, by the metre. I'd often heard that people went out of their way for this specialty, and once, driving home from some shopping trip, we stopped for a quick meal. The place was a hive of activity; cooks in white aprons prepared the dough, kneaded it, then rolled out pizza bases in large blocks. It was fun to watch. What an amazing number of diverse toppings there were: potato, onion, red and green peppers, eggplant, tomato and cheese. The shop was always crowded; people of all ages spent hours making up their minds.

"I think I'll have a pizza with capers and anchovies. No, maybe I'd prefer *prosciutto* instead of anchovies." A waiter stood patiently by as a young girl kept changing her order. "I know what I'm going to have," said her brother. "I always have the traditional pizza, the one with tomatoes and mozzarella. You can't do better than that." Similar discussions were heard all around. When each customer reached a decision, the chosen pizza was taken off its shelf and cut into a section of whatever size they'd requested.

Now I was to get to know another part of the town - the area where the Villa Maria clinic was situated. We rang the hospital to make an appointment. But I had much to learn. At this hospital it was not possible to make appointments. The doctor saw his patients on Monday, Wednesday or Friday mornings between nine and twelve. So, if I wanted to consult him, I must present myself at the clinic at nine and wait my turn. I tried to explain that, as I had to come a considerable distance, I'd like to be sure he'd have time to for me. But there was obviously no point in arguing, no-one was going to make an exception to please me.

On the occasion of my first visit, we left early in the morning, arriving well before nine. I imagined that if we got there early enough we'd be seen before anyone else. On entering the waiting room, however, I discovered that it was already full of expectant mothers. Most of them looked decidedly hassled. I looked at these women, all dressed in what seemed to be a local uniform. Despite the heat, they wore shapeless long-sleeved dresses made of dark, heavy material. There they sat, dark scarves tied tightly so that not a wisp of hair could escape. But what struck me most forcibly was the expression of long-suffering patience on their faces.

146

As each woman arrived, she was given a number and told to take a chair and wait her turn. I received a little disc with my number, and sat down in the waiting room. I was number twelve. Having brought a book with me, I tried to relax and concentrate on reading. After some time a door opened and a nurse appeared calling "*numero uno*". A woman in a black dress and scarf got up and followed the nurse. How long would it be before they got to number twelve? Patience has never been one of my strong points, and this situation didn't suit me at all. I knocked on the door where the nurse had disappeared, and asked whether I could go out for a cup of coffee in a nearby bar. "Go, by all means," said the nurse, "but you realise if you're not here when your number's called you'll have to start from scratch with a new disc."

And so I waited. And waited. But what could I do? When it was finally my turn to see the doctor, I was quite apprehensive. What was I doing in Vico Equense waiting to see some unknown doctor? What if I hated him, or he took an instant dislike to me? But fortunately Dr. Guida proved to be a pleasant man and seemed very competent. He reassured me that all was well, and sympathised with my obvious lack of enthusiasm at the long wait. "There's not much I can do about it," he said. "It's the system here, people are not accustomed to making appointments. They come when they need to see me, and they're prepared for a long wait. They wouldn't understand any other way of doing things." Each subsequent visit was the same. Some time later, when I had occasion to visit an eye specialist, I found that a similar situation prevailed in Sorrento. Again, nobody was going to bend the rules for me. I would just have to do as they did.

My first visit was in July. The previous year I'd had a miscarriage, and I was anxious that this time all should go well. Dr. Guida recommended that I be very careful; I must lead a sedentary life, especially for the first few months. He absolutely prohibited the use of steps.

"But how will I manage at home?" I asked. "The bedrooms are upstairs. I can hardly expect to have someone waiting on me day and night."

"I suppose you're right," the doctor conceded reluctantly. "We can't make life too difficult for you."

He thought for a moment, then announced a compromise. I was to be allowed to use the stairs in our house, but I should do this as little as possible. And most definitely, I must not spend my days clambering up and down the steep passages that constituted the thoroughfares of Positano. Since our home was situated so that innumerable steps had to be negotiated to go anywhere at all, I realised that the next few months were going to be very dull. I was effectively housebound.

Everyone rallied around. I certainly had plenty of help. Marietta was delighted that I was now obliged to sit around doing nothing. Stenio and my mother were happy to do whatever was needed. Friends came to visit. I reclined in the shade on our terrace, looking enviously at the suntanned people enjoying themselves on the beach below; swimming, sunning themselves in deck-chairs, eating delicious meals in the restaurant . I felt very sorry for myself. The days seemed never ending. Fortunately I had a good supply of books to read.

Although I had conscientiously studied Italian, reading the local papers and trying to increase my vocabulary a little each day, I still had a long way to go. Maybe some day I would be truly bilingual; this was the goal I'd set myself. The two languages had to become so completely interchangeable that I felt equally at ease in either one. I was sure this would happen eventually, but not today, tomorrow or even next month.

By this time my Italian was reasonably fluent, I could cope quite well with everyday conversation. But the written word was different. When it came to reading for pleasure rather than to improve my language skills, I chose books written in English. I had the impression that Italians express themselves more formally in writing than in speaking. Despite my increasing familiarity with the oral language, I still needed a dictionary by my side when reading. I kept coming across words I'd never heard. It wasn't much fun.

There I was, thoroughly immersed in a fascinating book, when suddenly I'd stumble over some perplexing word or phrase. I could say 'who cares' and keep on reading, but usually I felt obliged to interrupt my chain of thought and check the offending word in a dictionary. Since this tended to occur once or twice per page, I not only lost the thread of the story, but the whole process became repetitive, tedious and boring. So when I wanted to really enjoy a good book, I looked for something written in my native tongue. Perhaps this might be construed as cheating, but, I reassured myself, everybody deserves a little relaxation now and then.

I had wondered how I'd manage to find books to read; as far as I knew there was no library anywhere in the vicinity. It was hard enough to find a good supply of Italian books, let alone procure reading matter in another language. How would I survive? Reading has always been an essential part of my life. Just when I needed it, a source of unlimited literature turned up close at hand. I couldn't believe my luck. Who would have imagined that here in a foreign country, I'd find such an unexpected luxury. An endless range of English books that I could borrow whenever I wished.

This great good fortune came by virtue of the large expatriate community living in Positano. Among them were a number of English couples who, for a variety of reasons, had spent most of their working life in the tropics. When the time came to retire, they were often reluctant to return to England, preferring to make their home in a more temperate climate. Colonies of expatriates could be found in towns and villages along the Mediterranean coast, in southern Spain, Portugal, France and Italy. And a few had chosen to come to Positano. Although I could not claim to belong to the expatriate community, its members were happy to include me in their circle.

Many were the fascinating stories told about how each couple had selected their retirement haven, why they had chosen a particular place. But, basically, having become accustomed to life in the sun, they had no wish to spend their leisure years in Britain. "I can't imagine how I ever lived there," my friend Dorothy used to say. "It was so bleak and depressing. I hated the cold and wind.

149

And it never stopped raining." Southern Europe was close enough to allow them periodic visits to their family and friends in England. In the sixties, the pound sterling was strong, so life on a British pension proved relatively inexpensive.

We regularly met with a group of retired couples who had bought, built or rented houses in the town; most were English, others came from Germany, Scandinavia and America. The most complete library, a haven where I spent many happy hours browsing, belonged to Bill and Meg. Bill had been professor of history at an Indian university, and was an avid collector of books of all sorts. He had wonderful editions of old manuscripts, leather bound copies of the classics, and an enormous number of paperbacks. Bill was on several mailing lists, kept accounts at leading London bookstores, subscribed to English newspapers and journals, and religiously read every review he could find, ordering whatever took his fancy. The unreliable Italian mail drove him crazy.

"Just look at these," he exclaimed in disgust, striding angrily out of the post office. "Five copies of last year's journals, and not one for this year."

As for books ordered from London or New York; we all waited eagerly for their arrival, sharing his frustration as weeks passed without any sign of expected publications. The Italian mail was always held responsible, no-one even considered that the publishing company might be at fault. But, although such delays were disappointing, there was more than enough reading material to satisfy my needs together with those of all the other expatriates. Bill's interests were wide-ranging, and, once he and Meg had read all they wanted, they were more than happy to share their library with friends, taking pleasure in their role as principal supplier of English literature to our little community.

Another couple, also English, became close friends. Dorothy, in particular, effectively adopted me as a surrogate daughter. By a strange coincidence, her son had married an Australian and now lived in Perth with his wife and two children. Dorothy hardly knew her grandchildren; she'd only met them once or twice. Their principal contact was through polite letters written at Christmas and birthdays to thank for her carefully selected gifts. I'd met their daughter, who lived in the United States and came to see them occasionally. I knew how much they looked forward to her visits, always far too short.

We often met Dorothy and Allan for morning coffee in one or other of the local bars. There was invariably some Italian family group nearby, with toddlers climbing all over doting grandparents. I watched our friends. Allan smiled at the children, a few smiled back. Sometimes a little girl or boy came over to take a closer look. Neither Dorothy nor Allan spoke much Italian so they had difficulty communicating, but they so enjoyed watching the antics of other people's grandchildren. I wondered if their pleasure was tinged with envy. They'd have loved to have their own family nearby.

We became a substitute family for Dorothy. She looked on us with affection, knitted beautiful baby clothes and embroidered pretty little dresses for my children. She even made clothes for their dolls.

And so the months passed. The tourist season was in full swing, Positano was crowded, we had many visitors. Marietta enjoyed being in charge and produced wonderful meals. After the first few months, Dr. Guida relaxed his prohibition on my activities. I was allowed to venture out of doors, but not too far or too often.

In November my mother and I went to Rome with Adriana. I was thrilled to have a holiday, and above all a change in routine. It was stimulating to have an opportunity to go to the theatre, to participate for a time in the activities of a big city, to visit friends and see how the other half lived. And in Rome there were no steps, at least not in the streets. So I could go out and about without worrying too much.

\*      \*      \*      \*      \*

Simone was born in late February, on the last day of the festive season of *Carnevale*. This was surely a good omen. In much of

151

southern Europe, Carnival is a time of rejoicing, a happy and colourful celebration. The final day of *Carnevale* is very special, the French call it *Mardi Gras*, the Italians, M*artedi Grasso*. This name, whose literal translation is fat Tuesday, arose from the custom of parading a fat ox through the streets of Paris. The festivities begin on January 6th or Twelfth night, culminating in a final round of feasting, parties and masked balls. The climax is reached at *Mardi Gras*, a day to eat, drink and be merry; a day of fun and laughter in anticipation of Lent.

For the calendar of events, its timing regulated by the date of Easter, proceeds according to a predetermined cycle. The morning following *Martedi Grasso* brings an abrupt and dramatic change in mood. The churches are filled for the ceremonies associated with *Mercoledi delle Ceneri*, Ash Wednesday, heralding the start of Lent, and a period of fasting and penitence. The congregation, weary after their pre-Lenten activities, kneel at the altar while the priest rubs ashes on each forehead as a sign of penance and a reminder of mortality.

The most famous pre-lenten celebrations are in Venice, visitors come from all over the world to watch masked revellers cavorting in Piazza San Marco. But every town and village throughout Italy has its own *festa,* and Vico Equense was no exception. People wore masks, dressed in colorful costumes, and gathered in the streets, dancing to the accompaniment of music provided by strolling players and local bands. The motto is to have fun. Nobody loves a party more than the Italians. They certainly know how to enjoy themselves, generating an enthusiasm so infectious it's impossible to resist.

Mimi our favourite taxi driver had taken us to the hospital in good time. The clinic proved a good choice; not only because it was closer than Naples and the journey less intimidating. The atmosphere was relaxed, the staff pleasant, the doctor capable. The main complication arose when, just as we were due to go home, a late burst of freezing weather occurred in early March. Simone, like her sister, was a very small baby and we were advised against taking her out of doors while it was snowing. We had to stay at the hospital a few extra days. But this was a minor problem. Soon the sun shone, Mimi arrived, and we were on our way home, feeling extremely pleased with ourselves.

And so my baby was born to the sound of music, in fact it was impossible to sleep for the rest of the day. The whole town was out in the streets, bands played, children blew whistles, everybody was having fun. "*Sarà una bambina allegra*," she'll be a cheerful baby, everyone said. And she was.

# LEGAL WORK

Stenio was the only resident lawyer in Positano, a fact which had both advantages and disadvantages. He had studied law at the University of Naples, obtained his degree, then worked for a year in the office of a well-respected lawyer in Salerno. Having acquired some practical experience and the additional qualifications necessary for admission to his chosen profession, he opened a *studio legale*, a solicitor's office, in Positano.

As the only lawyer in town, he was much in demand. Most of his work involved local matters; *l'avvocato* was called upon to mediate in disputes, to advise on property settlements, to resolve and interpret matters relating to the law. Some of his clients, particularly those from the mountain villages, were illiterate; they required help in understanding any form of documentation. And in a country where bureaucracy is an integral part of life, there were forms to fill in at every turn.

Frequently he was paid in kind; at times a steady stream of people arrived at our house bringing home-grown produce. I would hear someone labouring down our side steps. When the door-bell rang I had a good idea what to expect. Waiting in the entrance I'd find a hesitant villager carrying a heavily loaded crate. The contents varied, sometimes the box contained a dozen bottles of wine or of freshly pressed olive oil. The quality of the wine was unpredictable, occasionally it was excellent, but certain samples tasted so raw as to be barely drinkable. Oil production was also highly individual, sometimes the virgin oil was dark-green and so concentrated it imposed its flavour on every other ingredient, no matter how hard we tried to disguise it. Cases of lemons and oranges, of tomatoes, onions and garlic arrived at our door; we were presented with whatever was in season.

The conduct of a legal practice in this part of the world was quite unusual. Although Stenio had clearly defined office hours, everyone seemed to think he was available twenty-four hours a day. Completely disregarding the *studio legale*, clients approached him when and where it suited them. I became accustomed to interruptions wherever we might be, at morning coffee in a local bar, dinner in a *trattoria*, shopping in one of the stores, or reclining on a deck-chair at the beach. I would hear someone say, "Excuse me, Signora. Can I just ask the advice of *l'avvocato*? It'll only take a minute." An hour later, they'd still be there.

"Why do you bother going the beach at all?" I couldn't help asking. There was my husband in his swimsuit, towel slung over his shoulder, going backwards and forwards between one litigant and another. But, in time I became resigned to the local variety of legal practice. After all, if he didn't worry, why should I? Stenio accepted such claims on his time as a normal part of village life. In fact I think he quite enjoyed the constant requests for assistance.

The court of law frequently sat in Amalfi. At other times cases had to be heard in Salerno. In certain trials involving court sessions, Stenio called upon Ruggiero Vasco, the lawyer with whom he'd studied, to appear in his stead. But often he would go himself, and he found these procedures both stimulating and enjoyable. Usually his clients did everything in their power to avoid appearing in the courtroom; he had enormous difficulty persuading the more diffident villagers to accompany him. He spent hours trying to convince them that their presence was essential if they were to have any hope of success. Eventually he managed to prevail upon most of these recalcitrant clients, but occasionally it proved impossible. The hardest to influence were those who came from the mountain villages. Stenio loved these people, and spent an inordinate amount of time and effort trying to help them. He was invariably paid in tomatoes, wine or other agricultural produce.

When Stenio had to go to Salerno, I often went with him, and enjoyed spending time in this pleasant coastal city with its panoramic ocean vista, mountainous background, and interesting medieval past. Leaving the lawyers to their work, I wandered through the well-kept parks, watching as ships were unloaded at the port. Consulting my history book, I learned that the town had been founded in the fifth century BC by the Etruscans, and that the twelfth century Norman conquest had ushered in a period of great prosperity. The intervening years were glossed over, perhaps the inhabitants had

155

been allowed a few centuries of relative tranquillity. The *Salernitani* were inordinately proud of their Medical School, established in the twelfth century. "Did you know we had the first medical school in Europe?" I was asked over and over again. Work commenced on the *Duomo* of Saint Matthew under the Norman ruler Robert Guiscard in 1076. An imposing medieval aqueduct was even older, its construction had been started by the Longobards.

In a more recent era, Salerno became something of a household name when its harbour served as a centre for invading Allied troops during World War II. Local fishermen proudly pointed out the beaches which had seen action.

"It all looks so peaceful now," said one of the old men, happy to have an excuse to reminisce about the past. "It's hard to believe what it was like during the war. That was a terrible time for us. We hoped and prayed the Allies would come, but when they finally arrived the fighting started, and we were caught in the middle."

I strolled along the waterfront watching groups of children at play. Back and forth they ran, collecting sand and pebbles in plastic buckets, while their parents smilingly looked on. Yet this calm and tranquil shore had been the scene of violent action. It was here that, as the tide of war started to turn against the Germans, Allied forces began a series of troop landings. In July 1943, an advance guard came ashore in Sicily, followed a few months later by further landings, first in Calabria, then in Campania. At about the time that Italy surrendered to the Allies, the lovely Salerno harbour became a battleground. From this strategic point, armed forces slowly fought their way north in pursuit of a retreating German army. Having seen innumerable films of British and American soldiers entering Italian towns to the joyful cheers of a welcoming civilian population, I felt overawed to be standing at the actual site where troops had disembarked.

We always had lunch with l'avvocato Vasco and his wife. I enjoyed going to their beautiful home, and Signora Vasco, a gracious hostess, always seemed pleased to see me. Luncheon was served at an elegantly set table, the meal a local specialty like *spaghetti con carciofi*, artichokes. Our hosts encouraged my interest in the history of their city.

"Over the centuries, this country of ours has suffered so much." said the *Signora*. "We've had an endless series of invasions, dominations, and wars; we've had earthquakes, tidal waves and other cataclysmic events. Successive civilizations have arisen along the shores of the Mediterranean, and their leaders have tried to extend their borders by expanding into our country."

At their suggestion I visited places of historical importance. On each occasion I made some new discovery. My knowledge of Italian history was minuscule, but I was determined to learn about the past, particularly in this area where I was now living. Greek temples, Roman ruins, Saracen invasions, Norman towers, medieval splendour; would I ever come to grips with the convoluted past of the Italian peninsula? Since I had assumed the role of tour guide for visiting friends, I really should try to increase my knowledge of local history. I kept making resolutions; I would study a little each day, or perhaps each week or month.

Legal practice in Positano was never dull; life as a lawyer was full of unexpected incidents. One day Stenio was in the court at Amalfi, presenting a case, when suddenly there was a scuffle outside. Officials were sent to investigate. There at the entrance to the courthouse was a fisherman, calling for *l'avvocato* and insisting he be allowed to enter. The court was adjourned for a short time. In came Giacomo *il pescatore*, holding up two small lobsters. "*Per l'avvocato*," he said. It turned out that Stenio had wanted to give me a surprise. Knowing my passion for lobsters, he'd asked Giacomo to get him one for that evening. The fisherman had done as requested, and was determined to deliver it in person.

Among the more bizarre events requiring a negotiated settlement was the case of the gypsies. A group of wandering gypsies had interrupted their travels to make ornaments for the church. Who had actually commissioned the work was a subject for dispute, to my knowledge the matter was never resolved. When the

157

decorations were finished, the priests said, "*Via, maledetti da Dio*," go away, you who are cursed by God, and refused to pay. I never heard what reply the gypsies made, no doubt it was too colourful for my ears. Stenio was called in, and went from one group to the other until he eventually managed to sort things out. The gypsies were paid, the priests never saw them again, and the crisis was resolved to the satisfaction of all concerned.

Legal action was also required when the proprietor of a small *pensione* was found in bed with one of the chamber maids. News spread rapidly, and the situation became extremely delicate. Everybody had an opinion. In such a small town there were long-standing feuds between families. At times considerable diplomacy was required.

To show their appreciation of Stenio's assistance, clients sometimes invited us to lunch. These were memorable occasions. The more prosperous tended to entertain outside the home, either in a restaurant or hotel. Such invitations were always appreciated and enjoyable. I was even more delighted when a grateful client happened to be a restaurateur. There was a good chance we'd be offered a specially prepared dinner in one of the better restaurants whenever Stenio settled a grievance to the proprietor's satisfaction.

But meals served in the homes of the simple people, those who worked long and hard to maintain a meagre existence; these were the experiences that stand out. For these feasts, the term lunch is a misnomer, it would be more appropriate to class such luncheons as banquets. I was always slightly nervous at being included, I felt a little out of my depth. First, the conversation was in dialect, so I was unable to make any real contribution. Secondly, I was invariably the only woman to sit at the table. The host presided over the proceedings. Other men were often present, adult sons, brothers, cousins, even close friends might be included. It was hard to know whether or not these guests brought their wives. Maybe they did. There were always plenty of women in the background. Women, however were not expected to share in the meal. Their role was to provide the repast. They slaved in the kitchen, served at the table, washed the dishes, but were most definitely not permitted to sit with the invited guests. Sometimes they stood in the kitchen doorway, watching anxiously to see if everyone was content, the diners were enjoying their food, or if extra assistance might be required.

The host was attentive and demanding. "Lina," he called in a peremptory voice. "I think the Signora might like more salad." Or "Can't you see *l'avvocato*'s glass is nearly empty?" I found it extremely difficult not to comment. My natural reaction was to retort, "Why don't you fill the glass and pass the salad yourself?" But Lina accepted her role, hurriedly refilling the wine glass and reaching for the salad. I, of course, refused to have any more salad as a matter of principle. But to everyone else, this was a perfectly normal way to behave. When the man of the house chose to invite visitors, his wife must be content to do his bidding.

And what feasts these were! What an astounding number of courses. No wonder the women had to stay in the kitchen. I could only guess at how many people were needed just to keep up the supply of clean plates. Two or three must have stood at the sink, continually washing an ever accumulating stack of dishes. We would start with *antipasto*, much of which had probably been prepared by the housewife during the previous summer. *Sottaceti*, pickles, made from home-grown vegetables: peppers, eggplant, green tomatoes, carrots, cauliflower, to name but a few. Salami, mortadella, anchovies, olives, all tasty and good. Next might be homemade *tortellini in brodo*, little circles of pasta painstakingly filled with meat or with cheese and spinach, and served in a meat broth or *consommé*. Perhaps we'd be presented with spaghetti in some extra special sauce. No-one would have considered offering anything as common as a *bolognese* or plain tomato sauce. Definitely not; this would not have honoured *l'avvocato*. The sauce had to be one that would be remarked upon and remembered. Because a neighbour might ask, "What *pasta* did Lina prepare for *l'avvocato*?" And it absolutely wouldn't do to reply '*spaghetti bolognese*'. That would constitute a *brutta figura* and the husband would lose face. Lina must produce a meal that was considered outstanding.

The *pasta* was frequently followed by some concoction based on offal. I was a little apprehensive at the thought, but to my surprise these preparations generally turned out to be excellent; liver, sweetbreads, kidney, all cooked in such a way as to disguise any strong and distinctive flavour. I had little previous experience of this type of food, and was impressed at how tasty it could be.

Next came the meat. This always worried me. Not only did I know that any form of meat was extremely expensive, I was also well aware that it did not constitute part of the regular diet. But meat there invariably was, either a fried pork chop, or an enormous portion of chicken, or a cutlet of the uninspiring *vitellone*, which I translated as tough and ageing cow. The portions were always large. One of the women would place a gigantic platter of king-size chips in front of me, while another brought a vegetable dish. Traditionally the accompaniment consisted of an extremely bitter variety of broccoli, definitely an acquired taste. Then came a mixed salad. And then dessert.

By this time I was almost ready to pass out. But the women were watching to make sure I kept eating. Not to finish what had been placed in front of me might be construed as an insult. And I certainly had no wish to offend our host, let alone his hard-working wife.

"Doesn't the Signora like my cooking?" she would say, half-jokingly. *"Non è buono, Signora? Forse c'è troppo sale? Vuole qualcos'altro?"* Isn't it good? Perhaps there's too much salt? Would you like something else? What a nightmare. How could I possibly finish this vast amount of food. And there was always someone hovering in the background waiting to refill my glass with potent home-brewed wine.

'No, just let me go home,' was all I wanted to say. But I knew how important it was not to offend, and I appreciated the effort and expense that had gone into the preparation of such a lavish feast. I was also genuinely fond of these kind people. They wanted to show their appreciation for all Stenio had done for them over the years. He looked after them well, and they wished to reciprocate, to

160

do something special to please him. But how happy I was when the coffee finally came, hopefully without cake. I breathed a sigh of relief. It was almost time to go home.

*       *       *       *       *

Stenio loved to visit the mountain villages. Life in these places was hard, the land mercilessly harsh and rocky. Access was difficult, we had to climb hundreds of steps, then negotiate narrow stony tracks. The mountain people must have wondered at their luck. Tourism had proved a bonanza for the town below. Location at sea level had led to financial success; everyone loves a beach resort, and land values had risen accordingly. But, despite the magic views to be seen by any visitor with the stamina required to climb to the hills, development had stopped at the coast. In the high country, people continued to live in small stone houses as their ancestors had done for centuries.

Daily life was a struggle. Most families had a little land where they grew vegetables: tomatoes, peppers, eggplants. *Pomodori*, tomatoes, formed a staple and essential part of the diet. Used all year, they were preserved in a number of ways. Women spent hours picking and sorting ripe fruit, bottled them whole or cut up, cooked and sieved them to form a paste conserved for the winter. Green tomatoes were pickled in vinegar and stored in airtight containers, ripe ones tied in bunches to be hung out and baked by the heat of the sun. Bright red clusters suspended beneath the eaves of an old stone house or wherever a spot could be found; how these welcome splotches of colour enlivened the drab grey surroundings.

I never ceased to marvel at the multitude of ways a tomato can be used; a meal that doesn't feature them in one form or other is almost unthinkable. In summer, with basil or fresh vegetables as a refreshing salad, with mozzarella in *insalata caprese, imbottiti*, stuffed, with rice, tuna or some alternative combination. In the villages, pasta is eaten at almost every meal. The myriad ways it can be served is inconceivable to anyone who has not lived in Italy. The vast majority of pasta sauces require tomatoes, either fresh or bottled. *Risotto*, fish and meat stews, so popular in winter, again we find this

161

ubiquitous fruit an essential ingredient. The poorer the meat, the more it tends to be disguised with *pomodori* and herbs.

Locally grown vegetables, carefully and lovingly cultivated in little garden plots, provide attractive and colourful meals. Fresh peppers, red, green and yellow, eggplants, zucchini, how good they are, separately or combined. Eaten raw, or cooked with onion, tomato and herbs from the garden, fried in batter, prepared as a pasta sauce. Recipes have been handed down from mother to daughter over countless generations. Chestnuts and walnuts, figs and pomegranates were readily available during the season. Fruit was eaten freshly picked; no-one even thought of cold storage.

The versatile grape was an essential accompaniment at mealtimes, both for eating and, of course, for wine production. Vines were everywhere, covered in late summer with thick clusters of grapes, red and green. The whole village participated in harvesting the fruit and preparing the wine. I must admit I never truly appreciated the resultant brew. Despite the enormous effort involved, the taste of local wine was not one I found easy to acquire. Try as I might, I could not bring myself to enjoy this cloudy beverage. Perhaps the wine was never kept long enough to allow it to mature. Certainly, the fresh, raw liquid tasted sour, disagreeable, and quite displeasing to my palate. I discreetly swapped glasses with Stenio when no-one was looking.

There were two little stores in Montepertuso. Mules were driven up and down the steps loaded with supplies; sturdy mountain people walked alongside, packs strapped to their broad backs and shoulders. Meat was rarely eaten. Although scrawny-looking chickens were always squawking underfoot, their principal function was to provide eggs. I really didn't want to eat the unfortunate birds, and tried to persuade our kind hosts that I loved their pasta and vegetables, but please, please don't kill a chicken for us.

A few proud villagers owned a cow. Brought up the mountain as small calves, these animals spent their lives in tiny stalls, just large enough to hold them. There was no available pasture, but on sunny days the cows were taken for a short walk, the only exercise they ever got. A few scraggy goats roamed around here and there, searching for food along the rocky mountain paths.

One of the local characters was Filomena, *la formaggiaia*, the cheese woman. Round-faced and jolly, my favourite cheese-maker had a deep voice and hearty laugh. "Come and see me," she always said. And so I made a point of going to her home on each visit. How she found space to work remained a mystery, somehow she managed to produce a variety of *formaggi*, using milk from both cows and goats. Shelves lined the walls of a small dark room behind the kitchen. Each shelf was stacked high with her output. Holding a large and threatening-looking knife, Filomena carefully examined her handiwork before cutting a slice and handing her selection on the knife blade for me to taste.

"Try this," she said, slicing off a hunk of sharp, hard cheese used for grating. *"Troppo forte per te?"* Too strong for you?

It was certainly tasty, I had to admit. The next was milder, resembling a *provolone*. Her specialty was a soft milky cheese, decoratively prepared and presented in small woven baskets.

*"Delizioso*, this is my favourite."

"Of course, all the foreigners like this one." She always insisted that I take one home, refusing to let me pay. How kind and generous these hard-working people were, and how hospitable.

I never discovered how Filomena had come to acquire her role, maybe it was a family tradition. I did try to enquire, but she only giggled in reply. Either my question was considered indiscreet, or she simply didn't understand.

My initial impression each time I arrived in the village square of either Montepertuso or Nocelle was that the whole place was filled with children. Perhaps there really were a large number, certainly those in the *piazzetta* were exceptionally lively. I was never sure; I did know that most families had at least three or four offspring, the older ones were called on to help when a baby was born. A tiny primary school catered to the local boys and girls. In the early days, schooling was compulsory only from the ages of seven to twelve. But as the years passed I noticed that more and more of the older children started to make the long trip each day to high school in Positano.

With the growth of the tourist industry, Positano was becoming a small and wealthy enclave. Increasing numbers of people opened hotels and restaurants, smart new shops were built wherever space could be found. The resultant commercial activity and growing demand for manual labour provided a welcome source of income for the mountain people. During the summer, men found work in shops and restaurants, in winter they were employed in the flourishing building trade. And for the first time in their history, paid work was also available for women. The fashion industry was reasonably well-established and boutiques began to spring up everywhere, forming a valuable source of income for any woman willing and able to sew.

# ROMAN HOLIDAY

When the Capri boat delivered its mournful farewell salute to summer, the sound of its siren heralded change. The high season was over, our glamorous life was about to be transformed into the calm, quiet days characteristic of winter. Now the *Positanesi* started to make plans for the following months. And my thoughts turned to Rome.

I needed a dose of city life now and then. Living in a village was great, particularly a glamorous one like Positano, bit I'd always been a city girl, and I did miss the hustle and bustle, the stimulation of a busy metropolis. Maybe my English colleague had a point.

Rome, the eternal city. Exciting, fascinating, magnificent, splendid. I can think of dozens of adjectives to describe my favourite city. Vibrant, stimulating, and absorbing, but also chaotic, noisy and congested. It's all these things and more, a gigantic treasure chest containing wonders from every epoch, an archaeologist's delight.

Thousands of books have been written about Rome. Beautifully illustrated picture books show monuments and churches. Art historians study the architecture, the bridges and sculpture; photographers delight in portraying fountains; experts argue about frescoes and paintings. Countless volumes describe its history, archaeology, and religion; travel guides examine the capital from every conceivable aspect, give information on museums and art galleries, offer advice on accommodation, language, and problem-solving. Literature can be found to suit every possible contingency.

But to me, Rome is a place where I love to be, where I feel alive and completely at home. I fell in love with the city on my first visit, and each subsequent Roman holiday has only served to increase my enthusiasm. Of course there are negative aspects, which I know only too well. Yet the moment I set foot in Rome I feel a thrill of excitement, a sense of happy anticipation. The moment I hear the familiar Roman accent, I'm convinced I've arrived where I

165

really belong. The feeling of euphoria is somewhat transient, after a few days the hassle level of everyday life begins to make itself felt, and I wonder. Maybe I don't belong after all? But it's great while it lasts.

In the early days I stayed in small *pensioni*. Many were family businesses and I was treated as part of an extended family. Like most young tourists I stayed near the central station, hardly the most interesting or beautiful sector, but enjoyable nevertheless.

As I became more familiar with the city, I discovered areas where the accommodation was more satisfactory and the surroundings more attractive. One little hotel I frequented was just around the corner from the Pantheon, that marvellous ancient temple, originally built to honour pagan gods, later converted into a Christian Church. Although this extraordinary building is massive, I habitually lost my way somewhere among the adjacent cobbled streets. It was so centrally situated, I knew exactly where it was. How could it disappear? Suddenly the Pantheon emerged in front of me, looming in confrontation as I approached from a side street. What a fascinating area! I loved to wander, to explore antique shops, window shop at smart boutiques, or just sit over coffee in one of the many bars.

A rambling *pensione* I came to know well was at the upper end of Via Veneto, just below the Borghese gardens. We breakfasted with earnest Scandinavians who took their sight-seeing extremely seriously. I watched them poring over maps and guide books as they sipped their *caffelatte,* planning the day's activity in meticulous detail. I was once like that. But I'd learned to relax, to enjoy the beautiful surroundings, to absorb the atmosphere. Sometimes I stopped to visit a church or gallery, but I did this when I wanted to, not when I felt I should. After a leisurely breakfast, I strolled along Via Veneto, the street of the American Embassy, of expensive, luxurious hotels. This was where the smart set congregated.

As the years passed my requirements changed. I could no longer come and go as I pleased, I was not a carefree *signorina* any more. I had responsibilities, a husband to consider. And once the children arrived, we needed a different form of accommodation. Ideally, I would have liked to rent an apartment, but this option was not readily available. I heard that an entrepreneur was about to provide serviced apartments on the Via Velabro, a street close to the *Foro Romano*, the ancient Forum of Imperial Rome. We investigated these apartments, and found them ideal.

And so, with my two little girls, I set off to spend a few weeks in Rome. Stenio came at weekends, my mother stayed for several days *en route* to her next destination. I was happy. My new-found Italian cousins were warm and welcoming, and I had other friends.

Each day we set off for long walks, Simone in her pusher and Adriana trotting along beside. The Roman Forum, central hub of the ancient city, was right beside us. Pillars and chunks of collapsed ruins lay on the ground. The children played among the ruins while I sat on a beautifully carved column of white marble, guessing where the fallen masonry had once been attached, trying to reconstruct the temples to their original splendour. Then we walked on towards the nearby Colosseum. But we confined our admiration to the exterior, leaving detailed visits to the masses of tourists for whom *Il Colosseo* was an obligatory stop.

One evening, after I'd fed and bathed the children and was about to put them to bed, I heard a commotion in the square below. Opening the window, I was alarmed to see a crowd of people shouting and waving banners. Why were they all looking up and gesturing at my window? Rushing to the phone, I called reception.

"What on earth's going on?" I demanded.

"Don't worry, *Signora*," said the man at the desk. "They're not looking at you. It's the apartment directly above they're watching. Peron, the ex-president of Argentina and his wife Isabella moved in this afternoon. The demonstrators are Argentinian exiles pressing for his return."

167

I wasn't so sure about this supposedly comforting reply. What if the situation became violent? *"Argentina, Peron, presidente."* Now I knew who the demonstrators were, I managed to catch a few of the words they were chanting. I closed the shutters and hoped for the best. Next day, entering the foyer with the children, I found myself surrounded by Peron's bodyguards. Like all Latins, they loved *bambine* and made an enormous fuss of us all. Forming an escort as we went out, they accompanied my two little girls, chatting to them in Spanish. Although I never met Peron, I sometimes I felt as though we were part of his entourage.

During this period, we started to think about buying a small apartment. Stenio and I both loved Rome. It was reasonably accessible, the drive from Positano took about five hours. But whenever Stenio had an opportunity to take a few days off and suggested we go to Rome, we were confronted with the major problem of where to stay. It was not easy to find family accommodation at short notice. An apartment of our own would solve this quandary.

We made enquiries. Friends introduced us to a charming lady, a *Marchesa*, who specialised in buying and selling houses. *La Marchesa* came to our Velabro apartment with a list of properties for sale. The first places she showed us were stately *palazzi* and villas.

"We're not American millionaires," Stenio felt obliged to explain. "We're looking for something small and functional, a *pied-a-terre,* just big enough to fit our family. We are definitely not looking for a luxury home."

Disappointed, but clearly still interested, the *Marchesa* promised to keep a look out for us. Every now and then she called with news of an interesting apartment. If it sounded at all promising, we agreed to have a look. We saw some weird and wonderful places. Old *palazzi,* large and spacious, have been subdivided, modernised and renovated over and over again by who knows how many successive owners. The end result is predictably haphazard, an amazing hotchpotch of styles and structures.

We were shown an apartment near the *Piazza del Popolo*, a lovely part of Rome. I was really interested; it would have been an ideal position. But the flat was odd; one huge room, ballroom size, with a tiny bathroom and equally minute kitchen. We visited apartments in Trastevere, each stranger and more quirky than the last. Many foreigners lived in this sought-after district; to buy here was certainly a consideration. But it was not to be; we saw one or two flats which were cramped and grubby, and a few that were absolutely splendid, their asking price way out of our range. Perhaps we'd never find anything, we'd just have to keep staying in *alberghi*.

And then one day the *Marchesa* arrived with a set of keys. "I've just been shown a flat, it's quite small and not at all smart," she said. "But maybe it's worth a look." We hopped into the back of her *cinquecento,* the tiny Fiat was a popular car, eminently suited to Roman conditions. Off we went, weaving in and out of traffic, until we came to a stop in Via Monserrato. I knew this street. It was a fantastic location, right in the centre of Rome. We were about halfway between the *Lungotevere*, the road that runs alongside the river Tiber, and the *Corso Vittorio Emanuele* leading to St. Peter's and the Vatican. In walking distance of *Piazza Navona*. In fact we were marvellously close to almost anywhere I would ever want to go. I couldn't believe it, here was a place suitable for us, just where I wanted to be. I held my breath.

The building was old and had been subjected to successive renovations. At ground level a large iron gate led into a cavernous area, the premises of a family business. Four apartments shared the block. We followed the *Marchesa* up the stairs to a small landing on the first floor, waiting impatiently as she stopped at a door, took a key-ring from her bag, and tried one key after the other. Finally she found the right one and opened the door with a flourish.

The apartment itself was nothing special; two moderately sized rooms, a small kitchen, and an even smaller bathroom. The entrance could be used as a third room if required.

The *Marchesa* looked at us enquiringly. "What do you think?"

Stenio made some non-committal remark. I said nothing, I'd been warned not to say a word. But I was sure it would suit us perfectly. The facilities were adequate, the price reasonable, and the position superb.

Over the next few weeks we negotiated a little, waited anxiously, and argued a lot.

"It's just what we want," I repeated over and over again.

"Be patient. You can't just agree to their first price."

Stenio couldn't believe I was so naive. Although I knew he was right, I never really became accustomed to the Italian system of haggling. Of course I realised the vendor always asked more than he expected. And we had to offer less than we were prepared to spend. But it was a nail-biting time. What if someone else entered the negotiating process? What if we missed out? *"Non ti preoccupare,"* don't worry. If he said it once more I'd scream. But we followed the rules, waiting through the required period of offer and counter offer. Stenio understood this method of bargaining. And eventually, to my great relief, it was all over. The deal was done. We became the proud owners of our own flat in Via Monserrato.

Never have I been so thrilled and excited. I knew that this small, simple, and slightly run-down apartment would give us untold pleasure. "Buying this place is one of the best things we've ever done," I kept repeating to anyone who would listen. And it was true. We found enough furniture to make ourselves comfortable. By a stroke of good fortune, a nearby store specialising in imported Danish furniture was about to have a sale. We bought an attractive table and chairs, some beds, and two comfortable armchairs. Now we had the *pied-a-terre* I'd long been seeking. We could come and go as we pleased. I wouldn't have to make a dozen phone calls, to hear the familiar, "Sorry, we're completely booked out next week." It was all there, ready and waiting for us to arrive.

\*       \*       \*       \*       \*

Via di Monserrato and the neighbouring Via Giulia are wonderful Renaissance streets. Every time I walked out the door, I was following in the footsteps of countless earlier generations. According to my trusted travel guide, I was living in what had been one of the most elegant thoroughfares of the sixteenth century Papal City. Who knew what important personage had inhabited our *pied-a-terre,* which once constituted only a small corner of some great *palazzo.*

Via Monserrato, named after a famous sanctuary in Spain, at one time served as headquarters for Spanish noblemen who'd left their country to join the entourage of two popes of the infamous Borgia family. Santa Maria di Monserrato was the Spanish national church.

The adjacent Via Giulia, inaugurated by Pope Julius II, was once a main artery of Rome. The wide and elegant street runs in a straight line for over half a mile, an exception in this precinct of narrow, winding lanes. Imposing palaces on either side have been split up into flats. Women come and go carrying their shopping, children hurry home from school, eager to dump school bags bulging with books in rooms which were once judicial and administrative offices of the Renaissance city. Admiring the noble facades, I had a mental picture of a time when people rode in carriages rather than cars or vespas. Did they enjoy life more than we do? Who knows.

Both streets lead to Piazza Farnese, whose crowning glory, *Palazzo Farnese,* is one of the loveliest architectural creations of the late Renaissance, and according to my guide book, a typical example of the sumptuous palaces built by popes for their families. Alessandro Farnese, later Pope Paul III, commissioned a number of architects, including Sangallo and Michelangelo, to contribute to the design. Like everything in Rome, the *palazzo* has had a series of owners. Today it belongs to the French government and houses the French Embassy.

Our apartment was at the unfashionable end of the street. We were in a section given over to restaurants, shops and small businesses. A few doors up, at the corner of the street, a series of inlaid tiles admonishes passers-by not to litter the ground with rubbish. Judging by the ancient script, the tiles have been in place for centuries, the message probably ignored since the day it was written. We always laughed when we saw street sweepers busily cleaning and tidying at that particular spot.

Further along, the street becomes wider and the villas more elegant. On my way to the market one brisk winter morning I was amazed to see a familiar figure coming towards me. It was Father Percy Jones, a face from my school days. A personality from the musical world of Melbourne, he had taught at the conservatorium, directed musical activity for the Catholic Archdiocese, and promoted opera and recitals. Seeing him stop in front of the tall and glossy timber doors of the English College, one of the most stately Via Monserrato building, I hurried up and introduced myself.

"You won't remember me," I said, as he turned in surprise, but I feel I know you well. I have happy memories of your visits to my old school. You were so enthusiastic and encouraging to our orchestra and choir.

"Delighted to meet a fellow Australian," he boomed cheerfully. "Would you like to have a quick look over our wonderful College? We can chat as we go."

We stepped through the hallowed doors into a spacious, imposing entrance hall with sweeping marble steps.

"This site has been a haven for Englishmen for six centuries." said Father Percy.
We're told that early pilgrims faced serious problems. Local innkeepers had a shocking reputation; theft, extortion and pillage were the order of the day. And so, in the Jubilee year of 1300, an entrepreneurial English rosary seller and his wife decided to convert their modest house into an English hostel. Ever since, English merchants and tradesmen have stayed here. During the reign of Elizabeth I, the hospice became a refuge for English Catholics, and a seminary for training priests. It still is."

172

The lovely old building was Italian baroque in style, but centuries of English living had left their mark. Reception rooms were hung with portraits of famous Englishmen, the enormous library was lined from floor to ceiling with leather-bound volumes, and the chapel dedicated to St.Thomas à Becket. Everything was maintained in perfect English order.

\* \* \* \* \*

Not far from Piazza *Farnese* is another of Rome's delights; *Piazza Campo dei Fiori*. Here every day is market day. And what a scene it is. A colourful marketplace, hectic, vibrant, swarming with shoppers, baskets over their arms, intently examining items on display. Shopping in the *Campo dei Fiori* was one of the joys of life in the capital.

One section was devoted to seafood. Vendors cut slices off massive swordfish, scooped out servings of shellfish, of *vongole e cozze*, clams and mussels; wrapped up glistening silver fish with staring eyes and names I never discovered, Some had been filleted, others left whole. Calamari, octopus, spectacular prawns. As a special treat we sometimes shouted ourselves to a feast of giant prawns.

Mouth-watering fruit and vegetables. Artichokes, peppers, and a bewildering number of salad greens. I never understood how to distinguish the various types, to me they all look similar, but one variety is utilised as salad, another, seemingly identical, is always steamed. Italians go crazy about mushrooms, in particular *porcini*. The first time I tried *funghi porcini*, I could hardly believe my eyes or taste buds. Large and fleshy, such a grilled mushroom constitutes a meal in itself, more like a steak than a vegetable.

Of course the *Campo dei Fiori* has a long history. In late afternoon, with the market closed and stands cleared, we saw the *piazza* in a different light. Until the fifteenth century, it had been used as a setting for floral festivities, hence the name 'field of flowers'. Then came a period when this beautiful square served as

173

the gruesome site where heretics were burned alive. In the centre stands a bronze monument to the philosopher Giordano Bruno, burnt at the stake after his writings were judged heretical by the Church.

Further on is *Largo Argentina*. At first sight this square seems unremarkable, passengers queue at bus stops, for this is a central junction of the public transport system. Looking closer, however, you see that the central area has been excavated. Here, well below street level, stand the remains of four Roman temples from the Republican period, rare survivals from the fourth and fifth centuries B.C. But it was difficult to concentrate on antiquity because the place was filled with hundreds of cats. Every stray feline in Rome must somehow find its way to *Largo Argentina*. Black toms and white kittens, big, small, fat, thin, never have I seen such a collection of wild and mean-looking animals in one space. Shiny eyes glint out of hidden crevices. Somebody must feed them. I was careful not to get too close.

When I wanted to buy clothes rather than food, I continued on towards the old ghetto. Once all Jews were compelled to live here, and most of the shops and businesses still have Jewish owners. This was the place to shop.

Roman women are exceedingly fashion-conscious. This became more and more apparent now we had our own apartment, and I could come and go on a regular basis. Each month I drove from Positano to the capital, sometimes I stayed a few days, sometimes a week. To my continual surprise, I found the prevailing fashion changed with each visit. I'd always thought Italians were individualistic, but, when it came to *haute couture*, this was not the case. Attending a theatre performance, I noticed the smart *signore* wore slim-fitting suits of fine wool, in white or palest cream. I must get a suit like that, I thought. A month later, not one white tailleur was anywhere to be seen. Suddenly olive-green jackets were *de rigueur*. How could I keep up? And did I really want to?

When I decided to buy a smart outfit, I developed my own technique. First I went to the elegant fashion district. From our flat I took a bus or walked to *Piazza di Spagna,* examining articles of

174

*haute couture,* checking the chic boutiques on Via Condotti and Via Frascati, gasping at the prices. Having established what I liked, I visited the ghetto. Usually I came away thoroughly satisfied, having purchased what I wanted at half the cost. If I couldn't find exactly what I wanted, I bought a length of fabric to take to Anna, my wonderful Positano dressmaker.

*     *     *     *     *

*Piazza Navona,* that most delightful and charming of all Roman squares is long and narrow, its shape corresponding to the stadium of Domitian which originally occupied the site. It still looks like a racecourse. The *piazza* has long been a centre for public entertainment. In Roman times people flocked to see chariot racing and athletics, in the Middle Ages there were tournaments and bull-fights. The strangest public display was the water festival, a curious custom which started in 1650 and continued for almost two centuries. On Sundays during the hot summer months, the fountains were allowed to overflow until the flooded square was deep in water. Parties were given in surrounding houses, bands played, and the aristocracy drove slowly through the little lake in gilded coaches, splashing water and throwing coins to watching children.

Today the *piazza* still has its annual festival; the acclaimed Christmas fair which culminates in the coming of *La Befana* on the feast of the Epiphany. In the preceding weeks, *Piazza Navona* is filled with wooden stalls displaying Christmas decorations, in particular figures for the Nativity crib. On the fifth of January, eve of the Epiphany, which also happens to be my birthday, the large square can hardly hold the crowd as Romans come, young and old, to buy toys, admire the decorations, and, above all, to celebrate.

By day and night, *Piazza Navona* is the place to be; the restaurants and bars are well patronised, the best ice-cream is served, the coffee is excellent. Romans and tourists come to admire the three fountains, particularly the central Bernini masterpiece. Artists sell paintings of Roman landmarks, others draw instant portraits of anyone prepared to sit still for a few minutes, while caricaturists make a living sketching passers-by. The *piazza* is like a magnet, attracting tourists and locals, schoolchildren and business people, women pushing prams, couples strolling arm in arm on their *passeggiata*. On summer evenings bands play, jugglers and fire-eaters perform.

When it was time to go, we strolled back to our apartment through a maze of streets, dodging vespas and motorbikes. Car horns tooted in narrow passageways. People live all around, between churches and monuments, above shops and small businesses. I came across unexpected jewels; tiny outlets selling lovely old prints, an antique shop whose proprietor was a fascinating storyteller, a Romanesque church. I never knew what to expect, but I did know I was lucky to be living here, in the historic centre of Rome.

On summer evenings we often went to the nearby *Piazza della Chiesa Nuova,* named after a 'new' church, built in 1575. Two restaurants have pride of place, their tables and chairs almost filling the large square. We became regular visitors at one of these establishments; the waiters recognised us and came to anticipate the meal I invariably ordered. *Paglia e fieno,* literally straw and hay, is a typical dish. Thin strips of green and white pasta - spinach provides the colouring - are served in a sauce of peas, ham and cream. Next came *vitello tonnato*, a specialty for which the chef was justly acclaimed. Prepared by marinating braised veal for several days in a tuna-flavoured mayonnaise, this was a delicacy. And a side salad of Roman greens. I rarely changed my order, it was so perfect that I hesitated to try anything else.

Most of the local wine is produced in the Alban hills, south-east of Rome, the region known as the *Castelli Romani*. Castel Gandolfo, where the Pope has his summer residence, is one of the *Castelli*. Helen and Marco lived in this picturesque area, and we often met for Sunday lunch at Frascati, the setting for a traditional culinary delight.

*Porchetta*, roast pork. Suckling pigs roasting on braziers in the central *piazza* and by the roadside. On a winter's day the tempting aroma carried for miles; we always arrived starving, to join other groups standing in line. Lunch at Frascati followed a prescribed set of rules. First we had to wait our turn while a chef carved large, juicy portions from a roast. Having bought all we could possibly eat, we set off to find the local bakery. Another perfume, that of freshly baked bread, led us to a nearby shop. We selected a round loaf. The next step was to find, among the crowded wine bars on either side of the road, one where there was room to sit. Long wooden benches were aligned on either side of narrow tables. People sat tightly crammed together, munching *panini* with *porchetta*. Eventually a group of friendly locals squeezed even closer to make room for us. Once we'd found a seat, we cut our crusty rustic bread in slices and made king-sized sandwiches. Waiters brought carafes of Frascati, the local wine. We sat for hours, enjoying the succulent pork sandwiches, sipping our wine, and joining in conversation with our neighbours.

*    *    *    *    *

My sightseeing went through phases. For a time I visited cathedrals, and churches, some famous, others relatively unknown. I have no idea how many thousands there are, nor how many I visited. The starting point was the *Basilica di San Pietro*, St. Peter's, with its enormous Bernini designed *piazza*. I always find the basilica deceptive. On first impression it seems quite large, but not until I actually entered the portico and proceeded through one of the five doors did I realise that large is not the appropriate word. It's absolutely huge.

You can walk around Rome day after day, guide book in hand, because every street is a repository of history. But you can't do this forever. I preferred to explore my immediate surroundings. I walked to the vast, rectangular *Piazza Venezia*; one of the busiest traffic centres. The austerely beautiful *Palazzo Venezia* was appropriated by Mussolini as his headquarters. Films about the Fascist era featured regularly on television, scenes showing the dictator declaiming to massed crowds had become a familiar sight. I recognised the balcony where he used to stand to give his stirring orations. In striking contrast is the nearby Victor Emmanuel monument. Built of white marble, ornate, with innumerable statues, it is mockingly referred to as 'the wedding cake'.

*Il Campidoglio*, is the most famous of the seven Roman hills. Here, six centuries before Christ, the Romans built the great temple of Jupiter. Famous for its geometric paving and design, the Capitol was the work of Michelangelo. In the centre, Marcus Aurelius rides his bronze horse. Brides battle with tourists to have their photo taken in front of this massive sculpture. Whenever I visited the Campidoglio I was amazed by the number of girls, displaying every conceivable style of wedding dress, who stood smiling at new husbands while cameras clicked all around.

I did all the tourist things. I threw coins in the Trevi fountain. It must have worked for me as I returned many times. I can't imagine that everyone is equally fortunate. Hordes of visitors toss coins into the fountain at all hours of the day and night. Surely they don't all come back! Tourist coaches crowd the little square, stopping just long enough for passengers to be photographed throwing money into the water. Who knows where it all goes. Like Gregory Peck in 'Roman Holiday' I gingerly placed my hand in the *Bocca del Leone*, the Lion's mouth, hoping my fingers would still be there to pull out. If you've told a lie, your hand will be snapped off, or so tradition says. I was never sure of the time frame for safety. How recently did the lie have to be told, was there a time limit?

*     *     *     *     *

Much as I loved Rome, there were moments when I felt uneasy. In the 1970s political unrest was rife in Italy, terrorist acts became more and more frequent, politics dominated the news. Life in Positano continued in its usual tranquil way, but in Rome I felt an underlying tension, a presentiment that all was not well.

Almost directly opposite our apartment was a restaurant known for its *cucina casalinga*, home cooking. We ate there frequently; the food was good, the owners friendly, and the cost hardly more than I'd spend for a meal at home. We became friends with the family who owned it, and I often went with the children for a quick evening meal. As I was leaving one evening, the proprietor came up, holding a plastic bag.

"Put your handbag in this," he said. "You shouldn't go out in the street at night carrying a handbag. That's asking for trouble."

"You must be joking," I said I surprise. "You realise I only have to cross the road."

"I'm not joking, Signora. We've had a few unpleasant incidents lately. Please be careful."

Not far from us, on the *Corso Vittorio Emanuele*, was a small *profumeria*, perfume shop. Displayed in the window were a range of items; such shops sold not only perfume but also costume jewellery, toiletries, and cosmetics. I often stopped on my way home, sometimes to buy a few things, sometimes just for a chat. I liked the cheerful, smiling couple who ran the shop. One day I noticed that the door was tightly closed. Disturbed, I rang the bell, and was even more disconcerted to see the worried face of the proprietor anxiously peering out the window.

"What's going on?" I asked.

"We've had a terrible experience." Cautiously opening the door, he let me into the shop, bolting it behind me. His wife appeared and they started to speak at once. "A couple of men broke in last week, took all the jewellery and threatened to tie us up if we protested. It was shocking." They'd obviously been severely traumatised by their experience. Now they wanted to sell their business and move elsewhere.

At about this time I noticed that armed guards were posted outside every bank. A system was set in place whereby entry to any financial institution was closely monitored. You had to ring a bell, wait until a sliding door opened, then stand in a small entry chamber until another inner door slid open. All this before you were permitted to enter and approach a teller.

It was a time of terrorism, of hijackings and kidnappings. In Italy it was the time of the Red Brigades, a left-wing terrorist group.

I personally had a few bad experiences. On one occasion I was driving to the airport to meet my mother, who was due to arrive from Australia. As I approached, I became aware that something was seriously wrong. There were police cars, fire trucks, ambulances. A pall of black smoke could be seen rising above the runways. It was frightening. I managed to park somewhere, and started hurrying towards the terminal. Pandemonium reigned. Thousands of people were streaming the other way, running in panic towards me. "What's happening?" I kept asking, but no-one stopped to answer. By sheer coincidence, I suddenly saw my mother. Never have I felt more relieved. She had no idea what had happened. "Everyone was pouring out to the car park, so I joined them." Knowing I was coming to meet her, she'd been worrying about me. Later we discovered that an American plane had been hijacked by Arab terrorists. The hijackers, their demands refused, had blown up the plane on the tarmac, killing all hostages.

On another occasion, I was driving Helen to the station. She'd had dinner at our house, and was on her way home to Castel Gandolfo. We had just turned into *Piazza Venezia* when we saw, to our horror, a mass of protesters, about ten abreast, marching towards us, shouting and waving banners. I've never been so scared in my life. I have no recollection how we managed to extricate ourselves from this predicament. But somehow we did. We were lucky. I heard horrific stories. Neighbours told us that a group of young toughs had jumped their car. They'd locked themselves in, and waited, terrified, until their tormentors finally decided to let them go.

Incidents like these made me stop and think. I loved being in Rome, but was this period of violence a temporary phenomenon, or would it always be like this? Sometimes I felt homesick for Australia.

# LE FESTE

The year was punctuated by the dates of important *feste*. I soon came to know our local feast-days, but Stenio assured me that each Italian region has a cycle of its own. Traditionally, he explained, in the days when life was based on agriculture, the annual calendar had been regulated by seasonal requirements. The year revolved around the cultivation of crops. There was a time for planting and a time for harvesting. Families worked long hours on their small farms; Sundays and *feste* were the time to socialize with their neighbours.

The annual cycle was further regulated by dates of religious significance. Over the centuries, important events on the liturgical calendar, days like Christmas and Easter, became associated with particular ceremonies. In the weeks preceding these solemn Christian festivals certain rituals were observed; Advent was a time of preparation for the birth of Christ; Lent a period of penitence leading to Good Friday, was followed by the Resurrection on Easter Sunday. The festive calendar continued its traditional course through the year, with days of devotion to the Madonna, feast-days of important saints, and anniversaries of national importance. There were saints of local significance, each district had its own parish, its special patron saint, and its individual *festa*.

I loved the preparation and excitement associated with each feast. The rituals to mark special days, the particular food to be prepared; all this was new to me. Marietta was my guide, a responsibility she took extremely seriously. She made sure the Bella household conformed with the specific protocol required for each occasion. Checking that everything was ordered well in advance, that I went to the right church, bought appropriate gifts and wore suitable clothes, Marietta ensured that I couldn't possibly do the wrong thing. One of her recurring fears was that I would make '*brutta figura*'. Literally an ugly figure, this widely used expression is best translated as cutting a bad figure or making a fool of oneself. I hope I never did make *brutta figura* in this context, certainly I respected local traditions and appreciated the role Marietta played in smoothing our way through the potential minefield of correct procedure.

181

*    *    *    *    *

Christmas, *Natale*, was a lovely time in Positano. With the tourists gone, life returned to the simple ceremonies practised for centuries. Traditional celebrations reflected the religious significance of Christmas. Every church had a *presepio*, crib, portraying the birth of Christ in Bethlehem.

There must be thousands of cribs in Italy, but each has its own individual touch. I was constantly impressed at the imagination shown by artists and sculptors in creating the Nativity scene. Figures were modelled in clay, in wax, carved in wood; some were brightly painted in elaborate detail, others were delicate and subdued. By some magic, each reproduction, in its own way, conveyed an atmosphere of peace and serenity. I lingered in the various churches, examining the figures, absorbing the feeling of tranquillity, marvelling at the gentleness of the images.

Most cribs had a background of *papier mache* mountains. A path meandered through a pastoral landscape to a stable. Here the birth of Christ was reverently recreated. Statues of Mary and Joseph stood on either side of Baby Jesus sleeping peacefully in a manger. Other figures were included in the tableaux; angels and shepherds, birds and trees. Typically an ox and donkey waited patiently behind the Holy Family; sometimes the three kings appeared to celebrate the momentous event.

In the principal parish church of Positano, *il presepio* was very intricate. Each year it was lovingly unwrapped a few weeks before Christmas, and the sculpted figures carefully put in place. Parishioners lighted candles and placed them before the Infant in his cradle. But this was only one of many cribs on display. Another very special *presepio* was exhibited in the old church beside the *Piazza dei Mulini,* a venue much loved by children. Here a marvellous Nativity image came alive. Some resourceful engineer had set up a highly original system whereby, once a coin was inserted in a slot, a magical train of events was set in motion. Hundreds of tiny coloured lights switched on simultaneously and the village came aglow. Water gushed out of a tiny creek. I loved to watch the children's faces as they gazed in fascination at this amazing apparition.

Many households, particularly in the South, had their own *presepio*. According to tradition, the practice dates back to St. Francis of Assisi. Some figures brought out year after year were very old, and had been displayed for centuries. Creation of these *pastori* has become a form of folk art. In recent years, many families, yielding to outside influences, included a Christmas tree among their decorations. But the traditional crib still retained pride of place in most of the homes I visited. It was customary to leave the Nativity scene in place until the Epiphany, when the three Kings were expected to arrive with presents for the Baby Jesus.

Midnight Mass was a very special event. The church was full, the congregation hushed and expectant. A choir sang Christmas hymns and carols, the priest in colourful vestments celebrated High Mass. Then a procession formed. First came the celebrant followed by a number of altar boys who always managed to look like cherubs - I invariably recognised a few I knew to be surprisingly unangelic! The villagers walked behind, singing carols at the tops of their voices. Leaving the Church they went out into the winter night, winding their way slowly down the hundreds of illuminated steps to the waterfront.

Each region of Italy has its own Christmas traditions. In many small towns the Nativity scene was portrayed by actors performing in the principal streets and squares. One year we spent Christmas in Rome. The streets of the city were decorated, the air festive, and the crowning glory was my favourite square, *la Piazza Navona,* which had become a Christmas marketplace. I was admiring the Nativity figures and deciding what to buy when I became aware of delightful music approaching. I turned to see a pair of strolling musicians. One man sang a local Christmas song, another accompanied him on what looked to be a type of bagpipe.

"*I zampognari.*" Stenio was thrilled to hear the haunting music. "They come from the Abruzzi, and most of their songs are

*Abruzzese*. It's traditional for them to play in Rome and all over Italy. That strange-looking instrument is called a *zampogna* or *cornamusa*. It's made of goatskin and is, I believe, rather like a Scottish bagpipe. The wooden flute we call *la ciaramella*. And you know what they're playing."

| | |
|---|---|
| *Tu scendi dalle stelle,* | You come down from the stars, |
| o *Re del cielo,* | O King of heaven, |
| *e vieni in una grotta,* | and come into a cave, |
| *al freddo e al gelo.* | in the cold and frost. |

"Isn't it lovely?" Stenio said as we stopped to listen to the haunting, nostalgic tune. "It was composed in the eighteenth century by a Neapolitan priest, Alfonso de' Ligouri, who founded the Redemptorists. He was a poet, painter and writer. He was canonised by Pope Pius IX."

During my early years in Italy, Christmas was a time for religious observance, a day for rejoicing at the arrival of *Gesu Bambino*, Baby Jesus. The exchange of gifts was of minor importance. The Epiphany, on the sixth of January, was the day for giving presents. But as the years passed, there was increasing pressure for change, for conformity with other European countries, and even more with the American way of life. This trend had started with the influx of American soldiers during World War II, and was becoming more pronounced each year.

Shops began to display a wide range of gifts, decorations for the Christmas tree made their appearance, and the festive season grew more and more commercial. The figure of *Babbo Natale*, Father Christmas, carrying a bag filled with gifts, became increasingly familiar. Children, watching American films and television, expected a visit from *Babbo Natale*. Anxiously they waited for him to come down the chimney. And of course, he did come. On Christmas morning they found he'd filled their Christmas stockings and left presents for them.

*     *     *     *     *

The traditional day for presents, the Epiphany, celebrates the visit of the three kings, or Magi, to the Christ Child. On this day *La Befana*, an old woman who rides through the sky on a broomstick, was supposed to come to each house. Legend recounts that *La Befana* was invited to accompany the three wise men on their journey to visit the newborn babe in Bethlehem. She was so busy cleaning her home that she felt obliged to decline. She told the wise men to leave without her, promising to catch up with them as soon as possible. But the old woman left it too late, and, by the time she finished the housework, the wise men had long gone. Frantically running after them, still carrying her broom, she began, magically, to fly astride the broomstick. But she never managed to find either the three kings or the Christ Child. And so *La Befana* keeps on searching.

*La Befana* is usually portrayed as a benevolent, curved old woman with a hooked nose and pointed chin. On the eve of the Epiphany she rides through the skies carrying a sack full of presents. She rewards good children with sweets and chocolate, those who've been naughty receive pieces of charcoal as punishment. Children hang a stocking by the fireplace; in the morning they wake to find it filled with gifts. But no-one gives charcoal any more, instead, every child, good or bad, finds their stocking bulging with shiny black hunks resembling charcoal. These bulky black objects are, however, no longer a source of deprivation. Made of hard sugar with black food colouring, they are quite delicious.

As a sign of welcome, it was customary to leave a meal of sausage and broccoli, and a glass of wine for the old woman. About twenty years ago, the Italian government proposed that the Epiphany should no longer be a public holiday. Such was the outcry that the government was obliged to beat a hasty retreat.

As local habits changed, parents found themselves in a quandary. Unwilling to disappoint *i bambini* eagerly awaiting their expected gifts, doting mothers and fathers ended up with a double requirement. What a bonus for the children, two days devoted to presents!

*     *     *     *     *

Food forms an essential part of Italian culture, so it's hardly surprising that each festival has become associated with particular things to eat. Again the traditions are regional, but I was never sure what was customary in Positano. Everyone had a different idea. Christmas was special, all agreed, but what food was appropriate? Some said chicken, others fish. Every Italian, however, from whatever region or province, knows exactly what to provide for dessert.

On Christmas Eve, most *Positanesi* sat down to a dinner of fish or seafood, whatever was available. But the main event, which served to while away the hours until Midnight, was still to come. Following the dictates of tradition, every household prepared to fry *zeppole*. These sweets, made solely of flour and water, were fried for only a moment. Families waited eagerly, savouring the odours emanating from the kitchen, as the *zeppole* were immersed in oil, then quickly removed and covered with honey and vanilla. Marietta introduced us to *zeppole*, and I had to agree that this specialty, cheap and easy to produce, was really a treat.

We all enjoyed the typical Christmas cakes: *panettone, pandoro, panforte*. The names are variations of the word *pane,* bread. Thus *panettone* is a large bread, *pandoro* is golden, *panforte* strong. Most common is *panettone*, made from leavened sweet dough and filled with raisins, sultanas and candied fruit. Shaped like a tower, and packaged in square-based cartons, *panettone* is a familiar Christmas treat.

*Pandoro* is eaten by the angels in paradise, they say in the Veneto. Originally from Verona, *Pandoro* is high, star shaped, and softer than *panettone*. It looks golden because it's made with lots of butter, and has no sultanas or candied fruit. My favourite is *Panforte,* a specialty of Siena. The base reminds me of Communion host, the surface is powdered with sugar, and the dough is gingerbread and honey, with candied fruit, nuts and spices.

Last but not least is *torrone*, a nougat of nuts and honey. And lots and lots of sugar. *Torrone* can be hard, soft, or chocolate coated, whatever the form, children love it. So do dentists; their clinics are filled with patients after each holiday season. And of course, whatever the sweet, it must be accompanied by *spumante*, the sparkling dessert wine.

Traditional New Year fare was one of the few Italian delicacies I found singularly unappealing. *Zampone* or *cotechino* with lentils is not my favourite food. My recipe book describes *cotechino* as a spiced sausage made from a coarse mixture of pork skin, lean meat and fat, and seasoned with cloves and cinnamon. *Zampone*, a stuffed pig's trotter, is similar but larger, and is regarded as a symbol of abundance. These sausages can weigh up to a kilogram, and require prolonged cooking, after which they're cut into slices and served with lentils. Lentils symbolise money, so everyone eats as much as possible, hoping to become rich in the New Year.

After dinner, tables were set up to play *tombola*, a form of bingo. At midnight everything stopped. There were always fireworks somewhere nearby, so we all trooped out to watch. Wherever we were, and whatever the weather, the fireworks were spectacular. Then corks popped as bottles were opened, and we filled our champagne glasses with *spumante* to toast the New Year.

*     *     *     *     *

All my life I'd looked forward to Christmas. How I missed the traditional turkey and ham, how I lamented the fact that such traditional Christmas fare was not available. It never occurred to me that Stenio might get tired of hearing how wonderful it all was in Australia. And so, on one memorable occasion when I was very pregnant, he decided to gratify me. He went to the local butcher and told him about my longing for poultry. Italians have great respect for pregnant women. They say that if a pregnant woman desires a particular food and her wish is not fulfilled, the child will be born with *la voglia*, a birthmark. I don't know whether anyone really believed this, but I heard stories of men paying vast sums to get peaches from Africa in mid-winter. If that was what their wife wanted, she must be satisfied at all costs. Better to make sure their child would be born without defect.

And so the word went around. *La Signora dell'avvocato* must have a duck for Christmas.

"Don't worry," the butcher said to Stenio. "I'll get you a duck. If the Signora wants roast duck, she must have it. I certainly don't want to feel responsible if your baby is born with *la voglia*."

And, sure enough, he managed to provide us with a duck. Imagine my surprise when Stenio proudly turned up on Christmas eve holding a precious bundle. But this particular bird, to my dismay, had not been cleaned or plucked. It was very much alive, and making a lot of noise. Neither of us had experience in killing, cleaning or removing feathers. Fortunately we had Marietta, who knew how to do everything. And we did have a lovely Christmas dinner. Even more important, Simona, when she arrived, had no sign of a birthmark.

Another memorable Christmas came several years later. By now we had two excited little girls, as well as house guests from Rome. Everyone had cooperated in preparing for the festive occasion. The tree sparkled, the table was set with green foliage and red candles. I was convinced that everything was under control. With great attention to detail, I'd planned a traditional dinner, or as close to it as I could get. Having decided to offer my guests a choice of roast pork or duck, I'd ordered the meat well in advance, giving Salvatore plenty of notice. This time I was forewarned, and had ensured the poultry would be delivered cleaned and plucked.

It promised to be a wonderful day, snow had fallen on Christmas Eve, a most unusual event, and the air was crisp and fresh. The children had woken early in anticipation of the big day. There were the usual questions.

"Will Father Christmas know where to come? Will he know what we want? How can the reindeer get down the steps?"

After the early morning excitement had died down, I went downstairs to start preparing. As I came into the kitchen, the lights blinked, and I realised, to my horror, that there was no electricity. This was quite a frequent occurrence; in bad weather or windy conditions, we were accustomed to power failures. But today was *festa*, everyone was on holidays, including the workmen employed by the power companies. Who would fix the faulty line? What a disaster! What a fool I'd been to install an electric oven. How would I cook my roast dinner? Stenio, sensing I was about to become hysterical, had a brainwave.

Doesn't your mother have a gas stove?" he asked. "I know mine does, she flatly refused to have an electric oven. I'll ring them right now."

Luckily they both lived close by. I hurriedly prepared the meat, peeled potatoes, cleaned vegetables. It began to rain. Stenio set off up the steps, carrying the duck in its roasting pan to my mother, then came back to take the pork in the opposite direction. At midday my mother appeared in a heavy overcoat, carefully picking her way down the slippery steps, and carrying a hot oven dish with roast potatoes. Stenio followed with a steaming joint. Next my mother-in-law knocked at the door. "You'd better hurry before the pork gets burnt," she said. In fact it was cooked to perfection. All was well, we had a delicious meal. But it took a few hours for my stress level to return to normal. And even longer for the power to be restored. Owing to the holiday season, we remained without electricity for four days. They were cold days. We had no heating and no hot water. It was bad enough for us, but even worse was the embarrassment I felt for my freezing guests.

\*     \*     \*     \*     \*

*Pasqua,* Easter, was a time for prayer, but also a time for feasting.

189

Good Friday was a day of mourning. The sombre rituals associated with this occasion were quite extraordinary. Naples and the surrounding areas had come under the rule of Spain in the fifteenth century; Spanish domination continued for several centuries. Certain religious ceremonies, in particular those associated with Holy Week, were presumably incorporated during this period.

In late afternoon, a procession of black-hooded, black-caped figures made their way to the parish church of Santa Maria Assunta. The church was packed, the congregation silent. Followed by his acolytes, the priest entered and proceeded slowly to a side altar where an enormous crucifix hung above him. The crucifix was solemnly lowered to the ground and held erect by four of the hooded men. I watched in fascination as the priest removed nails from the hands of the dead Christ. The yellow, lifeless arms fell limply, to hang loosely at either side. Next the priest took out the heavy nails holding the feet to the cross. The legs dropped sharply down. It was frighteningly realistic. To the accompaniment of dirge-like music, the body was gently lowered into an open coffin. I found it disturbing to watch this graphic re-enactment of the death of Christ, a sobering experience, sombre and macabre.

The coffin with its lifelike corpse was now raised by pall-bearers and placed on a stand. The priest very slowly made his way out of the church, followed by pall-bearers carrying the body. More hooded men and boys fell into line, then the whole congregation joined in behind. Slowly the cortege filed out of the church and made its way through the village streets. The procession moved at a funereal pace, two steps forward, one step back.

Stenio was waiting for me after the service.

"You look as though you've seen a ghost," he said.

"Well that's exactly how I feel. I know you told me what to expect. But I never imagined anything so agonizing, so gruesome. I don't think I could ever bring myself to live through such a melancholy experience again."

190

*     *     *     *     *

Two days later it was Easter Sunday. Bells rang, the sun shone, everyone rejoiced. We all went to church to take part in the festive Mass celebrating the Resurrection. Coming home, we stopped *en route* to greet friends. We'd hidden Easter eggs in the garden before we left, now the children couldn't wait to get home and start their treasure hunt.

Easter, of course, has its own culinary tradition. Lamb is the standard dish, for the previous week we'd seen lamb carcasses strung up outside every butcher's shop. Inside we had to thread our way carefully between baby lambs dangling head-down from the ceiling. I couldn't believe how small they were, accustomed to the leg of lamb sold in Australia.

*Torta pasqualina*, a tart filled with ricotta, must be served. In our region a particular specialty was *pastiera napoletana*, a pastry made with ricotta, candied fruit, and wheat soaked in milk. Eggs are used in Easter baking to symbolize life, fertility and birth. One of my Calabrian friends described her childhood recollections to me.

"In my town Pasqua was a time for presents and for really rich food." she said. "They put whole eggs in bread or on a biscuit paste. My mother used to arrange fifty-one eggs on pastry. Her mother and grandmother had done the same. It was an ancient tradition."

"Why fifty-one?" I couldn't help asking.

"I really don't know." She looked surprised at my question. "I never thought to ask. Next time I go home I'll see if I can find out."

Shops are full of marzipan fruits in marvellous shapes and colours, pears and peaches, cherries, slices of water melon, bananas, pineapples, figs. I loved to decorate the table with a selected arrangement, but I felt it was a shame to eat them. They were delicious, but why upset my colourful display by eating the ingredients?

A traditional gift is an Easter lamb, made of sugar and almond paste. Small or large, depending on how much the giver can afford, they're all richly decorated and quite ornate. For those who don't want a marzipan lamb, there are chocolate hens and doves. Most important of all is the *Colomba Pasquale,* yet another type of *panettone*, orange-flavoured, shaped like a dove, and covered with crystallised sugar and almonds. No table setting is complete without the *Colomba.*

Easter eggs had been in shop windows for weeks. They were different from the eggs of my childhood. Inside was a 'surprise' which varied according to price; cheap eggs contained plastic toys, cards, or some little gimmick. But, for those prepared to buy an expensive egg, the possibilities were endless. They might find a watch, a silver brooch, a picture frame. I was told that people went to endless expense to have special gifts enclosed in chocolate for their girlfriend, wife or lover. I have to admit that no-one ever gave me a hand-made Easter egg.

*    *    *    *    *

The second of November is All Souls' day. On this day people remember loved ones who have died. The whole village goes to the cemetery carrying flowers and candles to place on the graves of deceased relatives and friends. High up above the town, this final place of rest is set in a magnificent position, providing the best view that Positano can offer. There is an air of tranquillity, an atmosphere imbued with peace and serenity.

It was not easy to reach, however. Villagers and mourners had to climb thousands of steps. Coffins had to be carried halfway up the mountain, so that to be a pall-bearer, although no doubt an honour, was extremely onerous. There was talk of building a road, both undertakers and mourning relatives found the climb difficult and would surely welcome the prospect.

192

The majority of emigrants who left Positano went to New York. Many did well there; a few made their fortune, others were less successful. But whatever their circumstances, most migrants never lost their feeling of nostalgia. Many returned to pass their twilight years in the village where they were born. Others wanted their bodies brought back to be buried. How to find space in the already full graveyard was a recurring problem.

The feast of All Souls honours the memory of all who have died, and is a day of great importance. I joined in the local ceremonies, climbing the mountain with the crowd of villagers carrying white chrysanthemums. In Italy, the chrysanthemum is the flower associated with funerals and cemeteries, and vast numbers are especially cultivated for this annual event.

As evening approached, large yellow wax candles, protected in wide holders, were lit and placed, together with the flowers, by the side of each grave. In honour of the deceased members of the community, the cemetery, illuminated by thousands of candles and visible from almost every home in the village, was aglow with light. It was a sight to behold, a spectacular never-to-be-forgotten scene.

# LANGUAGE PROBLEMS

Every day I learned something new. A few new words to add to my vocabulary, a slight improvement in pronunciation, the correct way to use a certain pronoun. "*Brava, brava,*" said the *Positanesi*. How well I was doing, I congratulated myself. It wasn't nearly as hard as I'd expected.

When I first arrived in Italy, I could barely make myself understood. I knew how to ask elementary questions. 'Where is the toilet?' 'Will it rain tomorrow?' 'Would you like a cigar?'. I'd acquired a random selection of phrases, some more useful than others, but I badly needed to extend my repertoire. Each day I tried to learn a few new words and at least one irregular verb. Why were there so many tenses and conjugations, how would I ever know what was required? It was hard enough to understand the regular verbs without being constantly confronted with exceptions.

Gradually I gained a little confidence. At times I still struggled to make myself understood, but people no longer looked completely bewildered when I tried to communicate. On my way to the post office, the bank, or the local bar, I prepared appropriate phrases or sentences in advance. The local shopkeepers, friendly and encouraging, appreciated my efforts. Often, if they weren't too busy, they asked me about life in Australia. Sometimes we talked about their jobs, their families, their plans for the future. I can't say I understood every word, but I could follow enough to make an occasional sensible comment.

"Your Italian gets better every day," said Patrizia, the friendly girl who worked at the store, as she weighed out the fruit and vegetables. Italians are extremely helpful and responsive to foreigners trying to learn their language. "How well you speak," they say encouragingly. "You've learned so much in the short time you've been here." I became accustomed to such compliments. And of course I believed them.

But then, suddenly, I seemed to hit an invisible wall. From one day to the next, and contrary to all expectations, I stopped

194

making progress. My burgeoning self-confidence was rudely shattered. Why was this happening? I'd been so satisfied at my steady improvement; so pleased with myself. Maybe I wasn't doing so well after all.

Certain things were difficult. Although I coped reasonably well on a one-to-one basis, I had trouble in a group. Dinner parties were a nightmare. At first my companions made an effort to speak slowly and include me in the conversation, but as the evening progressed and they warmed to their theme, they forgot all about me. Once everyone around the table started talking, I was lost within minutes. The more animated the discussion, the more perplexed I became.

Television was another problem. I made a determined effort to follow the daily news. National television was excellent, offering a comprehensive coverage of world events. I listened carefully as expert journalists discussed and analysed news items, but I could never be sure I'd really grasped what they were saying. Feature films, documentaries and quiz-shows were easier to follow; it didn't matter if I missed the odd word.

Movies presented unexpected difficulties. Any suggestion that we go to the cinema filled me with apprehension. What if I didn't understand? But I discovered, to my surprise, that I could follow the dialogue reasonably well. As long as the actors had actually spoken Italian during filming, it wasn't difficult at all. English and American pictures were another matter. How could this be? Since foreign productions were usually dubbed into Italian, the only conclusion I could draw was that I was lip-reading.

It was distressing to see 'Becket' on TV. I had long been a fan of Richard Burton. What a magnificent voice he had, how beautifully he spoke! There he was on the screen in front of me, declaiming some wonderful speech. But instead of the deep and resonant voice of my expectations, I was shocked to hear a stream of almost unintelligible words issuing forth in dull, undistinguished tones. It was dreadful.

Answering the phone was another trial. It was disconcerting to pick up the receiver and hear a barrage of words emanating at incredible speed. Once again I realised how much facial expression contributes to communication. This probably explained my awkwardness on the phone. It was hard to speak to someone you couldn't see. I made excuses; the line was bad; there was too much background noise; the person had a strange accent. And I kept hoping it would be easier next time.

But the real test, I was told, is to think in both languages. 'You can't believe you've mastered a language until you stop translating words and sentences.' I knew this was true, all the experts said so; yet here I was, congratulating myself on my steady improvement, while my mind jumped backwards and forwards from Italian to English. Until I learned to control my head, I'd never be able to speak fluently, nor to take part in conversations and discussions. Somehow I had to overcome this hurdle. But how could I make the transition? Would it occur automatically? All our bilingual friends had managed, why couldn't I?

It did happen. By some extraordinary form of osmosis, the required factor X, for want of a better name, slowly seeped into my consciousness, to lodge in whatever part of the brain is associated with words. One day I was struggling, the next, I was starting to feel at ease in my new language. I became more fluent, less hesitant, less liable to translate each thought into English. It became natural to respond to a question immediately. Had I started to think in Italian? I set myself little tests. Walking along the street, or driving alone in the car, I tried to analyse my thought patterns. The end result was confusion. Recalling how you think is not easy. And then one memorable morning I woke to find I'd been dreaming in Italian. I could actually dream in either language. I felt a remarkable sense of achievement. Maybe I was finally on the way.

Children have an innate ability to learn languages. The younger they are when exposed to different sounds, the more receptive they appear to be. I was fascinated to observe the behaviour of my own infants. Once the moment came for their first words, they spoke in Italian and English simultaneously. Not only did they pronounce the words perfectly, without any trace of accent, they also knew which language was appropriate. Talking to my mother or me, they spoke English; if Stenio or Marietta appeared they launched into Italian without a moment's hesitation. I couldn't help feeling a little jealous. I'm sure there must be a scientific explanation for the ability of young children to learn so easily. I put it down to having an uncluttered mind. And to the complete and wonderful absence of self-consciousness associated with childhood.

*     *     *     *     *

Each language has its own rhythm. Even in Australia I'd been aware of regional differences. Accents and intonation vary, as does the stress on certain words. People from certain parts of the country talk more slowly than others. Farmers are known for their country drawl. Americans living in Australia gradually acquire the vernacular of their host country, but they never lose their original accent.

A feeling for rhythm applies even more when adopting a new language. Intonation, inflection, structure, phrasing; so much is involved. I'm sure a good ear for music is correlated with language skills. My New Zealand friend Christine was a good example. A gifted musician, Christine had won a scholarship to study singing in London and Vienna. Along the way she met and married a Neapolitan, and now lived in Naples. Although I had a wider vocabulary, and possibly a better grasp of grammar, her Italian sounded better than mine. Her accent was less pronounced; she spoke with a melodious cadence I could never manage. In fact I had to admit that my New Zealand friend could almost pass for a native Italian.

At the opposite extreme was one of my neighbours, a German lady who'd lived in Positano for forty years. *La tedesca*, the German woman, as she was known, was a formidable lady. Diminutive in size, with short cropped white hair, piercing blue eyes, and an unexpectedly deep voice, *la tedesca* understood Italian perfectly, but her conversation was quite eccentric. Having resolved early in her stay that she wouldn't bother about grammar, she stubbornly insisted on using verbs exclusively in the present tense.

197

"Tomorrow I see you; last week I go to Naples; this morning I eat toast for breakfast." Tenses were irrelevant as far as she was concerned. And nobody seemed to mind. *Positanesi* are tolerant; if *la tedesca* chose to maintain her idiosyncrasy, so be it.

In some ways I didn't blame her; the verbs are incredibly complex. I struggled with innumerable tenses: the perfect, imperfect, past perfect, past remote, not to mention the future, the conditional, and the all important subjunctive - I'd been told an educated person must know how to use the subjunctive correctly. I was determined to conquer those irritating verbs. But I had a particular problem of my own. My personal struggle was with nouns. Try as I might, I continually put the wrong endings on words. Somehow I could never come to terms with the fact that all nouns have a gender. Why should they? Wood, *legno* is masculine, table, *tavola*, feminine; *libro*, book, is masculine, *carta*, paper, feminine. I could find no logical explanation. How can anyone guess the gender of a television set? Masculine words generally end in -o, feminine in -a. But not always, again there are exceptions.

Language expresses the culture of a people. And, on an individual level, the way people talk reflects their personality. As I became more familiar with everyday words, and more attuned to a sound pattern, I noticed that my way of speaking was undergoing a change. An involuntary reflex, perhaps triggered off by the same factor X, now came into play. My ability to communicate appeared correlated with certain unconscious changes. I was modulating my speech to sound more like a 'real' Italian. I was using my hands to express what I wanted to say. Italian is a language of gesticulation and I'd begun to pick up local mannerisms. Certain phrases are commonly associated with a particular movement. Talking with the hands is not mandatory, but specific gestures do convey a meaning. The listener understands without any need for words.

In Italian a variation in tone can serve to indicate inquiry. *Andiamo al cinema* may denote 'We're going to the pictures', or 'Are we going to the pictures?' depending on the intonation. When asking a question, the voice rises on the last syllable. I experimented with the intonation required to make a sentence interrogative.

The addition of a suffix is frequently used to alter meaning. *Casa*, house; *casetta*, little house; *casaccia*, ugly house; *finestra*, window; *finestrone*, large window; *finestrina*, little window. Australians abbreviate Christian names as a sign of affection. Here, I discovered, they do the opposite. To the popular name Giovanni, John, fond parents add a diminutive, calling their son Giovannino, little John. But then, at some later stage, long names tend to be shortened once again. So the *ragazzino*, little boy, progresses from Giovanni to Giovannino and finally becomes known as Nino. My mother-in-law adopted this custom, calling her grandchildren Adrianina and Simonetta. Fortunately there was never any suggestion of Nina and Netta.

*    *    *    *    *

Gradually I began to feel more relaxed in social situations. At times I managed to join in dinner party conversation. This wasn't easy. Not only did I have to understand and express myself, I also had to make myself heard. I had to break into someone else's discourse and talk in a loud voice. My companions were usually so animated, and the discussion so lively, that considerable effort was required to make any impression at all. Sometimes I wondered whether I'd have to change my personality as well. Perhaps I'd become more Latin in temperament, more sparkling and vivacious. I wouldn't mind at all, in fact I'd be delighted at such a change.

'Every action results in an equal and opposite reaction'. This was a law I'd learned at school. Now I observed the law in action, as I found, to my dismay, that as my Italian improved, my English started to deteriorate. I was disconcerted to notice I was beginning to construct sentences in the Italian way. It didn't sound good. I acquired a habit of ending a sentence with 'no'. For example, '*Piove, no?*' This sounds fine, but when I said to visiting English friends, 'It's raining, no?' or 'Last night's concert was excellent, no?' they looked at me strangely.

English-speaking friends like Carol and Diana made similar slips. I suppose this must be typical of expatriate communities.

Certain expressions, for which there is no exact equivalent, become indispensable. *Simpatico* is a lovely word. It's impossible to find a literal translation. The dictionary supplies adjectives such as nice, pleasant, agreeable. But *simpatico* means much more. A person is *simpatico* when you get on well together and enjoy each other's company. Another marvellous expression is *magari*, to signify 'if only' or 'I wish this were so'. *Magari* is said in a particular tone of voice, with an ever so slight shrug of the shoulders.

Many English expressions are just as difficult. I never discovered a satisfactory way to say 'looking forward to'. Such untranslatable words find their way into a type of mixed language, easily understood by fellow expatriates, but unintelligible in other environments. On a more general scale, terms like 'il weekend', 'il barbecue', and OK, have infiltrated Europe. Since Italian food enjoys world wide popularity, we all eat *pizza, pasta, mozzarella,* we drink *cappuccino*. In Australia, *caffelatte* has become extremely popular. Given the Australian tendency to abbreviate words - unlike Italians who like to add endings - *caffelatte* is referred to as *latte*. As a result, Australian coffee drinkers assume that *latte* means white coffee. I can imagine the amazement of tourists who order a *latte* in an Italian bar and see the waiter arrive with a glass of milk.

Idioms are peculiar to their own language. To us, they proved a source of much hilarity. Stenio had a habit of translating figures of speech. One of his favourite phrases, '*non è ne pesce, ne carne,*' it's neither fish nor meat, could be relied on as a conversation stopper. 'I don't know whether you'd like Jack, he's neither fish nor meat,' left his listeners totally confused. The reverse is true, of course. Try saying in Italian, 'wait for a rainy day'. Or any one of a host of picturesque expressions; 'water off a duck's back'; 'it's raining cats and dogs'; 'burning the midnight oil'. I was occasionally tempted to adapt an Australian figure of speech, but the result was never good. People just looked puzzled and perplexed. "Drop me a line' might be an appropriate recommendation to a person about to go fishing, but it's definitely not suitable when suggesting a friend should occasionally write a letter.

In time my Italian became as fluent as English. As the years went by I felt reasonably proficient. But despite my increasing facility with the language, I never managed to lose my accent. It was so frustrating. As soon as I opened my mouth, someone would say, "*La signora è inglese?*" I found this really annoying. Even more irritating was the reaction my accent provoked among the sales staff of large department stores. The national chains, Upim and Standa, are represented in most Italian cities. And for some inexplicable reason, these shops made a habit of employing young girls who took delight in patronising me.

When I approached a salesgirl with a piece of merchandise to ask, "*Quanto costa?* she would barely glance in my direction. "*Cinquecento lira';* was the reply, enunciated slowly and distinctly, as she counted out on her fingers the numbers: *uno, due, tre, quattro, cinque.* How maddening, how very disappointing. I felt like throwing whatever I'd planned to buy at the annoying salesgirl. But I realised the girls, accustomed to tourists, were only trying to be helpful. Couldn't they tell I spoke as fluently as they did? Obviously not.

*      *      *      *      *

The longer I stayed in Italy the more I became aware of its extraordinary linguistic complications. Italian is a beautiful, melodious language, but it varies enormously throughout the peninsula. Some people speak Italian. Some speak dialect. Many speak both, choosing one or other depending on the circumstances.

Each district has its own particular dialect. I have no idea how many dialects there are, but I do know that many are almost like separate languages, bearing little resemblance to one another or to Italian. The situation is complicated even further by distinctive regional accents. Sicilians and Venetians both speak Italian, but their accents vary markedly. To a novice like me, these strong accents presented one more dilemma, was I listening to Italian or to a local dialect? In time I learned to identify the more obvious accents, to distinguish whether someone came from the north or south. Finer

201

distinctions - whether an accent had originated in Verona or Brescia - were quite beyond me.

"Why does it have to be so complex?" I complained. I'd had a difficult morning trying to follow the conversation in a nearby village. Their odd mixture of Italian and dialect had left me feeling bewildered. It was hard enough to understand their Italian pronunciation; I couldn't cope with dialect as well.

"They're trying to include you in the conversation," Stenio said, hoping to cheer me up. "It isn't easy for them either. Normally they'd just speak dialect. You realise, of course, that before schooling was compulsory, these village people had no opportunity to learn the national language."

"But today every child learns Italian."

"Yes I know. It's really just an excuse. And we can't do much about our accents. You should know, you're always telling me about your accent problem. But I can't explain why we're so proud of our dialects. It's not just *Napoletani*. We're all the same, we Italians. Determined to hold on to every bit of our local heritage. You'll just have to get used to us, I'm afraid."

Italians dialects go back a long way, further even than Latin. Barbarian invasions, foreign domination, centuries of geographic isolation; all these factors no doubt played a part in regional speech patterns, which are as much a part of local colour and identity as are geography and parochial customs. Not until Italy was unified in the nineteenth century did the need for a national language become imperative. It was decided that the literary language of Florence should be spoken throughout the nation.

*Napoletano* was the dialect I heard every day. Although it became familiar and I understood the odd word, I never learned to follow it completely. Nor did I attempt to speak it. Stenio enjoyed talking *Napoletano* with his father and brother, and with friends. At home, however, they always spoke Italian, otherwise his mother would have been excluded. But many local families, even in homes where children had married non-Italians, talked exclusively Neapolitan, using Italian only on formal occasions. This led to a bizarre situation where foreign women picked up dialect rather than Italian. Ilka, an Austrian, was a case in point. Having married a *Positanese* and produced a tribe of children, she worked with her husband in a bar near the beach. I often heard her as I passed, holding forth in the broadest and most colourful language imaginable. Neapolitan has some particularly evocative swear words, and Ilka knew them all.

# CHOOSING THE RIGHT MOMENT

The walnut tree was heavy with fruit. The nuts ripened in late summer, and were collected a few weeks later. At the appropriate time, men came to beat the branches, so that the mature fruit fell to the ground. But unfortunately, although branches of this enormous tree overhung our bedroom balcony, the tree was not ours. It belonged to the owners of the property below.

Walnuts are enclosed in a green sheath or hull. When the fruit is fully ripe, the outer covering splits open and falls off, revealing a hard brown shell. I'd never before come across newly picked walnuts. Full of expectations, I cracked the shell and tasted the young nut. It was really bitter. Then I realised that the kernel was enclosed in a membranous skin. Why was this skin so bitter, I wondered. Nature has devised ingenious ways of protecting and propagating plants. Presumably there must have been some reason why, in the course of evolution, the walnut kernel was provided with its particular shield. It was easy enough to strip off the offending membrane, more difficult to remove the stain from my fingers. The underlying core was white, tender and mouth-wateringly delicious.

Walnuts bought in a shop are completely different. There's no need to peel anything off; the protective skin has usually disappeared. But the kernel, although still good to eat, has lost much of its initial tender, delicate aroma. And the nuts are often yellow and oily. At least I learned how a really fresh walnut should taste.

Walnut collecting became a challenge. I never knew the rules. Were we entitled to the fruit within reach? We watched them slowly ripen outside our bedroom window. I studied the heavily laden boughs, looked closely to see whether the hulls were beginning to split. If I succumbed to the temptation and picked the nuts too soon, the sheath clung to the shell and the fruit rotted without ripening. If, on the other hand, I waited too long, the beaters came, knocked all the nuts down, and I was left with nothing. I could hardly ask the proprietor of the property below when the beaters were due to arrive. I knew that early September was the time.

Sometimes I won, sometimes I lost. It was a guessing game, a matter of luck.

\*     \*     \*     \*     \*

One of my claims to fame was the fact that I introduced passion fruit to Positano. *Passiflora edulis*, to give it its botanical title, is a climbing evergreen plant which produces a spectacular flower and delicious fruit. The flower is many layered, at its centre is a cross, hence the name passion flower. The fruit, dark purple when ripe, is originally from South America, and is extremely popular in Australia. As a child, one of the pleasures of late summer was picking the fruit off a vine in our backyard, and eating as much as I could possibly manage. But I'd never seen passion fruit in Italy.

My mother's friend Di was a keen gardener. On one of her visits I mentioned the sad lack of passion-fruit in my life.

"Next time I come I'll bring some seeds," she said.

And sure enough, the following summer Di presented me with a packet of seeds collected from her own garden. By this time I had managed to obtain a tiny garden plot where I was allowed to grow whatever I wished. I planted a few seeds in front of a north-facing wall.

I waited impatiently. Would the seeds grow in this part of the world? How would they cope with a change in seasons, with summer in July instead of January? And a completely different climate. Time would tell.

In due course, the seeds germinated to produce tiny seedlings, which developed into what looked like the real thing. The following year, a few buds emerged. They looked perfect, lovely, exotic *passiflora*. I waited for the flowers to develop into fruit. But nothing happened. The blooms dried and fell off, but no fruit appeared. Perhaps it was too early, perhaps the vine needed time to settle in. Maybe a plant didn't bear fruit in its first year. But the next year the same thing happened. This time there were a number of flowers, but again they dropped off. I was so disappointed. I spoke to friends who purported to know about gardening. They're not being fertilized, they told me. They probably need some particular insect or bird to effect cross-pollination. Perhaps we don't have the appropriate vector in this country. There was talk of a bird called a colibri supposedly responsible for pollinating passion fruit. I was prepared to believe anything.

If nature couldn't do the job, I decided to help. I borrowed an old paintbrush from my father-in-law, and proceeded to brush pollen from the stamens of one flower to the stigma of another. I've since discovered that passion fruit is bisexual, so my efforts were probably superfluous. However, I followed this routine on a daily basis, watching the progress with keen anticipation. To my increasing frustration, flowers continued to drop off, no fruit appeared. And then one day, to my delight, I saw a tiny green swelling forming at the centre of a flower. I was so excited, I ran inside to tell the children and Marietta. They all came out to look. Day by day the green fruit increased in size, but before it had fully ripened, it dropped off. Eventually, however, an occasional fruit did mature, and, after a few years I could boast that my vine was producing fruit. I gave a sample to all my friends. They were enthusiastic, complimenting me on my perseverance and horticultural skills.

In Australia, the most popular of all desserts is known as pavlova. Named after the famous ballerina Anna Pavlova, the assumption is that this sweet should be 'light as Pavlova'. It's really a large meringue filled with cream and fruit, commonly passion fruit. Stenio had tasted pavlova in Australia, and was most impressed. Now he expected me to produce passion fruit pavlova as a matter of course. But unfortunately, despite the fact that all my Australian friends assured me their recipe was foolproof, I was an absolute flop as a pavlova maker. No matter how carefully I whipped the egg whites, how slowly I beat in the sugar, or what other ingredients I added, I never managed to achieve a satisfactory result. It looked all right when I put it in the oven. But at some point the mixture started to weep, the egg white seeped away, and I ended up with a sticky shrunken mess. I filled the sticky meringue case with cream (unpasteurised) and passion fruit. Stenio told our guests this was typically Australian, and I smiled graciously. Fortunately none of our visitors had the slightest idea how a real pavlova should look. They made suitably polite comments, and I accepted their compliments.

*      *      *      *      *

We shared our house with geckos. I didn't mind the lizards. Lizards abounded; darting across the terrace, flitting through the garden, sunning themselves on paths and steps. But they didn't come inside. Occasionally a lizard might stray through an outside door, to hurry out again as quickly as possible. Geckos had no such inhibitions. And I didn't want them in my home. To me they were fat, ugly and unaesthetic. Stenio and Marietta laughed at my aversion, having grown up to regard geckos affectionately as normal household companions. Could I help it if I found them repulsive?

Lizards flitted around during the day, but at night they disappeared. Geckos, on the other hand, emerged after dark. During the day they sheltered out of view. At dusk, I'd look up to see one clinging to a wall. In general, they stayed outside, but apparently they felt equally at home in my sitting room or bedroom.

One morning Marietta was cleaning the entrance hall.

"Maybe we should dust behind the mirror," I suggested, lifting one of my favourite antique pieces from its hook on the wall. Set in a lovely frame of carved wood, this was one of the treasures I'd discovered in Carmine's Minori *antiquariato*.

"I'll take it, Signora." Marietta hurried over, snatching the mirror from my hands. Perched on the back, hidden from view, was an enormous gecko. Marietta knew me well. She realised I'd drop the mirror in horror the moment I saw the gecko. Grateful at her intervention, I watched as she opened the door to the terrace, shook off the offending reptile, and carefully wiped both frame and mirror. Replacing it in its customary position, she smiled at me encouragingly. I felt ashamed to be so stupid.

207

When we were building the house, there'd been considerable discussion about where to locate the hot water service. Someone had come up with the bright idea of utilising the empty space beneath the stairs. The heater could be accessed by opening a small wooden panel to the left of the staircase. In early summer I began to notice tiny baby geckos, small and transparently pink in colour, darting across the stairs as I went up. The climax came one evening as I was running the children's bath. To my dismay, I found a baby gecko floating in the water. I couldn't cope with baby geckos. This would have to stop. Everyone else thought it was hilarious, the funny story of the week. Eventually I prevailed; the empty space behind the heater was tidied and blocked off. And the geckos presumably felt obliged to move their nest elsewhere; no longer did I cross paths with their offspring on my staircase.

*     *     *     *     *

And then there were bees. Raffaele, my father-in-law, loved his bees and was proud of his honey. He was oblivious to my broad hints about the inconvenience of picking fruit or vegetables in the upper terrace garden, the risk to his little granddaughter who accompanied me on my fruit picking visits, and the general discomfort and unpleasantness of fending off angry buzzing bees whenever we passed their hives.

But this was a minor, if irritating problem. A confrontation of major proportions was yet to happen. My laundry was downstairs under the house, two terraces below the vegetable garden. Each day I went down the steps to put clothes in the washing machine, or to fold and put away the clean laundry. One fine summer afternoon I arrived home from the beach unexpectedly early. Going downstairs to hang my wet bathing costume on the line, I was surprised to find the door closed. Unsuspectingly, I opened the door, to see Raffaele and his two sons surrounded by a swarm of buzzing bees. They looked up, startled to see me. Stenio and his brother seemed like schoolboys caught in the act.

"What on earth are you doing?" I yelled.

"Close the door," Raffaele shouted back. "Can't you see we're extracting honey? There are enough bees in here as it is. We don't want the whole hive to get in."

I was speechless with shock. How dared they use my clean, tidy laundry as a honey house? And without telling me. It was pointless to stay and argue. I would only be stung. But I couldn't believe they would ignore me in this way.

That evening Stenio was most apologetic, sorry I was upset. I had the impression he thought it was all a bit of a joke, and that I was over-reacting. But neither he nor the other two really understood how I felt. For them it was a practical solution, they needed a closed area to extract honey and my laundry served the purpose.

I never managed to convince them that I was entitled to have a say in my own house, even if I was a woman. I don't know where they took their hives in following years, I didn't ask and I wasn't told. I'd never particularly liked honey, and this incident put me off for ever.

\*     \*     \*     \*     \*

It was nearly lunchtime when the doorbell rang. I opened the door to find four attractive, suntanned young girls, casually dressed in shorts, T-shirts, and Positano sandals. They stood there happily smiling at me. Even before they said a word I could tell they were Australians.

"We've finally found you," they all said at once.

I'd become accustomed to strangers appearing at our door, with the customary explanation that some friend or other, often someone I barely knew, had told them about us.

"Jack said we must come and see you while we're in this part of the world. He said you'd be thrilled to have visitors from Australia." Often I wasn't sure who Jack was.

Such callers were a mixed blessing. Friends usually wrote to tell me if they'd given my address to potential visitors. This was fine, in general I enjoyed meeting people from home. If I'd been informed in advance, I was more than happy to invite them for a meal. But it could become too much, particularly in midsummer when we were busy and often had a house full of guests.

In this case, however, I was pleased to meet the girls. It was late October, I had plenty of time, and the parents of one were family friends. They had lunch with us. Marietta was her usual capable self, managing to rise to the occasion and provide an excellent meal at short notice. My unexpected guests were full of enthusiasm. They'd been travelling for several months, and were now heading back to England to look for jobs, hoping to return to southern Europe the following summer.

"You don't know of any jobs here?" asked Megan, who seemed to act as organiser. "Do you think we could find work in a shop or travel agency. Or maybe there are families interested in having an *au pair*?"

Many Italian families employed *au pair* girls. The idea was a good one. A family with young children took in a foreign girl. Usually, her duties were limited to looking after children; she was not required to do housework. In exchange, she received free food and board. The system was mutually beneficial, the *au pair* was encouraged to speak English to familiarize the children with the language. And at the same time, the foreign girl had the opportunity to learn Italian, and to experience the way of life in another country.

Suddenly I had a brainwave. I was expecting my second baby in February, and I'd wondered how I would manage in summer with two small children. Would I be confined to the house? Here was a perfect opportunity. We had a spare room downstairs; a pleasant room with a small bathroom and balcony overlooking the sea. Perhaps one of the girls would like to stay with us for a few weeks. She'd be free during the day, but if we wanted to go out in the evening, we could ask her to baby-sit. The more I considered the idea, the more it appealed. I might as well suggest this option and see what they thought.

"How fantastic. I'd love that." Again they all spoke at once.

"Let's think about it for a while. I'll have to discuss the idea with my husband. It wouldn't happen till about June. Then, if one of you still wants to take up my offer, I imagine it would suit us perfectly."

They started to discuss the prospect. One of the girls was going home to get engaged, she'd been missing her boyfriend. That left three. No doubt they'd sort it out. Maybe they'd decide against it. There was plenty of time. Megan seemed the most enthusiastic, she definitely wanted to spend a summer in Italy. We passed the afternoon chatting, I heard about their travel adventures and their future prospects. They were good company. Eventually it was time to say goodbye. We agreed to keep in touch.

The following June, Megan arrived as promised. By this time Simone was about five months old. The arrangement worked beautifully; we all got along extremely well. Megan was good with the children. Now we could go out for dinner whenever we wished. Or meet friends for after-dinner coffee in one of the local bars. We were usually home quite early. This suited our baby-sitter; her social life didn't start till late. She could go out after we came home. An unforeseen complication was the fact that Megan, an attractive, friendly young girl, was an enormous success with many of our male friends. Suddenly acquaintances, previously seen infrequently, found ingenious excuses to visit us constantly.

Megan stayed a few months. Having established the format, we decided to repeat the experience. Each year we found a suitable girl. We never had the slightest problem; news of the Australian lady offering board in return for baby-sitting spread rapidly, and I was besieged by young women wanting to move in. We had quite a series; American, English, Irish. In general the system worked successfully. But, as with Megan, problems arose as a result of romantic entanglements. The 'au pair girls' had a habit of attracting

211

admirers. In one case, our resident help disappeared for over a week, coming back when it suited her. In another, a rejected suitor kept vigil at our door, trying to enlist my support and refusing to go away. One year we had an American called Linda, who, after an unhappy romance with a man from Praiano, packed her bags and left in floods of tears. Next day a delightful English girl, by an extraordinary coincidence also called Linda, knocked at the door, offering to take the place of Linda number one. We didn't even have to remember a new name. I tried taking on an older woman, hoping to avoid romantic entanglements. But age proved no deterrent.

*    *    *    *    *

Each of our *au pair* girls in turn became part of the family. It was surprising, given the limited duration of their stay, that we developed such close relationships. I enjoyed the company of this succession of young girls, and tended to adopt the role of mother figure or counsellor, listening to the latest saga, offering useful advice. On evenings when we dined at home, we often invited the current *au pair* to join us. And, if possible, we included them when guests were invited. On these occasions, Stenio usually took charge, his cooking provoking its usual acclaim. The girls were amazed that a man should be a gastronomic expert. By now I'd become accustomed to the enthusiasm of Italian men for everything associated with food. I developed a theory about the culinary differences between men and women which I used to expound at dinner parties.

"You men don't realise what it's like to be a woman," I started, stating the obvious. "In our society, most women are obliged to prepare the family meal each day. They don't have the time or inclination to be creative. Men, on the other hand, cook for their own enjoyment. They don't have the everyday worry of 'what on earth will we have for dinner tonight.' Cooking isn't part of their daily routine. On the contrary, they do it for fun. They love preparing food, and expect to be praised. How often are women complimented on their cooking? They're just doing what's expected."

No doubt, my argument was a generalization and oversimplification, but it provided a controversial topic for dinner party conversation.

*      *      *      *      *

An invitation arrived in the mail. The pleasure of our company was requested at a luncheon to be held on a Sunday in late January at the Hotel Sirenuse, the premier hotel in Positano. We were invited to participate in 'the feast of the pig'.

I couldn't help laughing. Formal invitations were a rare event in our lives, and I'd been surprised when I opened the envelope to find a printed card. What could it be? Not in my wildest dreams would I have expected to be invited to a *festa* to celebrate the raising and slaughtering of a pig. For this was the theme of the luncheon.

I couldn't wait to show Stenio this bizarre communication. He wasn't nearly as bemused as I'd expected. It was not so unusual in Italy, he explained. Farmers do kill pigs and invite their friends to share in consuming the resultant bounty. This particular event, however, was a little out of the ordinary, he had to admit. Our prospective host, Ruggiero, whose name I'd never heard, was a legal acquaintance from Naples, an old friend he rarely saw.

"Would you like to go? Shall we accept?"

"Why not? It'll certainly be a new experience. But why would a colleague of yours want to organise such a strange event?"

A few days later Stenio came home with a detailed description of the circumstances leading up to the forthcoming social occasion.

"I had a chat with Ruggiero this morning," he said. "He's really pleased with himself. According to him, this luncheon will be the event of the year."

213

It had all started on a normal working day. *L'avvocato* Ruggiero had stopped to visit a small farm outside Naples. The farmer proudly showed him a litter of new-born piglets, and Ruggiero, on a whim, decided to buy one. He spent some time examining the cute little animals, and chose the most appealing.

"I'll pay you to raise it for me," he told the farmer. "Add up your costs for feeding, fattening, and looking after the piglet till it's ready for slaughter. When it's fully grown, let me know."

When the time came, the farmer contacted his patron.

"You're sure it's all in order, the liveweight, condition, and whatever else you have to check?"

"*Certamente*, you'll be really happy. You've selected a perfect specimen. It should be excellent."

"Wonderful I'll leave the details to you. At the right moment, go ahead and kill the pig, then prepare it as usual. I'll let you know where to deliver the finished product."

And our host-to-be happily set about finding a suitable venue and preparing a guest list. This was to be a party to end all parties.

In the meantime the farmer slaughtered the pig. He was an old hand at pork production, he'd done it all many times before. But on this occasion he took extra care. *L'avvocato* had paid him well, and he wanted to do a perfect job. So our farmer gathered together his two sons and a few trusted helpers. On the appointed morning, the unfortunate pig, which by now was strong and powerful, was led to the slaughter.

Since life had never been easy on small farms, a system had been established whereby neighbours called on one another to assist whenever there was a heavy workload. Now the whole family plus neighbours gathered to take part in the prescribed activities. The carcass had to be cleaned and de-haired before the experts, using their sharpest knives, proceeded to cut it into sections. The amount

214

of food produced by this one, unlucky animal was incredible. As well as chops and other cuts of meat, a bewildering array of by-products included sausages, salamis, sweetbreads, kidneys, hams, the lot, as in the old saying, 'Every part of the pig was used except the squeal'. The intestines were cleaned to be used as sausage casings. The women were responsible for ham production.

Eventually the great day arrived. A little unsure of how to dress for the occasion, we settled on what might be described as smart, casual. I put on a new trendy pants-suit usually reserved for dinner in Rome. Stenio wore his 'city clothes'. At the appointed time, we arrived at the Sirenuse, to be met in the foyer by the *Marchese* Sersale. The *Marchese* was quite a character; his family owned the hotel, but were not normally in the habit of personally receiving guests. Obviously this was a special occasion, not much happened in midwinter.

I was always pleased to be invited to the Hotel Sirenuse. The entire hotel was a showpiece. Exquisite pieces of antique furniture stood here and there, the walls were hung with valuable paintings in elaborate gold frames. We were ushered into the grand dining room. How elegant it all was. You'd think we were about to celebrate a brilliant society wedding. Hothouse flowers decorated elaborately set tables. No expense had been spared.

I was introduced to our fellow guests; I didn't know a soul at our table. In fact, although there were an enormous number of people, I hardly knew anyone at all. Never mind, it would be interesting to meet a new group. I assumed they were from Naples, and would include a few entertaining personalities. By this time I'd met enough Neapolitans to expect idiosyncrasies, and to anticipate the heated discussions that arose as a matter of course whenever Neapolitans gathered together.

We made polite conversation until the food started to arrive. Once the first course was served, I thought it would never stop. There was no printed menu, and I had no way of knowing how many courses there would be. At one stage I really believed the luncheon might go on for ever. Waiters appeared, setting a plate in front of each diner. Then came the next, and the next; the meal rolled on and on in successive waves of meat-filled platters. How could anyone eat so much?

First we had an *antipasto* of *prosciutto* and salami. I enjoyed that. Then in rapid succession we were served sweetbreads, liver, kidneys, sausages, spareribs, chops, chips and salad, roast fillet of pork. I'm sure it was all excellent and no doubt superbly cooked, but I was unable to judge; each course followed its predecessor at such a pace that I was left with a blurred and fuzzy memory. How one pig could provide such a quantity of fillet must remain a mystery. Finally we came to the dessert, a highly prized delicacy. Known in dialect as *sanguinaccio*, it can best be described as chocolate mousse to which pig blood has been added. Hardly appealing, and by this time I believed I'd never be able to eat again. Maybe I should become a vegetarian.

I didn't have to worry about making conversation. There were no engrossing philosophical discussions. There was no opportunity to think about anything other than how to survive the onslaught of food. Although my table companions managed better than me - they probably felt less intimated, having been to similar functions before - they also reached saturation point, perhaps a little later than me.

Between courses we listened to toasts and speeches. As the interval between each course was so brief, the speeches continued while waiters bustled to-and-fro. Our host Ruggiero, who was perfectly charming, despite his inclination to destroy his guests by overfeeding, gave a detailed description of the life and death of the animal we were devouring. By now I'd developed a certain fondness for the unfortunate pig, I could only wish it were still alive.

At long last coffee arrived, accompanied by titbits which nobody touched, and it was time to make our farewells. Waiting in line to thank our amiable and generous host, I wondered how I would manage to walk home.

"Nothing would ever induce me join in a 'feast of the pig' again," I announced, as we slowly trudged up the hill. It was nearly dark and very cold. I felt an overwhelming sense of relief.

"Thank God it's all over."

# SCHOOL

Schoolchildren wear smocks known as *grembiuli*. Worn by both girls and boys, smocks eliminate the need for a school uniform. With a pleat at each side, a round collar, long sleeves and buttons down the back, the pinafore is designed to look like a short dress. I thought compulsory overalls an excellent idea; they served a dual purpose: providing protection for clothes worn underneath, and effectively minimising peer group pressure. Since no-one can see through the smock, it's impossible to tell who's wearing the latest fashion, or whether their outfit is up-to-date. No doubt the peer group will still find areas to exert influence, but at least parents needn't cope with daily demands for money to spend on school clothes.

Little children look adorable in their white *grembiulini*. A coloured ribbon, tied in a large bow in front, is a distinguishing feature. I was never sure how the colour was determined, it seemed a function of age and seniority. In kindergarten, the ribbons were pale yellow or mauve, at primary school bright blue. Once a child progressed to middle school, the prescribed overall changed from white to black. I imagine that mothers breathed a sigh of relief, when, after years of laundering, their children moved on. Black smocks might be drab, but they are certainly less demanding.

The time came for us to make enquiries about the local kindergarten. With my two little girls, I set off one morning to investigate. *L'asilo*, the nursery school, was situated near the point of entry to Positano, just before *la Chiesa Nuova*. We drove around the town, parked the car, and entered the foyer of a grey stone building. An old woman was sweeping the entrance. She looked up as we climbed a flight of stairs to our destination.

"You can't come to school yet," she said, smiling at the children. "It's holiday time."

"We've just come to have a look."

"Well knock at the door and go in, the nuns must be inside somewhere."

We did as we were told. The kindergarten consisted of two very large rooms on the first floor of a slightly dilapidated old edifice. Double doors opened to an enormous balcony. The first thing I noticed was the bright *terrazzo* paving; irregularly-shaped coloured tiles were arranged at random to produce a cheerful picture, well-suited to a children's playground. A slide stood in one corner, opposite was a table covered with plastic toys. My children were fascinated by a set of purple skittles. I could see they wanted to play.

"Look at the view," I said, trying to distract them. "Can you see our house from here?"

As we stood waiting, we identified familiar landmarks in the town below. Eventually two very young nuns in long black traditional habits, their hair hidden behind a wimple, joined us. I introduced myself and the children.

"I'd like the girls to go to kindergarten," I said by way of explanation. "In Australia, where I grew up, we started when we were quite small. It was really a place to have fun. What's the system here?"

I still had much to learn. It took me a long time to understand that no-one likes to be told how things are done elsewhere. In fact it usually causes resentment. I had a similar experience in Melbourne when I had the temerity to suggest that some Italian custom might serve a useful purpose. *Le suore*, the sisters, clearly didn't want to know about nursery schools in other countries, nor did they show any inclination to discuss their daily routine with me. I did discover that the beautiful terrace served as a playground. What happened when it rained, I wondered. But I had the sense not to ask.

The older nun explained the various options available to pre-school children. They could stay for the morning and go home for lunch. If they wished to stay longer, the sisters provided a *minestra*, a soup or light pasta. The meal was followed by a siesta. Afterwards the children could play until their parents were ready to pick them up. Marietta took a dim view of any suggestion of lunch at the kindergarten.

"But *Signora*, surely you wouldn't let *le bambine* eat the stuff they cook there," she said, appalled at the prospect.

When I appeared unmoved by her vehemence, Marietta tried another approach.

"What would you like for lunch tomorrow?" she asked them temptingly. "I'll prepare your favourite pasta. Or *minestrone*. Perhaps you'd prefer *polpettine*, rissoles?"

As she ate with the girls each day, she knew their preferences. Lunchtime had originally presented a problem. Having prepared the meal, Marietta served us at the dining room table, then went to eat by herself in the kitchen. I often invited her to join us, but she was shocked at the idea.

"No no, *signora*, that wouldn't be proper. I wouldn't feel right."

The problem was resolved when we bought a little table and chairs for the girls. The new bright-orange furniture fitted perfectly into a corner of the dining room near the kitchen. Now they could sit comfortably beside us while eating their meal. One day Marietta drew up a stool as she helped cut the meat, bringing her plate to their table. This became a daily habit, solving an awkward situation to everyone's satisfaction.

"We'll see," I told Marietta, when she continued to worry about the kindergarten food. "When the time comes we'll decide what to do."

Adriana and, at a later date Simone liked the idea of going to 'school'; particularly the opportunity for playing with other children. Both attended pre-school for a limited period.

Term started in September. On the appropriate day, we drove around the town in a state of eager anticipation. This was an important event, my daughter's first day at 'school'. I was a little apprehensive at the prospect of leaving my little girl with the nuns. But there were lots of new girls and boys, some happy and excited, some tearfully clinging to their mothers. I was surprised to find the daily activities were almost like primary school. The children learned a lot, after a few months Adriana had made considerable progress in reading and writing. To my mind, what they didn't have was fun. My conception of kindergarten - a little learning, a lot of play - was not the prevailing situation. I decided not to interfere. The best solution was to leave it to the children, if they wanted to go, fine; if they preferred to stay at home, that was fine too.

But when, a year later, the time came for Adriana to go to primary school, I was forced to point out that situation had now changed. The option of going only when you felt like it was no longer valid. *La scuola elementare* was compulsory. Children attended six days a week. They left early in the morning and came home for a late lunch. As the primary school was not far from our house, I accompanied my young daughter up the steps each morning, and stood watching as she set off to join her fellow pupils on their daily walk.

Again, what impressed me was how much they learned. I couldn't believe it. The first year syllabus included a history, admittedly brief, of the Sumerians, the Phoenicians, the Egyptians, the Greeks, and the Romans. And this was only the start. Every afternoon they had several hours homework. It was certainly commendable, but to me it seemed a shame. After all, they were only little children. I couldn't help thinking nostalgically of the school I'd attended at the same age - the facilities, the playgrounds, the sense of space. We may have learned less in primary school, but we definitely had more fun.

The text books used in the *scuola elementare* were really impressive. Entitled '*Come; Quando; Perchè*', 'How, When, Why', they were beautifully illustrated, featuring splendid reproductions of famous paintings and sculptures. Each book was divided into sections; religion, history, civic education, geography, science, grammar, and arithmetic, all skilfully presented to arouse interest and invite further study. I spent hours absorbed in these school readers, and I learned a lot. I have the greatest respect for the authors of such delightful and instructive books.

*     *     *     *     *

Pietro the plumber stopped me in the street one morning.

"Can I call around to see you later?" he asked. "I have a request to make."

We agreed on a time, and I continued on my way, wondering what he could possibly want. Having spent many frustrating hours trying to contact Pietro whenever we had a plumbing crisis, it seemed amazing that he was trying to fit in with me. I was intrigued and curious at this unlikely turn of events.

He arrived on time, again most unusual, smartly dressed and looking important. This was an official visit. As we sat down with a drink, he cleared his throat and proceeded to announce the reason for his visit.

"My wife and I," he began, "have long been concerned that our children are missing out on a whole range of activities. City children have so many options. We've discussed this problem with friends, and we've come to the conclusion that we have to do something about it."

"We've decided to form a committee." he went on. "We're still discussing what to call ourselves. The idea is to organise a series of activities for the children of Positano. We've found a venue, that old disused hall you pass every day on your way to the *centro*. This is going to become 'the leisure centre'. It's actually owned by one of our group, so it shouldn't cost too much." He paused for a moment. "We wondered if you'd like to join us?"

"I'd be delighted." I replied without the slightest hesitation. "I think it's a great idea. My children may be a bit young, although possibly Adriana could join in. What sort of activities are you planning?"

"Well this brings me to my next request." Pietro looked a bit embarrassed. "Helga's agreed to give ballet classes and Marie Louise has offered to teach painting."

I knew the women he'd mentioned, Helga was an ex-ballerina from Germany, while Marie Louise, who'd grown up in Marseilles, spent her days painting in a small studio she rented near Praiano. What did he want from me, I wondered. I didn't have long to wait.

"I've been delegated to ask if you'd be prepared to give English classes."

'Why not?' I thought. It would be good for me to have some regular commitment, and it would certainly be a challenge. I'd never before taught children - nor adults either, for that matter.

"I'd be happy to give it a try," I heard myself saying. "If it doesn't work out, we can always stop."

We discussed the probable ages of the children involved, the size of the classes, the level we could hope to attain. There was really no way of knowing how many might enrol.

On my next visit to Rome I went to an English bookshop. After browsing through the vast range of material devoted to English teaching, I selected a few books, and came away with some idea of how to approach this new enterprise. I wanted the classes to be fun. In my opinion, the children already had far too much homework for their age. Their school work was demanding. I determined that my lessons would be interesting and stimulating, but at the same time relaxing.

In due course the activities centre was set up by the enthusiastic group of concerned parents. Voluntary helpers were coopted. Everyone agreed the objective was to develop skills previously unavailable to our children. There was considerable discussion, however, about which subjects should be given priority.

English turned out to be one of the most popular classes. I found myself teaching a group of twenty children: fourteen girls and six boys aged from eight to fifteen. It was not easy to find a common denominator with such a discrepancy in age. I had my work cut out trying to keep everyone interested.

For the end of the year concert, I taught my class a little poem I'd enjoyed as a child. *The Wind on the Hill* is a verse from the delightful *Now We Are Six* by A..A. Milne.

No-one can tell me
Nobody knows,
Where the wind comes from,
Where the wind goes.

This was a great success, everyone liked the short and snappy lines. We practised and practised, reciting the lines so often that each child knew them off by heart. Maybe the accents were less than perfect, but we all thought it sounded great. And so did the parents.

\*    \*    \*    \*    \*

"Why don't we have a fete?"

The activities centre had been functioning for a few months. Its organisers, delighted at the enthusiastic response to their initiative, realised they needed to keep up the momentum. A meeting was called to discuss the next step. Money raising was a major priority. Despite the generous contribution of voluntary helpers, it became apparent that unavoidable expenses would be incurred. The building was in need of repair; a coat of paint would certainly brighten it up. There were printing costs, and expenses connected with administration and postage. How could we raise funds without constantly appealing for donations?

Lisa, one of the ringleaders, had grown up in New York. She and her husband, both children of Italian migrants, had met and married in the United States. Visiting relatives in Positano, they'd decided to remigrate. They opened a jewellery shop; Lisa divided her time between looking after their two little boys and helping in the shop.

Now she gathered a group of foreign wives including me, hoping we'd take part in fund-raising.

"Let's make this an international effort. I remember our school fairs; they were great fun."

Having experience with jewellery, Lisa offered to run a stall selling beads and necklaces, bracelets and brooches. Some she could make herself, others would be donated by the shop. Katrina, a German girl, volunteered to organise a children's clothes stand.

"I'll join you," her Austrian friend Veronica joined in. "I like sewing, maybe we can make dolls' clothes as well."

Two Swedish women had married brothers. Both enjoyed knitting, now they proceeded to discuss what garments would be popular among visitors to our fair. Should they knit scarves, gloves, pullovers? It depended on the time available. I wondered how long it took them to finish a jumper.

I was next in line. I racked my brains. What was typical of Australia? Suddenly I thought of lamingtons. Conjuring up a vivid memory of fetes at school, of arriving home with sticky hands after gorging myself on home-made cakes, I came to a decision.

"What about a cake stall. My contribution will be a surprise. Would anyone like to join me?"

225

Carol and Diana said they'd help supply cakes for my stand. We became more and more enthusiastic; ideas began to flow. Jackie, a hockey-playing Canadian, suggested a section devoted to sport. A date was set, notices were circulated. I went home and told Marietta I would have to take over the kitchen on the appointed day. I warned that it would be messy, but neither of us realised quite how bad it was going to be.

Lamingtons consist of small squares of sponge cake covered with chocolate icing and coconut. To make a few is relatively easy. But to produce a large quantity, I discovered to my dismay, is a daunting undertaking. How many sponges should I bake? I had no idea whether the fete would attract large numbers of people, nor whether anyone would want to try my sweets.

When the time came, I borrowed a couple of extra large cake tins, and baked several square sponges. Allowing these to cool, I proceeded to cut each block into small cubes. Here I encountered my first problem. It proved difficult to cut uniform sections, the freshly baked cake was soft and crumbly. Well, too bad. The pieces wouldn't be perfectly even. Next I made an enormous quantity of chocolate icing. I dipped each square into the liquid icing, then rolled it in desiccated coconut. What a mess. Bits of sponge dropped into the icing, which rapidly became unusable. I ran out of coconut. Marietta stood by, ready to help; making up more icing, hurrying out to buy more coconut from Palatone. Above all, she cleaned up after me.

"*Brava Signora*," she kept repeating. She was thoroughly enjoying herself. I could imagine her entertaining family and friends for weeks with stories of the Signora's baking.

Eventually, after what seemed the longest day imaginable, I had a kitchen bench covered in row after row of lamingtons. Together we wrapped them in groups of four, six and eight. Next day Carol, Diana and I set up our stall. They'd put considerable effort into their contribution and had certainly done their share of work. Our table was filled to overflowing. We were an enormous success. My lamingtons were the talk of the town.

"They're absolutely wonderful. Why don't you make them more often?"

"I'm thrilled you all like them. But don't think this is going to be a regular feature. Because I don't imagine I'll ever make them again."

And, despite frequent requests, I stood firm. Never again did I make lamingtons. But I was secretly happy that my contribution was so well-received.

*    *    *    *    *

At some future date, decisions would have to be made about the children's schooling. This was a problem we often discussed, a problem we would have to face. Once the three years at the *scuola media* had been completed, a moment of truth would arise. When I tried to visualise our life twenty years on, or even ten, I drew a blank. Where would we be? It would depend on the children.

After middle school, students had to choose a direction. This would occur regardless of where we lived. I had yet to master the complexities of the Italian system. Senior schools offered a wide range of options. Of course I knew that *il liceo* was the generic name for a state secondary school. I'd heard countless discussions of the relative merits of *il liceo classico* and *il liceo scientifico*. Classical and scientific subjects were taught at both; the former offered a more detailed study of the classics, including Greek and Latin, the latter specialised in science. In addition, various institutions provided courses formulated to develop particular skills. *Il liceo linguistico* was for students majoring in languages, *il liceo artistico* offered art courses. *L'istituto magistrale* was designed for aspiring primary schoolteachers. At Amalfi a highly-regarded institute catered specifically to young people hoping to pursue a career in the tourist industry. At one time Stenio had been on the staff, teaching legal aspects of tourism. He believed the course was excellent.

All these colleges prepared students for matriculation. At the end of four or five years, depending on the curriculum, students took a school-leaving examination, emerging with a certificate of *maturità*. Having obtained this certificate, they were eligible to proceed to university.

Originally, we'd planned that once the children reached senior school, we'd move to Rome. I'd listened to endless conversations about the well-known *Licei*. Obviously, all were not equal, a few were reputedly outstanding. Many of our friends came from Rome, and had long-standing perceptions about one or other *Liceo*. They argued for hours. Had the academic standards altered over the years? Was it when Professor X retired, or perhaps when Professor Y moved to another school? These matters were examined and dissected in minute detail.

Since students were obliged to attend the school nearest their home, parents sought to live in certain prescribed areas. A system was perpetuated whereby families chose their home according to available schooling. This was the case even at primary level, where the Montessori schools were highly regarded. Maria Montessori had developed programs to stimulate learning attitudes in small children. Young married couples discussed the merits of various schools long before their children were born or even expected. Some of our friends, from the moment a baby was due, set about organising their lives in relation to sought after schools. As the children's education progressed, the demand for preferred schools and the perceived needs of pupils became more of an issue.

In view of our intention to educate the children in Rome, I listened with considerable interest to these discussions, and began to draw my own conclusions. Times were changing, however. We were extremely conscious of the prevailing tense political situation and sporadic outbursts of violence.

Coming to grips with Italian politics is not easy. Even Italians had trouble following the ups and downs of their politicians. So how could I possibly understand the complex plays that occurred, the coalitions that formed and broke up, the trade unions divided along political lines. The country seemed to function despite its politicians.

In the post-war period, three major political parties, the Christian Democrats, Socialists, and Communists had dominated the Italian scene. Although the conservative Christian Democratic party had long been dominant, it had rarely been able to govern in its own right, and had been obliged to form unstable coalition governments with smaller centrist parties. In 1962, the Christian Democrats undertook a controversial initiative, known as the 'opening to the left', joining in coalition with the Socialists, a move that proved unpopular among many of its hard core supporters.

Strange as it might seem in a Catholic country, the Communist party regularly recorded the second largest number of votes at national elections. Italian Communists gradually distanced themselves from hard-line Soviet-style policies, taking up a more moderate 'Eurocommunist' approach. Their electoral success steadily increased, until the Christian Democrats maintained ascendancy by only a small margin. During this period, the Communists gained control of many local and regional governments, but were unable to obtain a national majority.

Political unrest and instability were aggravated by terrorist groups, both of the extreme right and extreme left. The Red Brigades, a Marxist-Leninist group, formed in 1969, had arisen out of the student protest movement of the late 1960s. Its aim was to create a revolutionary state and separate Italy from the Western Alliance. At the same time, neo-fascist extremists contributed to escalating urban terrorism.

A neighbour of ours was a *professore* at one of the more prestigious Roman high schools. The *liceo* where he taught had become highly politicised. He couldn't believe the scenes that occurred. A number of senior students aligned themselves with one or other political party, becoming belligerent supporters of the ideology of either left or right. There was a time, our neighbour told us, when the police appeared every afternoon to prevent pitched battles between students at the end of the school day.

229

Even in the *scuola media* of Positano, politics became a factor. The recently appointed school principal, a lady from Milan, was a convinced Maoist. Many parents were horrified at the radical teaching she favoured, and its possible effect on their teenage children. Shopping at Palatone I overheard shocked mothers discussing her latest controversial statement.

"Did you hear what *la professoressa* told the class yesterday?" they said to each other in tones of disbelief.

The more we listened to parents, to their constant worries about education, the more we began to wonder. The educational system in Italy was excellent, there was no doubt about that. But who could tell how the political situation would evolve. Should we rethink our plans for the future?

I remembered my childhood in Melbourne, where schoolboys worried about sport rather than politics, where terrorism was not a problem, where left and right referred to traffic, not to extremist groups.

I'd become accustomed to the fact that Italians considered Australia a distant paradise.

"How amazing," they said when I told them my nationality. "Why on earth should an Australian choose to live in Europe?"

Maybe they were right.

# FAMOUS PLACES

About once a week I went to Sorrento. It was only a short drive, and I could always find a reason to go. Like Capri, Sorrento had been a resort long before the days of mass tourism. Several of the old and gracious hotels, built at a time when only the idle rich could afford to travel, have remained relatively unchanged. Our favourite was an elegant old establishment with a magic view.

I liked to imagine guests sweeping through the imposing entrance in horse-drawn carriages, clattering along a driveway lined on either side by perfumed orange groves. Perhaps they stopped in some sheltered alcove to admire the marble statues and gently flowing fountains. Waiting to greet them in the cool and spacious foyer stood the major-domo, resplendent in a dark-green uniform bedecked with gold braid. Alighting from their carriage, visitors were escorted along a series of cool, wide corridors to their luxurious suites. Crossing the room, the porter threw open French doors to reveal a balcony overgrown with wisteria, and a vista of olive groves, vineyards, and volcanic cliff tops plunging down to the *Golfo di Napoli*. Mt. Vesuvius loomed large in the distance.

Such flights of fancy were prompted by several enormous paintings which dominated the reception area. Set in ornate gilt frames, two splendid tableaux recalled scenes of past glory, providing a charming picture of contemporary costumes and manners at a time when life was lived at a slower and more relaxed pace than today. Depicting an earlier generation in cheerful holiday mode, the artist had captured the air of well-bred gentility and polite refinement common to society in the early twentieth century.

The reception rooms were a connoisseur's delight. Highly polished antique furniture, a handsome gilt-edged mirror, a fireplace lined with decorated tiles; all were relics of a gracious past. Carefully selected ornaments adorned the marble mantelpiece; a Capodimonte figure of an elegant cavalier, a stylish decanter, a Venetian-glass vase filled with flowers.

Today, the hotel still stands in its luxuriant garden setting. Lemon trees in terracotta pots embellish the entrance, the cool and spacious reception area has remained unchanged. But instead of horse-drawn carriages, the driveway is filled with chattering groups of tourists piling out of buses. The atmosphere of elegance and sophistication has given way to scenes of bustling confusion, tour leaders are in command, instructing clients to collect their bags, follow the signs, and walk in line.

"This way please," they call in English, German, Japanese, or whatever language is appropriate.

The town itself, perched on the cliffs of the Sorrento peninsula, has maintained its role as a celebrated holiday destination. The main street is always filled with people, the daily *passeggiata* proceeds unaltered year after year. Restaurants, beach bars, and cruise boats do good business, boutiques and shops cater for the steady stream of visitors. Cameos, corals, embroidered linen, ceramics, pastries, ice cream, all are arranged in displays to tempt the most hardened traveller.

Inlaid woodwork or marquetry, using wood of different kinds and colours, is a local specialty. Developed into a highly intricate art form during the Renaissance, marquetry has long been a Sorrento tradition. I wandered along the narrow side street where skilled artisans still ply their trade. Shop after shop sells every imaginable object that can be made with inlaid wood: tables, chairs, chess-boards, boxes, wall-hangings. The work varies in quality; certain workshops display exquisite woodwork, others produce articles 'made to a price'.

Sorrento is famed for its food and excellent restaurants. My favourite was *O'Parrucchiano* - an untranslatable dialect name. Situated at the far end of the long main street, *O'Parrucchiano* was enormous, extending over three levels. Always packed with people, the restaurant did a roaring trade. I made a point of arranging my trips to include lunch; in time the meal became a principal feature of my weekly outings.

As a regular client, I was cordially welcomed whenever I appeared.

"You'll have the same as usual, Signora?," asked the waiter, conducting me to my preferred table. Handing a menu to each person, he recommended the specialty of the day. Perhaps the fish, or, if we preferred, *i fegatini;* today the chicken livers were even better than usual. But I knew better than to indulge myself by ordering whatever took my fancy. Two specialties of the house were irresistible. The first was home-made *gnocchi;* individual portions served in small metal dishes, sizzling hot, covered with tomato sauce and sliced mozzarella, and baked so the cheese melted into the *gnocch*i. I've tried to repeat this technique, but whatever the chef did is remarkably difficult to reproduce.

The second treat was yet to come. I rarely ordered dessert; it was usual to finish a meal with fruit. But here I couldn't resist, I had to have profiteroles. They were fantastic, the best I've ever tasted. Perfect choux pastry filled with a delicate cream and bathed in rich chocolate sauce.

Most of the regulars had a preferred menu. Everyone argued about the chef's principal talent. Was it his mastery in preparing fish? No, no, of course not; you obviously haven't tried the *involtini,* beef olives. But on one thing we were all in agreement. *O'Parrucchiano* was an exceptionally good restaurant.

*     *     *     *     *

Over the years, the little towns of Sorrento and Piano di Sorrento have steadily grown and expanded until they became virtually continuous. Row after row of apartment houses line newly constructed streets, the outskirts extend further and further, resulting in an unplanned urban sprawl. Progress, coupled with a large increase in population, has converted two charming villages into a vast, sprawling suburbia.

While I might deplore the demise of the little villages, I had to admit that the resultant provincial town was extremely convenient for shopping. Usually I stopped first in Piano di Sorrento, where the weekly market offered excellent value. The shops were well-stocked and the goods considerably cheaper than in Positano. On one of my shopping trips I happened to look in the freezer cabinet. There, to my surprise, I beheld packages labelled 'New Zealand lamb chops'. Marietta was not impressed.

"Frozen meat? Why should we eat chops that have come all the way from New Zealand?"

Stenio agreed with Marietta. So much for New Zealand lamb. In fact the chops really weren't very good. Maybe they'd been in the freezer too long.

The only food I bought in Sorrento itself was *mozzarella*. One particular shop was known for its excellent *treccia*, plait. In what was apparently a local custom, strips of milky white cheese were plaited together to produce a distinctive mozzarella. The best was that prepared from buffalo milk.

Sometimes we went to the cinema in Sorrento. Current films were shown, and it was a welcome excuse for an outing on a bleak winter's day. Occasionally we saw a play or attended a concert. I enjoyed wandering the streets around the centre, where life still proceeded at a leisurely pace.

In particular, I was fascinated to observe the time-honoured, traditional way of shopping. A cart trundled by filled with produce: bread, fruit and vegetables, groceries. I stopped to watch. The driver called out in a singsong voice, announcing what he had for sale. A window opened on the third floor. A head emerged. The vendor stopped, looked up, and a shouted conversation ensued in dialect. The dialogue went on for some time. Eventually, after considerable haggling, the two parties agreed on a price and the deal was concluded. Then, to my amazement, a basket attached to a long rope was lowered from the upstairs window. The vendor weighed out the goods and popped them into the waiting basket. I looked up again to see the customer hauling her end of the rope. Up went the basket with its load. The travelling salesman moved on to find another client. At what point money had changed hands was unclear to me. The whole operation was conducted like clockwork, the players knew the rules.

*      *      *      *      *

Mt. Vesuvius was part of my life. We saw it from Sorrento, Capri and Naples, a peaceful slumbering giant. Yet this volcano had once buried two ancient cities in ash and mud, preserving them as if frozen in time. In the days of the Roman Empire, Pompeii and Herculaneum were popular summer resorts. Wealthy Romans built villas in the fertile countryside. In the year AD 79, both towns were destroyed. Mt. Vesuvius erupted, belching forth steam, lava and flames; burying all around it under a mass of ash and lava. It's believed that much of the population escaped, but at least two thousand people died. The devastated cities were never rebuilt. In fact they were forgotten. Not until the eighteenth century did a well-digger come upon a marble statue from Herculaneum. A few years later, traces of buried Pompeii were discovered by a peasant working in his vineyard. These finds aroused the interest of archaeologists.

Carefully excavated and virtually intact, the ruins give a vivid picture of the daily life of a citizen of imperial Rome. We walked along streets whose stepping stones show ruts worn by chariot wheels, stopping at the forum of Pompeii with its temples and theatres, the Basilica (ancient law court), the amphitheatres and baths. Further on are *vicoli* where shops and houses once stood. Notices of community interest, election slogans and advertisements for shops to rent are still visible on the walls.

The sumptuous villas of the rich are distinguished by wall frescoes, mosaic floors, and tiny sleeping quarters designed for servants and slaves. Most spectacular is the house of the faun, named for its delightful bronze statue of a dancing faun, and decorated with magnificent mosaics. Narrow alleyways reveal districts where the lower classes lived. On each visit I noticed something new, bronze tools used in a tannery, millstones for grinding grain outside a bakery, ovens at a potter's workshop, wine jars on the counter of a wine shop. Paintings, statues, mirrors, and

235

small objects including coins, pens, and ink bottles, are displayed in the *Museo Archeologico di Napoli*. The celebrated dancing-faun statue is also there.

Herculaneum has been better preserved than its neighbour, perhaps because it was buried at greater depth, perhaps because it was under volcanic mud rather than the stone and ash that covered Pompeii. Experts suggest that the owners of Pompeii houses may have returned to dig out their valuable possessions, while those from Herculaneum had no hope of digging through the twelve or more metres of volcanic material covering their homes. Whatever the reason, excavations have revealed wonderful treasures, including the remarkable discovery of thousands of rolls of papyrus manuscript.

One day I'd taken friends to Pompeii. Fancying myself as a tour guide, I was explaining some detail when a voice interrupted my discourse.

"You don't happen to be Australian?"

I turned to see a tall young man dressed in jeans, coke in hand, looking at me expectantly. I reluctantly agreed that I was Australian.

"Thought I recognised the accent," he said. "Do you know if Essendon won last Saturday?"

I couldn't believe it. Here we were, in this marvellous outpost of Roman civilization, and all my fellow Australian wanted to know was the result of a football match in Melbourne. I was sorry to disappoint him. Although I came from Melbourne, the home of Australian rules football, I'd never been a football fan. And I'd been away a long time. We had a chat, however, and he and his friends seemed really happy to have met someone from home.

In July, theatrical performances were given in the ancient amphitheatre of Pompeii. One evening we went to see a production of the Greek tragedy, Medea. It was a fantastic performance, the actors excellent, the setting magnificently appropriate. I was feeling quite overcome by the sense of occasion, when suddenly, in the midst of some stirring oration, a train thundered by. A true anachronism, causing everyone to dissolve in laughter, it brought us back to reality. It had been fun to imagine, for a few hours, that we were back in ancient Rome. But at the end of the evening, we counted ourselves fortunate to return by car to a home equipped with modern amenities.

Some people visit Mt. Vesuvius itself. The crater of the volcano is still active, steam can be seen venting from its walls. I'm told the bay of Naples looks sensational from this height. I personally had no wish to climb to the top of a volcano. The last eruption was in 1944, and scientists believe that further eruptions are a distinct possibility. I was happy to leave this particular tourist attraction to others.

*    *    *    *    *

Paestum was next on my list of obligatory attractions for visiting guests. South of Salerno, in the middle of nowhere, stand three magnificent temples. Wonderfully preserved, these monuments to the Greek presence in southern Italy look out over the sea. As in Greece, the temples face eastwards so that the rising sun will awaken the statue within. Doric was the preferred style in the Greek colonies, and Paestum, constructed from local limestone, represents a perfect example.

Paestum has always been shrouded in mystery. Founded in about 650 BC, some say it was built by Dorians expelled from their native city of Sybaris. Originally called Poseidonia, it was a famous centre of *Magna Grecia*, the Greek colonies in southern Italy. The Romans arrived in 273 BC, Saracens invaded many centuries later. In time the place was abandoned and left to become a mosquito-ridden malarial swamp.

Like Pompeii and Herculaneum, Paestum was rediscovered in the eighteenth century. But unlike the ancient Roman cities, which are perpetually filled with sightseers, the temples of Paestum are often deserted. This is how I prefer my tourism, free to wander where I choose, without guides or throngs of people disturbing the tranquil atmosphere. Free to follow the city walls, which extend for about five kilometres. With walls like these, it must have been a highly prosperous colony. Maybe I'll find some treasure.

Nearby is a museum; interesting, and again not crowded. The shelves are filled with objects excavated in the surrounding areas, bronze pots, sculptures, painted figures, and a multitude of fragments. Who knows where and how they were used. A few signs attempt to interpret the shards, but I was never satisfied by the explanations.

RAVELLO

# PERSONALITIES

Positano abounded in unusual characters. People considered eccentric in a more conventional environment were here not only accepted, they were regarded as fascinating and special. Outstanding examples were a couple known as *gli ultimi esistensialisti*, the last existentialists.

Rudy and Valli were a striking pair. Valli had grown up in country Australia, become a dancer, and moved to post-war Paris at the age of nineteen. Valli had long, tangled bright red hair, tattooed hands and feet, a diamond tooth, and lots and lots of make up. She wore layers of brightly coloured skirts, matched with a shirt, vest, and assorted scarves, all in vibrantly contrasting shades. Chains of jewellery adorned her neck, wrists and ankles.

She had met her partner Rudi, an Austrian architecture student, in Paris. Rudi was tall and thin, his long dark hair tied in a pony tail, his characteristic feature an enormous moustache. They lived for some years in existentialist Paris, in the quarter of Saint Germain des Pres, at the time of Jean Paul Sartre, Juliette Greco, and Yves Montand. Valli was much in demand as a night-club dancer.

In 1958 the couple came to Positano. Together they lived in a mountain cabin. Some said their home had started out as a cave, others believed Rudi had adapted a derelict house. Certainly their abode was short on modern conveniences. There was no gas, electricity, or running water, while the concept of a television set or motor-car probably never entered their heads. Having acquired a few sheep and chickens, they continued to collect animals, until they were surrounded by a veritable zoological garden. There were sheep, goats and rabbits, chicken and geese, cats and dogs, a donkey, a pig, a few foxes and a turtle. Their ideal, we were told, was to live according to nature.

"You've got a long climb ahead of you," I said to Valli, meeting her one evening on her way home.

"You're right," she replied. "We're living the way we always wanted. But I must say it's hard to get up the mountain on a night as warm as this."

Every now and then complaints were made; the donkey or goats were eating plants, chewing the bark off trees, destroying the vegetation. It was feared that the menagerie of animals, if left to run wild, might irreparably damage the environment. Letters were mailed to the superintendent of police in Salerno, to the mayor, even to the *Questura di Napoli*, the police-headquarters. Officials were sent to investigate. At various times one or other authority made an effort to evict the unconventional couple. The matter attracted considerable publicity, articles were published in the local press, and in newspapers and magazines throughout the country. But Rudi and Valli were well-liked by the *Positanesi*. Moreover, they'd become something of a tourist attraction. They were allowed to stay.

Valli was a gifted artist. Her characteristic ink and wash drawings consisted of intricately embellished stylized figures representing exotic animals, demons, men and women. In addition, she was an accomplished sculptor. Her work was displayed at several successful exhibitions in New York.

*　　*　　*　　*　　*

Communes were springing up along the Amalfi coast. It was the time of hippies, of flower people. Long a haven for writers and artists, in the sixties Positano became a gathering place for the beat generation. It was a perfect setting, the climate temperate, the surroundings beautiful, the people friendly. As an added bonus, *Positanesi* were tolerant of foreigners and their foibles.

A motley array of nationalities: Americans and Scandinavians, French and British, Australians and New Zealanders, were represented among the newcomers, usually but not always young, who set up and lived in communities along the coast. Among them were creative artists, actors, novelists, musicians; some stayed a few months, others settled in for years.

Mandy was an Australian girl who designed and fashioned clothes, selling them at local markets. We were bound to meet; living in a small place it was inevitable we'd become aware of our shared accent and recognise each other as compatriots. Mandy had a daughter, Melissa, a delightful little girl with auburn hair, a chubby face, and an infectious grin. They lived in a commune near Praiano, where Melissa was the darling of the group, a sort of mascot to be fussed over and petted. Despite being the constant centre of attention, Melissa remained cheerful and unspoiled. Mandy invited us to meet the companions who shared her home, a heterogeneous and constantly changing population, all of whom adored Melissa.

Occasionally we went to one of their parties. I never knew what to expect. One evening we were introduced to an American couple, known as J.C and Meg, who had started a school for painters in Positano. Having left their home in Atlanta, they had no desire to return, and were casting around for a way to make a living in a congenial environment. Their enterprise, set up in an abandoned house converted to a studio, was successful for a time, attracting would-be artists from a diversity of backgrounds. Happily teaching their craft, they gathered disciples around them, forming the nucleus of a new community. Finding accommodation for their students was not easy, particularly in summer. As many as possible were lodged in the studio; every available nook and cranny was employed. But at times the numbers exceeded the available space, and students had to find rooms in nearby houses.

The art school and its American protagonists were a conspicuous feature for several years. The children of J.C and Meg, two little boys with bright blue eyes and a mop of blonde hair, attended the local school. At first, the pale, fair-haired American boys stood out as strangers. But after a time, tanned from hours of playing in the sun, they became virtually indistinguishable from all the other children. Once they learned to speak dialect and acquired the habits of their mates, the boys felt perfectly at ease.

A complete extrovert, J.C. was ideally suited to his role. He established a workable relationship with expatriate artists living in the area, prevailing on them to give an occasional talk to his students.

241

Bjorn, a flamboyant Swedish painter, was one such artist, happy to impart a little of his expertise in a good cause. An interesting man who became a good friend, Bjorn was kind and generous, always willing to oblige, particularly if approached the right way. A little flattery went a long way with Bjorn. Having lived all over the world, he settled in Positano for a variety of reasons. The paramount attraction, he said, was the scenery, which served as a point of reference for his paintings. The relaxed lifestyle was appealing, and there was always hope that international visitors might buy his work. I bought one of his paintings, a pastel fantasy of flowers and shapes. Vassili, his companion of many years, was born in Corfu, and had worked in New York, establishing a reputation as a playwright.

One evening we were sitting over coffee at a nearby restaurant when a woman, seated at an adjoining table, started a conversation. This often happened, many of my enduring friendships began in this way. Jake, Margot, and their three daughters became regular visitors at our Via Fornillo home. An Australian family, they'd made a decision to take the children out of school and travel around the world. Matters of importance were discussed by all concerned, children and adults alike, put to the vote, and determined by mutual agreement. The parents conscientiously took it in turn to give the girls lessons each day, reasoning that an understanding of life in other countries would serve them better than conventional schooling. After extended periods in Indonesia, Mexico, Spain and Africa, they rented a house in Positano for a year. The children dressed in clothes picked up here and there, usually in markets. A pretty eight year old daughter had acquired an outfit in maroon velvet embellished with gold braid that she wore winter and summer. Theirs was a happy family, and I listened with interest to descriptions of the adventures and experiences that had come their way.

Positano became a focus, a meeting ground for an international, itinerant population. A few became my friends, but my world was not theirs. I fancied myself somewhat as a trailblazer, convinced I was leading an exotic, unconventional life. But in the eyes of the hippie community, I realised, my role was perceived as that of traditional wife and mother. And from my perspective, although I enjoyed our meetings and discussions, which tended to centre on self-analysis and philosophical rhetoric, I often felt we were on an unequal footing. Why was everyone else so articulate, so sure they were right? Why weren't they prepared to listen to another point of view, mine in particular? Was it because my life seemed boring compared to theirs?

\*     \*     \*     \*     \*

Halfway down the steps to the *spiaggia principale*, main beach, in a charming little whitewashed house, lived the Creighton-Browns. Dick had been a pageboy to Queen Victoria. As a young man he fell in love with Margit, a pretty Austrian girl he met on a skiing holiday. They married, and their life together had been interesting and varied. Having lived in so many countries they'd almost lost count, retirement presented them with a problem. Where should they live? Margit made the decision. They would spend the years of their retirement on the Mediterranean coast.

Dick had been a senior executive with Elizabeth Arden, and spoke of Miss Arden with respect and admiration.

"Miss Arden wanted to set up a salon in Sydney, you know." Dick was fond of telling the story.

"Would you go there, Dickie?" she asked me, "I know it's not the most exciting place in the world."

"Margit and I talked it over. It could be a worthwhile experience, we decided. And, of course, you didn't say no to Miss Arden. So we set off, not knowing what to expect. It was the 1930s, you know. We had to go by flying boat; there was no other way to get to Australia. The trip took over a week, with overnight stops in fascinating places. When we finally arrived, we were astonished to find that Sydney was such a beautiful city. No-one had told us about the harbour. We were delighted we'd agreed to go there, particularly after we managed to rent a house with a harbour view. But then, just as we were settling in, war broke out in Europe. We were caught, unable to return."

243

During their enforced stay, Dick and Margit came to know a circle of interesting Australians. I could imagine that the tall, slender, English gentleman with his charming and sophisticated Austrian wife would be welcome guests at any social gathering. By the time the war ended they'd acquired a collection of memorabilia, including paintings by well-known artists.

Margit enjoyed entertaining, and we were frequently invited to their home for drinks. Our visits followed a format which never varied. We walked in to be greeted by a circle of British expatriates. Seated in comfortable chintz armchairs, under framed photographs of Dick's family and prints of English hunting scenes, they sipped whisky and expectantly awaited our arrival. I knew what was about to happen, and sure enough, as soon as we walked through the door, I heard a familiar sound. Our host's idea of fun was to play a recording of a laughing kookaburra, timing it to start the minute we arrived. All the guests thought it was a great joke. After a while these recurring scenes of hilarity became tiresome; I had to remind myself they were well-meant.

Along with other members of the British community, the Creighton-Browns faced a difficult situation as the Italian *lira* gradually increased in value relative to the pound sterling. The buying power of their pension underwent a progressive decline; the cost of living rose. Part of the reason for our frequent invitations was their hope that we might buy a few paintings from their Australian collection. Although I was sorely tempted, we never did. Having recently inherited a number of my father-in-law's works, we had trouble finding places to hang the paintings we already owned. In our home, with its eye-catching architectural features, wall space was hard to find. It seemed every available inch of hanging space had been filled.

"Where on earth would we put it?" asked Stenio, when I suggested we buy an Australian painting. One, a Margaret Preston composition of waratahs in a vase, was offered for about thirty dollars. Why didn't I buy it?

*     *     *     *     *

Representatives of the Italian nobility, an impoverished aristocracy in decline, were included among our persons of note. *La contessa* Marina, descendant of an exalted and princely line, was one of the most fascinating people I ever met. Her ancestors had come from Spain; among the illustrious forebears a pope, several cardinals, and two generals had pride of place. Whenever I visited a well-known art gallery, I stopped to inspect portraits of Marina's antecedents. How strange it was, to look at the face of a long-deceased cardinal, and recognise features of the Marina I knew. Her heredity was evident in the characteristic facial features and in her bearing.

Marina grew up in Naples in an atmosphere of incredible luxury. She often talked of her childhood home, a *palazzo* with sweeping marble staircase, walls lined with paintings by Rembrandt and Franz Hals, rooms furnished with priceless French antiques. Her family had been absentee landlords, their vast holdings in Calabria administered by estate managers. Over the years, the trusted overseers enriched themselves at the expense of their patrons, until the day arrived when the landholders no longer received any income at all.

Marina had hardly a penny to her name, nor had she the vaguest idea how to live within a limited income. What she did have, was a bubbling personality and wonderful sense of humour. Loved by all who knew her; her extensive circle of friends were genuinely concerned at her situation and anxious to help. No-one ever referred to her financial circumstances, that would have been bad taste. Many of her close friends were wealthy, and made it their business to contribute to her well-being in whatever way they could. An importer of beautiful fabrics regularly sent rolls of representative samples. Marina designed extravagant gowns from lengths of material, another friend arranged to have the designs made up. A third member of the group showed the finished product at a fashion parade held in the gardens of her private villa. All the invited guests bought at least one outfit, and the proceeds went to Marina. Unfortunately, Marina usually spent the money immediately, buying

245

an enormous bottle of French perfume or other totally extravagant item.

My mother often invited Marina to eat with us. A delightful *raconteur*, she told of a world that no longer existed, of the exploits of her forebears, revealing glimpses of the mores of the aristocracy, and of a social system no longer relevant. Modest in many ways, "Don't call me countess, my name's Marina," she had, nevertheless, an undeniable aura that attested to her noble lineage; an awareness of her position, and the obligations it imposed.

The tiny home Marina rented was quite primitive, with an outside toilet, running water but only just, and cooking and storage facilities which could only be described as sub-standard. Unfazed by her circumstances, Marina behaved in character with her background and upbringing. Together with my mother, I occasionally called at her home. Marina received us in the manner of a gracious hostess. A charming companion to all and sundry, she was nonetheless defensive of her place in society. Close by lived a *principessa*, a lady whose lineage was Neapolitan. Despite the opposition of her family, the princess married a Danish painter. Their financial situation were considerably better than those of Marina. Whenever *la principessa* was mentioned, Marina turned up her nose in disdain.

"*Parvenue*", was her haughty comment, "she gives herself such airs. Can you believe the title was conferred on her family less than three hundred years ago? And she expects to be addressed as *principessa*. Doesn't she realise she's making a fool of herself?"

\*     \*     \*     \*     \*

And then there was Peppino. No description of Positano's memorable characters would be complete without him. He had a gift which gave pleasure to all who heard him, the gift of making music. Neapolitan songs, to the accompaniment of the guitar, were his specialty. With an infectious smile, an easy-going personality, and a delight in the lyrics and melodies of his homeland, it was hardly surprising he should be one of the most popular men in town.

What a joy it was, on a balmy summer evening, after the sun had set and the fishing boats were slowly wending their way out to sea, to participate in a singsong *alla Napoletana*. Such musical occasions were sometimes prearranged, at other times we unexpectedly came upon a group of *Positanesi*, sitting in a circle at the beach or in a waterfront bar, singing with gusto and swaying in tempo to the music. At its centre was Peppino, strumming away at his guitar. Eyes sparkling, full of fun, he sang a few numbers, smiling at his audience, encouraging them to join in the chorus, happy at the enthusiasm he aroused. Occasionally someone asked Peppino what he'd like to play, but he didn't care; his aim was to make his friends happy.

"*O Marenariello*," called one of his mates. "Caterina, please play Caterina," begged another. "It's my turn, I've been waiting all night for '*E Spingole Francese*'."

Everyone had their favourite. I liked them all, even though I had trouble understanding the words, which were, of course, in dialect. Neapolitan songs have wonderful, sentimental melodies. I'd been accustomed to recordings made by famous Italian tenors, many of whom came from the north. Such recordings are undoubtedly excellent, and I'd always enjoyed distinguished renditions of *Santa Lucia, Funiculi', funicula'* and other well-loved songs. But until I actually heard local exponents, I hadn't realised there was an extra dimension known only to those who really understand the genre.

Although the famous tenors used dialect words, something was lacking. You had to be Neapolitan to sound the part. In addition to facility with the vocal score, the timbre of the voice is all-important. It must be light and husky, almost crooner-like. One of the outstanding performers, recognized as a master of the category, was Sergio Bruni, whose voice was ideally suited to *canzoni Napoletane*. Peppino's voice was similar to that of Bruni. No wonder he was in demand.

Often after dinner at the home of friends, the assembled company decided they wanted music.

"I'm sick of listening to records," someone would say. "Let's get Peppino." And they all smiled in anticipation.

A few guests set out in search. Eventually someone triumphantly appeared with Peppino and his guitar. As word spread, more and more people arrived; in no time the house was overcrowded and the party spilled out of doors. Glasses were passed around, wine was poured. We sipped our drinks and hummed along with the music. *Vino rosso*, I was told, was an essential ingredient, enhancing the genial mood of the gathered entourage.

"*Povero* Peppino, nobody's given him a drink. What a selfish lot we are."

Peppino was swamped by apologetic mates, eagerly offering to fill the glass of their hero. Now and then he interrupted his repertoire to stop for a glass of wine, but Peppino's satisfaction was derived from the enjoyment he engendered. He was a delightful person, gentle, thoughtful and unassuming, happy to give pleasure to friends.

# FAREWELL

Nothing lasts forever, say the *Positanesi*. And now this truism was about to apply to me, and to my life in *via* Fornillo. Why did we decide to leave? There were so many reasons.

Important decisions, those which have the capacity to affect an entire future, are obviously not made in a hurry. We often discussed our future. Should we spend the rest of our lives in Italy? Or would it be wiser to return to Australia?

The political unrest in Italy concentrated our minds. We became increasingly aware that the time had come to reach a conclusion. We agonised for weeks and months, but in reality the question had been occupying our minds for years.

Our main consideration was the children. Where should they go to school? What would be best for them? It seemed that their future would be more secure in Australia than in Italy. And on that basis we made our decision. We would move to Australia.

For me it would be a return to an environment I knew. For Stenio the whole process would certainly be more difficult. Yet he was enthusiastic. He had thoroughly enjoyed his previous visits: the hospitality of the people, the friendly, relaxed atmosphere, the wide open spaces. Friends had entertained us royally, ensuring that we had a wonderful holiday. But we couldn't expect this to continue once we became permanent residents.

"Life will be different, of course it will," Stenio assured me repeatedly. "But we'll be all right, don't worry."

Always an optimist, he made light of potential problems. If he was so confident, so sure he could happily effect a fundamental change in lifestyle, why should I be apprehensive? Hopefully he'd manage to find a satisfying occupation, a job suited to his skills and training. We realised that the longer we waited, the harder it would be to establish ourselves in a new country.

249

The same was true for the children. The younger they were, the more easily they'd fit in. We should go while they were little, at that carefree, innocent age while they were still adaptable and open to change. On this we were in complete agreement. The sooner we set off the better, from every point of view.

Is it wise to move back home with a new family? This was a frequent topic of discussion among friends who, like me, had married Italian men. Each case was different, as in all marriages there was no definitive pattern. Why should there be? Attitudes varied from one extreme to the other. Some were completely happy with their life in Italy, others were always discontented. The majority lay somewhere in between. A few of my friends had long dreamed of returning to their native country. Those who did go met with varying degrees of success.

Changing countries is always an adventure, a voyage into uncharted territory. There are no established rules. A certain parallel can be drawn with the migrant experience, although the problems are considerably diluted. In fact they're halved; one partner may feel uprooted, but the other's there to smooth the way.

Jackie, one of my close friends, had recently moved with her husband and teenage children to her home-town in Canada. She returned miserable and disappointed when the whole undertaking went wrong. While her husband was supportive in every way - the idea of going had in fact originated with him - the children refused to adapt. They hated school in Canada, and made no effort to fit in with a new and different set of values. Language problems were an important factor, as were the demands of a strange school curriculum. The children were more advanced than their classmates in certain subjects, behind in others.

But the main problem, I gathered, resulted from their interaction with the local teenagers. They couldn't handle the peer group pressure. With a total lack of interest in the leisure activities of their fellow students, they never stood a chance. Poor Jackie, I could imagine her frustration. But what could she do? How could she change the negative attitude of her teenage offspring? This depressing situation went on for almost two years. Finally, the disillusioned parents could cope no longer with the long faces around them. They packed their bags and returned to Italy.

The net result was not good from any aspect. The children had lost touch with their friends and were assigned to a lower class. The husband's career had suffered as a result of his long absence. And financially, the whole enterprise had been disastrous.

We were determined that this wouldn't happen to us. Ours would be a positive step; we'd make sure of that. Adriana was seven years old, and Simone only four. In the previous year, we'd spent a few months in Melbourne, and they'd really enjoyed themselves. Our visit had been, to a certain extent, a fact-finding trip to investigate the likely outcome of a move to Melbourne. Now we were reasonably confident we wouldn't face insurmountable problems.

*    *    *    *    *

Ten years earlier I had moved everything I possessed from one side of the world to the other. Now I was about to repeat this arduous performance in reverse. But this time, instead of transporting my own belongings, we were dealing with the accumulated possessions of a household of four people. More, in fact. It was really a matter of two households and five people, because my mother was coming too. Having moved from one side of the world to the other to be with her only daughter, she was hardly going to stay on in Italy on her own.

Why couldn't I just wave a magic wand and find that we'd suddenly landed in Melbourne, house and all? *Magari* (one of those untranslatable words, defined in my dictionary as 'would to God'). But unfortunately I had no fairy godmother and this wasn't going to happen.

Moving house is traumatic. Nobody enjoys it, even if the move is confined to the same city; even within the same suburb. How much worse to change countries. But the difficulties, I'm convinced, are as much mental as physical. Once you get your mind around the idea, and persuade yourself it's going to be fun - you have to believe it - the problems tend to disappear. And so I made a resolution. Nothing was going to bother me. Our transcontinental relocation would be a challenge, not a problem.

Where did we start? Bureaucracy in Italy was alive and well; we had coped with tangles induced by State and Municipal Councils many times in the past. All matters pertaining to officialdom I left to Stenio; he was used to dealing with such issues on a daily basis for clients, now he would have to act on behalf of his own family. The same applied to any other requirement within the legal domain. This was his territory.

I assumed responsibility for sorting out the practicalities. Included were vexatious decisions about what we should take with us, what we would leave behind. This was easy, we'd just take everything. After all, once we arrived in Australia we'd have to completely restock a new home. So why leave things behind we'd have to buy again. We might as well take everything we possessed, even the brooms. Of course I'm exaggerating. Obviously there was much to dispose of; I had again accumulated a ridiculous number of expendable objects. Marietta was given first choice.

"Take whatever you like," I told her. "Give the rest to whoever you think can best use it. Please yourself. You know who needs what."

I was sure she'd enjoy making gifts. This was the least I could do.

When I first told Marietta we were leaving Positano she was devastated. She was, after all, one of the family. How could we leave her behind? Could she come with us? This was only half-joking. I know she seriously considered joining us in Australia. I was just as sad at the prospect of losing her. I'd become very dependent on Marietta; she knew as much about our daily habits, about the needs and desires of the children as I did. Possibly more. And she really loved the children. But, much as I would have liked

252

to take her with us, it was never really an option. I couldn't imagine Marietta in Australia. How would she cope with life in a large city, with the traffic, the supermarket, the suburban shopping centre? She'd be like a fish out of water, unable to go to Palatone to discuss the day's events. Or to meet with her large family, for apart from brothers and sisters there were aunts, uncles, cousins. How lonely she'd be removed from her familiar world. What would she do all day in a big city? She'd be absolutely miserable.

I contacted several companies specialising in international freight, asking them to quote on the cost of packing all our possessions and transporting them to the other end of the world. A few freight-forwarding firms had been recommended by friends. Although it seemed an enormous undertaking to us, it was really not so extraordinary. Diplomats were transferred to remote and isolated countries on a regular basis, as were company executives and businessmen. It happened all the time. Representatives of three well-known companies came to examine the situation. All three provided quotes, the first two seemed exorbitant, the third more reasonable. After considerable discussion, we chose the cheapest alternative. This proved to be a costly error. We should have known better, particularly as the company concerned was Neapolitan.

*    *    *    *    *

"We'll miss you, Signora," said Palatone's wife.

Everyone in the shop turned to look at me, interrupting their daily talk session.

"Is it true you're leaving?" they asked. "Are you really going back to Australia? It won't be the same without you."

"How will we manage without *l'avvocato*?" Silvia, who worked in the Post Office, looked at me reproachfully. "And the two little blonde girls, we're so used to seeing them skipping along on your daily *passeggiata*."

How warm and caring they were, these women. Many of them I hardly knew. Apart from a polite *bongiorno* when our paths crossed as we went about our daily business, we'd never exchanged more than a few words. And yet, despite my foreign accent and different ways, they'd accepted me. I'd become an honorary *Positanese*.

It was really moving, I could feel the tears coming to my eyes.

"We'll be back," I said. "We'll come back whenever we get the chance."

"But it won't be the same, Signora."

The same thing happened when I went to the *centro*. People stopped me on my way to the bank, in the tourist office, in the bar over coffee. Everyone asked similar questions. Were we really leaving? Why should we go so far away? Uppermost in their minds, I gradually realised, was a sense of mystification. How could anyone in their right mind choose to leave Positano voluntarily?

Admittedly they were all familiar with the concept that Australia was a semi-tropical paradise. I'd become accustomed to the standard reaction of Italians on hearing I hailed from Australia. "Why would anyone leave such a wonderful country?" But still, even if that far-away country was some sort of paradise, it surely couldn't compare with Positano.

The expatriate community was also perplexed. In recent years a few of their number had departed. But this was in the natural order of events. They were growing older and wanted to be close to their children and grandchildren. Others left for the simple reason that the cost of living had rendered Italy beyond their means. We didn't fit either pattern; we were young, and Stenio was a local boy. But although our expatriate friends were disappointed at the news of our imminent departure, they tended to be more realistic, understanding the rationale behind our move. "We'll miss you," they said. "But you're doing the right thing."

\*  \*  \*  \*  \*

The packers came. They took over the house. They were everywhere; in the kitchen, the bathroom, the bedrooms, on the terrace. I have no idea how many packers were in our house at any one time. Everywhere I looked I saw hands pulling objects out of cupboards, stripping reams of paper off enormous rollers, wrapping articles, packing odd-shaped parcels into cardboard cartons, stacking cartons one above the other. It produced an illusion of perpetual motion.

I'd told them to pack everything. And that's exactly what they did. "Not that," I exclaimed, rescuing a packet of tissues. I came upon a large, fat lady conscientiously wrapping our phone books in layer after layer of paper. "Don't pack the phone books," I said, grabbing one large volume. "Who do you think you are?" she snapped, snatching it back angrily. I couldn't stop her, the supervisor was nowhere in sight. She continued like a robot, packaging everything in sight.

"Why don't you go out?" said Marietta, looking at me sympathetically. "Go and have a cup of coffee. I'll look after things here."

The phone rang. Where on earth was it? It had probably been packed too.

For the last few days, we moved into a nearby *pensione*. We couldn't stay in our house. The beds had already been stripped, the sheets and blankets set aside. I went to relax in my room. But how could I keep away, I had to watch what was happening. In five minutes I was back again, ineptly interfering in a superbly managed operation.

Transporting our possessions from the house to removal vans was another logistic nightmare, similar to that I'd encountered in getting them there in the first place. Here the removalists wisely deferred to the skills of local *facchini*. Some of our furniture, particularly my highly treasured antiques, was extremely heavy. I

255

held my breath as I saw a large, solid, awkwardly-shaped *credenza* being passed from person to person up the steep and narrow stairway beside our house. Again, I could only admire the skill and dexterity with which these experts conducted the operation.

Eventually everything had gone. The trucks were loaded, the house was empty. Every trace of our existence had vanished. It was hard to walk around a house that had been home for years, to look at bare walls, to hear our footsteps echo through empty rooms. But enough of that. We hadn't been driven out. It was our own choice.

That evening, we were sitting over dinner, discussing our plans for the next few days, when the phone rang. The Naples manager of the international freight company was on the line.

"We've loaded your goods into containers," he said. "But we can't fit everything in."

"How do you mean?" we asked in trepidation. "What happens now?"

"I'm afraid we'll have to hire an extra container," came the unwelcome response. "There'll be an additional cost of course."

"How much?" He named a figure, an exorbitant sum. We'd been caught. The total cost was now more than that originally quoted by the other companies. We had to agree. We had no other option.

\*      \*      \*      \*      \*

How did we feel about leaving Positano? We were full of anticipation. We were moving to a new country, a new life. Even so, it wasn't easy to leave. The years in Positano had been happy ones. And we were about to undergo an enormous upheaval, a complete and utter change. We were about to start all over again. Now and then I had a moment of doubt. Were we doing the right thing? I'm sure Stenio wondered too. But we kept our hesitation to ourselves.

We had to say goodbye to family, to friends and acquaintances. Ten years is a long time, and I'd made some close friends. I was used to seeing Carol and Diana almost every day, I'd really miss them. And the genuine affection shown by people I hardly knew was really moving. There were emotional farewells. Again I wished the magic wand would wave us on.

Finally the day arrived, the day of our departure. We woke up bright and early. The car we'd ordered was ready and waiting. Our friend Mimi the taxi driver was going to take us to Rome. This time we didn't have to walk up any steps. Our *pensione* was on the road.

Yet I couldn't bring myself to hurry. I kept finding reasons to linger. I had to pack our bags, to organise the children. A few friends had gathered to wish us well.

Eventually I couldn't delay any longer.

"*Andiamo*," said Mimi.

We rounded the curve and Positano disappeared from view. I turned to take a last look at the mountains, at the houses and boutiques, at the spectacular coastline.

"We'll be back," I said.

And we have been, many times. But it's not the same.

# EPILOGUE

The Positano I knew no longer exists. I came at a time of flux. It was 1965, and, although the days of the simple fishing village were long since gone, traces of the old, traditional way of life still lingered. Time-honoured customs persisted, particularly among the older generation. On festival days children stood by watching as their grandparents followed ancient rituals. But each year brought change. I could see it happening before my eyes. More and more tourists arrived, word spread all too rapidly. And the lovely, sleepy little town moved slowly and inexorably into the twentieth century, undergoing a transformation that was gradual, relentless and unstoppable. Today Positano is recognised as a sophisticated and fashionable resort.

*    *    *    *    *

We did return. Stenio made the long trip more often than I, escaping the Melbourne winter to spend time with his family and savour the delights of the Positano summer. But we agreed that we had made the right decision, our readjustment to a new way of life had been reasonably smooth.

In 1985 Stenio began to feel unwell, with considerable pain in his hip. He was convinced that a few weeks in the Italian sun would solve his problems, and set off to enjoy a few weeks holiday with his mother and brother. He returned feeling no better, and was diagnosed with a very aggressive form of cancer. Sadly, he died six weeks later.

*    *    *    *    *

My home is full of memories of Positano. I have lovely antique pieces of furniture collected during our years in Italy. I am surrounded by paintings, lamps, candelabra, brightly coloured ceramics, all brought with us when we left. I treasure several of my father-in-law's delicate pastels, they are really exquisite. A life-size gazelle, executed in bronze, stands near my front door today; I feel it gazing at me each time I pass.

Over the years, much of my donkey collection has had to be repaired; legs, tails or ears glued on. A few have reached the point of no return, and sadly have been discarded. I know that I could buy more, but it wouldn't be right. My donkeys belong to the past, not the present.

Even now, after all the years that have passed, the Italian phase of my life stands out, an isolated interlude seemingly unrelated to the periods that came before and after. And yet, I know that this is not so. Life cannot be divided into segments. The Positano experience has become an integral part of me, and of my family.

*　　*　　*　　*　　*

Some years after Stenio's death, I remarried. My new husband, Ian, became accustomed to hearing my Positano stories. Not only did he listen, but he was really interested to hear about our life in Italy, and encouraged me to write about those years. A few years ago, we went together to Positano, and I introduced Ian to many of the places and people I had talked about.

One day we took the local bus to Montepertuso. What a change! In my day such a visit meant climbing thousands of steps! About twenty years ago a road was finally constructed, and the mountain village has now entered the twentieth century. Montepertuso has become an extension of Positano. The village is still charming; it now has several restaurants and appears quite prosperous. I recognised a few of the old faces; somehow they didn't seem to belong in the present day scene.

I walked slowly along the main thoroughfare, the little shops and dwellings on either side were still there. Arriving at the end of the village, I discovered to my dismay that the road was being extended to Nocelle. I followed the brand new road until it petered out in a tangle of bulldozers and excavating machinery. The quiet pastoral landscape of my memory had been shattered by an accumulation of heavy earth-moving equipment. The noise and clatter of road works totally destroyed the peace and harmony I had known. So much for progress.

Following what remained of the old path to Nocelle, I arrived in the *piazzetta*. To my delight, it was relatively unchanged; children still ran around barefoot, stopping to stare at us; chickens wandered underfoot. I found my way to the little restaurant. It was as I remembered, perhaps a little larger. I was about to introduce myself to the woman behind the bar when I noticed that she was staring at me in amazement.

"I remember you," she said, laughing with pleasure. "I was the little girl you always talked to. Mamma was so cross when we giggled at the way you spoke."

How thrilled I was to find that the shy little girl with the big brown eyes had followed in her mother's footsteps. How could I not have seen the resemblance? I recalled how she used to emerge from the kitchen carrying an enormous platter, almost as big as she was. Now she and her husband were running the family business.

Nocelle, at least, was as I remembered. I recently heard that the road has now been completed. No doubt the little huddle of houses will gradually be modernised, and the tiny township will develop and expand to accommodate the ever-increasing tourist trade. Few will regret this happening, certainly not the local population. But I prefer to remember it as it was.